The book offers an excellent and badly needed review of the several factors that affect competitiveness both in the Eurozone and more specifically in Italy.

Reading it is highly recommended to those who point at one single factor and concentrate their therapy on it only. They might make their labour market even more flexible than the German one but eventually they discover that labour productivity remains much lower than the German one because of the poorer training of their workers. They might do whatever is needed to make their firms and banks more competitive, but inadequately reformed public institutions keep producing negative externalities that reduce the total factor productivity of their economy.

It is a lesson mostly for Italy. A lesson that unhappily is still to be learned.

Giuliano Amato

Competitiveness in the European Economy

This book deals with the relationship between the competitiveness of countries in Europe and the analysis of macroeconomic imbalances. It focuses mainly on a European analysis, along with special studies of the German economy, which is rarely considered to be a cause for the current crisis. The book also compares Germany with Italy, providing a comparative perspective on structural reforms.

The first part of this book analyses macroeconomic imbalances based on a new framework from the analysis of the flow of funds rather than balance of payments, and presents an alternative measure of unit labour cost comparisons to investigate the relationship between imbalances and competitiveness. The second part is dedicated to the analysis of the trade performance of Germany and Italy and the sustainability of the German model in the EMU. The third part describes the reform policies implemented by Germany and their effect on imbalances; this includes wage moderation, the labour market reforms and weak labour demand. The final part explores the regional inequalities within Germany and Italy, providing useful lessons regarding fiscal federalism and regional banking developments.

In conclusion, a big part of the problems within the Euro Area is generated by the use of a wrong framework of analysis, where the EMU is considered as a fixed exchange rate regime and not a single country. This book provides an alternative view which holds at the core the relationship between sectors. It is stressed throughout the book that the German behaviour has contributed to the rise of imbalances between countries due to its growth model, not suitable for a big developed country in a currency union. This book also finds that stressing banking integration within countries helps to reduce regional inequalities, which has important implications for the management of Europe's future banking union and macroeconomic imbalances.

Stefan Collignon is a Professor of Economic Policy at Sant'Anna School of Advanced Studies, Pisa, Italy.

Piero Esposito is a Post-Doctoral Researcher at Sant'Anna School of Advanced Studies and researcher in internationalisation and international trade at Centro Europa Ricerche (CER), Italy.

Routledge studies in the European economy

Competitiveness in the European Economy

Edited by Stefan Collignon and
Piero Esposito

LONDON AND NEW YORK

First published 2014 by Routledge

2 Park Square, Milton Park, Abingdon, Oxfordshire OX14 4RN
52 Vanderbilt Avenue, New York, NY 10017

Routledge is an imprint of the Taylor & Francis Group, an informa business

First issued in paperback 2020

British Library Cataloguing in Publication Data
A catalogue record for this book is available from the British Library

Library of Congress Cataloging in Publication Data
Competitiveness in the European economy / edited by Stefan Collignon and Piero Esposito.
    pages cm. – (Routledge studies in the European economy)
    Includes bibliographical references and index.
    1. Germany–Economic conditions–21st century. 2. Italy–Economic conditions–21st century. 3. Competition–European Union countries–History–21st century. 4. Euro–History–21st century. 5. Business cycles–European Union countries–History–21st century. I. Collignon, Stefan II. Esposito, Piero.
    HC286.8.C665 2014
    339.5094–dc23   2013033350

ISBN: 978-0-415-71232-3 (hbk)
ISBN: 978-0-367-60095-2 (pbk)

Typeset in Times New Roman
by Wearset Ltd, Boldon, Tyne and Wear

Contents

Figures

Tables

Contributors

Dr Francesca Bartoli, Head of Economic and Banking Research, Italy Research, UniCredit, Bologna (IT).

Prof. Dr Stefan Collignon, Sant'Anna School of Advanced Studies. Piazza Martiri della Libertà 33, 56127, Pisa (IT).

Prof. Dr Sebastian Dullien, Hochschule Technik und Wirtschaft Berlin – University of Applied Sciences Fachbereich 3 – Wirtschaftswissenschaften Treskowallee 8, 10313 Berlin.

Dr Piero Esposito, Sant'Anna School of Advanced Studies. Piazza Martiri della Libertà 33, 56127, Pisa (IT).

Prof. Dr Ulrich Fritsche, Universität Hamburg, Fakultät Wirtschafts- und Sozialwissenschaften Fachbereich Sozialökonomie Welckerstr. 8 D-20146 Hamburg.

Prof. Paolo Guerrieri, Sapienza University of Rome and College of Europe, Bruges. Via del Castro Laurenziano 9, 00161, Rome.

Dr Gerhard Heimpold, Halle Institute for Economic Research (IWH), Department of Structural Change, Kleine Märkerstraße 8, D-06108 Halle Saale.

Prof. Dr Joachim Möller, Institute for Employment Research (IAB) Nuremberg and University of Regensburg, Universitätsstraße 30, D-93040 Regensburg.

Prof. Dr Torsten Niechoj, Rhine-Waal University of Applied Sciences, Faculty of Communication and Environment, Südstraße 8, 47475 Kamp-Lintfort, Germany.

Dr Zeno Rotondi, Head of Italy Research, UniCredit, Bologna (IT).

Prof. Enrico Saltari, Sapienza University of Rome and College of Europe, Bruges. Via del Castro Laurenziano 9, 00161, Rome.

Dr Mirko Titze, Halle Institute for Economic Research (IWH), Department of Structural Change, Kleine Märkerstraße 8, D-06108 Halle Saale.

Dr Denni Tommasi, Université libre de Bruxelles, Bruxelles (B).

Kristina van Deuverden, DIW Berlin, Mohrenstr. 58, 10117 Berlin.

Preface and acknowledgements

Competitiveness is a tricky notion. While it occupies a large place in public debates, competitiveness is nearly absent as a concept from most economic textbooks. Yet, for entrepreneurs it is a question of survival, and for many policymakers it is a convenient argument to justify unpopular structural reforms. Paul Krugman has argued that 'It seems far too cynical to suggest that the debate over competitiveness is simply a matter of time-honoured fallacies about international trade being dressed up in new and pretentious rhetoric. But it is'.[1] This book aims to clarify this debate and to separate the wheat from the chaff.

The contributions to this book were first discussed at a conference in July 2011 organised by Centro Europa Ricerche (CER) in Rome. CER is a research institute in applied economic analysis focusing on central issues of Italian and European economic policies. The conference brought together leading economists from Germany and Italy.

The initial conference and the subsequent book publication was financially supported by Ateneo Italo-Tedesco – Deutsch-Italienisches Hochschulzentrum, which aims at developing bi-national networks dedicated to higher education, scientific and technological cooperation between Italy and Germany, thus creating links between the educational, cultural, economic and entrepreneurial systems of both countries. Additional support was provided by the Embassy of the Federal Republic of Germany in Rome. We are grateful for the encouragement we have received, without which neither the exchange of ideas nor this book would have been possible.

Note

1 Paul Krugman (1996), 'Making sense of the competitiveness debate'. *Oxford Review of Economic Policy*, 12(3): 24.

Introduction

Stefan Collignon and Piero Esposito

Europe has been obsessed with competitiveness for a long time. In 2000, the Lisbon Strategy set the target of making the European Union 'the most competitive region in the world' within a decade.[1] Few people believe that it has succeeded. During the first decade of the euro, the north stagnated and the south boomed; in the second decade, it was the opposite. Before the crisis, unemployment rose from 3.6 to 5.2 per cent in Austria and from 2.5 to 5.3 per cent in the Netherlands. Germany went through a prolonged period of stagnation after its reunification: from 1990 to 2006, German unemployment nearly doubled from 5.6 to 11.3 per cent. On the other hand, it looked as if southern economies, especially Spain and Ireland, were rapidly catching up with the more prosperous member states in the union. The convergence of interest rates to German low standards had generated a boom in the south that translated into high growth, huge employment gains and also large current account imbalances. Unemployment fell from 11.3 to 6.1 per cent in Italy, from 21.3 in 1995 to 8.3 per cent in Spain. At the same time, Italy's current account position deteriorated from a surplus of 2.9 to a deficit of 1.3 per cent of GDP; Spain went from balance to a deficit of 10 per cent. Prices in the south increased more, and in the north less, than the Euro Area average. Then the crisis came. Suddenly the roles changed. Germany, which had implemented radical labour market reforms, rose like the phoenix from the ashes; the south fell into deep depression. Unemployment shot up in the south, but started to come down quickly in Germany (although not in the Netherlands or Austria). Noticing the differences in current account deficits, the conclusion was easily reached that the crisis countries must have had competitiveness problems, which were only 'masked' by excess demand during the boom (ECB, 2012).

How can competitiveness in the European Union be improved? The Lisbon Strategy wanted to make Europe fit for the knowledge society of the twenty-first century. It had formulated structural indicators, which all member states were supposed to achieve. After 10 years, the results were disappointing. This was partly a consequence of the *open method of coordination*, which had left it to member state governments to implement structural reforms, partly because the macroeconomic dimension, which had been originally the second pillar of the strategy, had soon been abandoned (Collignon, 2008). Instead, the policy focus was narrowed to labour market reforms. After the global financial crisis and the subsequent debt problems in the Euro Area, attitudes changed again. Debt and macroeconomic imbalances became the major concern, but aggregate demand was largely ignored and the increase of unemployment was linked to rigid labour markets.[2] To deal with imbalances, the European Commission set up a monitoring tool and created a new process to avoid macroeconomic imbalances, largely based on the model of the Stability and Growth Pact. It uses a scoreboard of 11 indicators with thresholds triggering an alert mechanism followed by binding policy recommendations. While the indicators include competitiveness variables like real exchange rates, unit labour costs, etc., the thresholds are primarily setting limits for current account deficits, while higher surpluses are asymmetrically tolerated. For example, alert thresholds for current account deficits are −4 per cent, but surpluses are acceptable up to +6 per cent. Given that imbalances within the currency area are always zero, this must imply that the Euro Area as a whole is aiming for current account surpluses with the rest of the world. Nevertheless, the focus on current account imbalances within the Euro Area has given a very particular flavour to the issue of competitiveness that privileges austerity policies.

No doubt, the global financial crisis of 2008–2009 has revealed structural weaknesses in the European economy and also in the governance of the currency area. The main economic problem is the unequal development of member states in the Euro Area. Capital flows have moved from relatively rich to relatively poor countries without evidence of fostering a sustainable process of real catching up. Before the crisis, peripheral countries had developed a credit-financed growth model based on high consumption (Spain, Greece, Ireland and Portugal) where investment was concentrated mainly in non-tradable sectors such as construction (Spain), tourism (Greece) and other services (Ireland). This model was responsible for the deterioration of current accounts and high dependency on imports. At the same time, core European countries (Germany and the Netherlands) chose export oriented growth as their model and increased their trade surpluses without, however, improving their growth performance.

With the advent of the crisis, the credit bubble burst and the southern boom collapsed. High uncertainties and risks of private and public debt insolvencies put a brake on bank lending and interrupted capital flows. Political mishandling has prolonged and deepened the recession in the southern member states of the Euro Area, and excessive austerity did not succeed in stabilising public finances. As a result of these policies, external imbalances were transformed into internal ones, with unemployment as the adjustment variable. The northern model became now the benchmark for successful economic policy. It was thought that Germany had improved competitiveness through structural reforms under the Schröder government and if others followed the example, they, too, would quickly overcome the crisis. However, the chapters in this book will show that this story is too simple.

The euro crisis has also revealed deep political problems. The causes and conditions of the crisis that are at the root of the disruptive economic imbalances were primarily interpreted through the ideological frame of neoliberalism. It was believed that structural reforms would empower markets to heal themselves. Hence, there was little need for proactive economic policies. This belief fitted the institutional arrangements of the Euro Area. European institutions are weak because they have little decision-making power and they have no power because they lack democratic legitimacy. During the crisis, the need for a more powerful instrument which could be used to implement austerity policies has become obvious. The answer was charging the troika with this task, although it lacks any democratic foundation and is often seen as the agent of a German *Diktat*. The only democratically elected institution of the EU, the European Parliament, on the other hand, has little power to influence or overrule the opinion of the most influential countries like Germany or France. This point became clear when the Greek crisis exploded. Germany did not want to pay for Greece, but ended up doing it anyway. Uncertainty regarding policy actions, i.e. whether or not to bail out the Greek debt, exacerbated the loss of confidence of investors and markets. This led to speculative attacks on bonds emitted by countries with high insolvency risks. Hence, the political uncertainties generated by Europe's fragmented polity were an important factor in the acceleration of the euro crisis (Collignon *et al.*, 2013).

Given the depth of the economic crisis, eurosceptics have suggested that peripheral countries should leave the Euro Area and depreciate their new national currencies. We will see in Chapter 1 that this is fallacious economic thinking. An exit would serve neither the periphery nor the core of the monetary union. It is therefore coherent with the functioning of a monetary union that the European Union treaties have no provisions for leaving the Euro Area. Nevertheless, there is an inconsistency between the dominant policy consensus in Europe, which reflects the preferences of surplus countries for export-oriented growth and puts the burden of the adjustment on deficit countries, and the need for more balanced growth. This inconsistency is embedded in the European Commission's Macroeconomic Imbalances Procedure and is causing political tensions without solving the economic issues.

The recent literature on the euro crisis discusses three explanations for the rise of macroeconomic imbalances: first, imbalances are the natural outcome of financial integration (Blanchard and Giavazzi, 2002; Schnabl and Freitag, 2012; Croci-Angelini and Farina, 2012; Collignon, 2012a); second, they are a consequence of wage bargaining and unit labour cost developments in member countries (Dullien and Fritsche, 2009; Brancaccio, 2012; Onharan and Stockhammer, 2013; Belke and Dreger, 2011; Collignon, 2012b); third, they were caused by external trade shocks, in particular from emerging economies (Chen *et al.*, 2013; Guerrieri and Esposito, 2012, 2013). In spite of the different starting points, most of these contributions share the idea that improving competitiveness is the key for rebalancing the European economy and restore growth.

But what is competitiveness? In general terms competitiveness is the ability of a country to compete in the world market. This definition does not translate into a well-defined set of indicators unambiguously linked to a country's performance. In general terms, competitiveness is a multidimensional concept which includes the performance of individual firms or sectors, the ability of the public institutions to provide a positive framework for the development of competitive productions and efficient markets, the ability to take advantage of the opportunities offered by the international economic environment and so on. The *World Economic Forum Competitiveness Report* and the IMD World Competitiveness Center (WCC) provide comprehensive surveys of different dimensions of competitiveness. Yet, as we will see in more detail in Chapter 2, aggregate indicators are not always useful for policy purposes.

The aim of this book is twofold. On the one hand, we attempt to provide a better framework for the analysis of European imbalances and the definition of policies aiming at the improvement of competitiveness in the Euro Area as a whole. On the other hand, the book provides a comparative analysis between Germany and Italy. We critically question to what degree the German model can serve as a benchmark for the rest of Europe. The German economy has gone through a profound transformation since reunification in the early 1990s. The Schröder reforms in the mid-1990s, called Agenda 2010, have become the glorious beacon of hope and inspiration for many commentators, but few policymakers have been able to imitate them. The Italian economy has had some interesting historical similarities with Germany, such as a high share of manufacturing and a relatively high export orientation, but today it is the country with severe growth problems and the lowest productivity increases in the Euro Area. Inevitably, there is a question if and what Italy could learn from the German reform experience. The different fates of the two countries since 2003 provide useful insights for defining policies to improve internal and external competitiveness.

The book is organised in four parts. The first part analyses the Euro Area as a whole, while the following parts are dedicated to the comparative analysis of the German and Italian models with respect to external trade (Part II), labour market reforms (Part III) and regional convergence (Part IV).

In the first chapter Stefan Collignon takes a look at how a monetary union works and what that means for competitiveness within the Euro Area. He emphasises that a monetary union functions in fundamentally different ways compared to fixed exchange rates in international economic textbooks and this fact requires a different interpretation of current accounts. Macroeconomic imbalances are better reflected in gross lending/net borrowing balances recorded in flow of funds statements than in international balance of payment statistics. This puts the emphasis on achieving balanced growth within the Euro Area rather than eliminating current account imbalances. However, growth requires investment and credit, so that restoring economic balance is not just a matter of relative costs, but also of risk–return considerations. Collignon therefore redefines competitiveness as the capacity to earn above average returns to capital, given equal degrees of uncertainty in the environment within which firms are operating.

In Chapter 2, Stefan Collignon and Piero Esposito take this approach into the arena of unit labour costs (ULC). They review the different definitions of competitiveness and propose a production function approach in which the output measures of competitiveness (trade and current account balances, market shares) are the result of the input measures such as relative costs of labour and capital, relative prices, productivities and profits. In this framework the authors propose a new competitiveness indicator for the Euro Area called CER Competitiveness Index (CCI), which takes into account not only the cost of labour but also the productivity of the capital stock and the profit rate. Starting from the simple assumption that competitive differences are reflected by the different profit rates, the CCI indicator reveals how much a country's ULC is overvalued or undervalued compared to the level which would ensure a profit rate equal to the Euro Area average. The econometric tests prove the higher explanatory power of this index compared to traditional measures.

Part II focuses on the relation between export performance and competitiveness. The two contributions (from Fritsche and from Esposito and Guerrieri) stress the fact that Germany is the winner among European countries as it has succeeded in increasing exports at the expense of the rest of the Euro Area and in particular of the Italian economy (Esposito and Guerrieri). The contributions focus on the German model in order to assess its sustainability within a currency union and the possibility of applying it to the other countries of the area.

In Chapter 3, Ulrich Fritsche argues that the German export-led growth model is not sustainable if the target is the well-being of the whole of Europe. This is because the beggar-thy-neighbour approach implied by the model causes unwanted structural divergences, which are magnified when the strategy of belt-tightening is implemented by the most advanced country of the area and not by a developing country. Fritsche advocates the end of the export-led growth strategy and an increase in German aggregate demand as a precondition for the rebalancing of the European economy. This would imply, however, a change in the European governance as beggar-thy-neighbours strategies are presently not punished and often not even part of policy debates.

The analysis of Esposito and Guerrieri in Chapter 4 supports Fritsche's conclusion that Germany has contributed to the emergence of imbalances. However, the authors show that the German success is not only caused by wage moderation and productivity growth, but also by an important transformation of the structure of German trade relations, namely production fragmentation and the penetration of fast-growing emerging markets. When comparing Italy and Germany, the authors find that the German high-tech industries have largely benefited from delocalising activities to Central and Eastern Europe, while this effect is null for Italy. In terms of trade integration, the main result is that the Italian trade balance has suffered from the overall growth of total trade, while trade integration with China and ASEAN countries has in addition displaced high-tech industries. By contrast, in Germany the growth of trade integration is associated with higher net exports, largely because of German specialisation on capital equipment. Esposito and Guerrieri conclude that copying German outsourcing and market penetration could be a good strategy for the other countries when seeking to mitigate imbalances. Nevertheless, they also stress that part of the German success is due to the creation of European monetary union, which implies, of course, that the euro's integrity needs to be preserved.

The third part analyses what is seen by many as the most important element in improving the German competitiveness: the Hartz reforms of the labour market (also called Agenda 2010).

In Chapter 5, Torsten Niechoj analyses the German model in order to assess whether wage restraint should be a policy benchmark for other Euro Area countries. He finds that labour market reforms are not the most important element in explaining the German success. The author argues that the coincidence with the end of the negative cycle in 2005 has overstated the advantages of the Hartz reform, especially because its ultimate effect was to create many low-pay, low-quality jobs and to increase part-time jobs, which had detrimental welfare effects.

In Niechoj's view the real causes of the German success are twofold: on the one hand, its lower inflation rate implied higher real interest rates in the first years of the euro, with the effect of reducing consumption and increasing the outflow of savings toward countries with a lower real interest rate (i.e. with higher inflation). At the same time, domestic investment was concentrated on exports, as wage restraint together with fixed exchange rates have boosted the competitiveness of German products. Both these factors have contributed to the rise of imbalances in the Euro Area.

The above argument is in line with the analysis by Collignon (Chapter 1) and Esposito and Guerrieri (Chapter 4), although it qualifies the mechanism by which the euro has turned Germany into the big winner in intra-area trade. Surpluses were achieved by excess savings and under-consumption. Niechoj stresses therefore the importance of demand effects for the German economy: stimulus measures implemented by the government immediately after the global financial crisis and the rapid recovery of the external demand from emerging economies have pulled Germany more rapidly out of the crisis than other Euro member states. He concludes that wage restraint should not be copied by other countries, while stimulus measures can be successful. This would mean that a change in the European attitude toward adjustment policies is necessary, while the German push for asymmetric adjustment in surplus and deficit countries imposes austerity on countries which are still in the midst of a recession.

In Chapter 6, Joachim Möller questions whether the Hartz reforms have destroyed the German model of social market economy. The standard interpretation sees the so-called Agenda 2010 of the Schröder government as the main factor for improving German competitiveness. It implied wage moderation and export orientation by manufacturing firms, but he finds that an additional factor for German success was the strong internal flexibility in German firms, especially during the global financial crisis.

Möller's chapter assesses the costs of reforms in terms of living conditions for the labour force and changes in industrial relations. He argues that the reforms succeeded in reducing structural unemployment, first, by creating low-quality, low-pay jobs regulated mainly by 'non-normal' contracts and, second, by hardening the conditions for accessing the social security network. These two tendencies have increased both labour market segmentation and income inequalities, in particular in terms of skill premia. These developments have weakened one of the pillars of the German model, namely the high level of solidarity, and may threaten the survival of the German model.

In Chapter 7, Enrico Saltari starts from a discussion of Möller's work and seeks to identify the causes for the poor success of the Italian labour market reforms. These reforms have started in the late 1990s, and although they may not yet be complete they resemble in many aspects the reforms of the Agenda 2010. Saltari finds two main differences: first, the Italian reforms have acted only on temporary contracts, while leaving the legislation for permanent contracts unchanged; second, the Italian reforms have mainly improved external flexibility, while the German model has a high degree of internal flexibility and this has helped to shield the country from the negative effects of the global financial crisis. Saltari concludes that the low effectiveness of the Italian reforms has to be attributed to the different economic structures and political contexts, factors which have little or nothing to do with the reforms themselves.

In Chapter 8, Sebastian Dullien reviews a variety of features of the German model with respect to labour market reforms and wage restraint, trade developments, and the evolution of domestic demand. Given this broad view, his work provides an integrated perspective of the main findings of Parts II and III of the book.

Dullien argues, similarly to Niechoj, that the effects of Agenda 2010 have been overstated as gradual changes in the German labour market had already started in the early 1990s. In addition, he argues that the country has benefited from more competitive positions in world trade. On the one hand, German specialisation in equipment and high-quality manufacturing met the demand of emerging countries, a fact that is also stressed by Esposito and Guerrieri; but on the other hand, the country's geographical position has allowed German industry to capture demand from high-income countries in Western Europe and from the integration of the new member states into the European Union. Additional factors are certainly wage restraint and the low growth of domestic demand, which has mechanically improved net exports. An interesting point is that domestic demand has been influenced not only by consumption but also by the low expenditure on investment, R&D and education, which confirms the analysis in Chapter 1.

Dullien concludes that most of the above-mentioned features of the German model cannot be exported to the rest of the area as some elements generate negative externalities for the partners and others simply reduce growth. Hence, the elements of the German model which can generate growth without negative consequences should be carefully selected.

The fourth and last part of the book deals with regional issues in Italy and Germany. This part is interesting for the better understanding of the two countries, but it also adds substance to the argument in Chapter 1 that monetary flows in a monetary union are one of the possible adjustment mechanisms in case of imbalances. The two countries have deep regional disparities in common, originating, in the Italian case from the historical backwardness of Mezzogiorno, and in the German case from the reunification and the relatively disappointing growth performance of the new Länder.

In Chapter 9, Kristina van Deuverden explains the implementation of fiscal federalism in Germany and its effectiveness in fostering regional development. Yet, in her view, German federalism suffers from several drawbacks arising from conflicts between federal and regional laws. In particular, the Länder have less tax-setting power than the federal government and they have high incentives to act as free riders by increasing their debt levels. According to van Deuverden, Italy and other countries should pay attention and learn from the German experience by, first of all, carefully defining the system of public finance in order to avoid free riding, and second, by setting up an easily understandable equalisation mechanism that does not overcharge single regions.

Gerhard Heimpold and Mirko Titze review in Chapter 10 the economic developments in East Germany after reunification and derive the policy implications for speeding up the convergence with the West. East German firms are characterised by low export orientation, small dimension, low level of private R&D and specialisation in labour-intensive productions. Additional problems arise from the lack of headquarters in East Germany and from the low potential for clustering. In this respect, the East German economy resembles features of the Euro Area's periphery.

Given this picture, the authors stress the role of policies favouring increases in firms' size, suggesting a restructuring of taxation in order to make it neutral to the firm's dimension. In addition, policies should favour the increase of skilled labour supply and demand. This objective could be fulfilled by transferring R&D activities from public to private institutions, with the additional result of filling the technological gap with West Germany.

In the final chapter of the book, Francesca Bartoli, Zeno Rotondi and Denni Tommasi describe the banking system and its integration in the Italian Mezzogiorno and discuss the possible lesson to be applied to banking in the *neue Bundesländer*. The authors stress the fact that the two regions share a high dependency on regional imports and external (i.e. non-regional) financing as well as a consistent gap in economic convergence. However, the lower integration of the banking system in East Germany, together with the appreciation of the deutschmark following reunification and the huge monetary inflows and transfers from West Germany have caused a sort of 'Dutch disease'. The integration of the banking system plays a crucial role in reducing the external financing of the regions by locally increasing private loans. In Italy, banks in the Mezzogiorno are integrated with those of northern Italy and the latter's market share in the Mezzogiorno is high, with the result of increasing the loans to deposit ratio without draining resources from south to north. By contrast, the German banking system provides lower support to the less-developed territories, in the new Bundesländer. According to Bartoli, Rotondi and Tommasi, the main lesson that Germany should learn from the Italian experience is the need for higher banking integration of the less-developed regions with the more-developed ones.

In our view, this is also a fundamental lesson for the Euro Area. As Collignon has shown in Chapter 1, the Euro Area is a fully integrated monetary economy, economically resembling nation-states, despite being financially fragmented and politically fractioned. Bartoli, Rotondi and Tommasi present evidence that monetary flows and private credit facilitated by the banking system have a much neglected role in a currency area, while government transfers may actually be one of the obstacles of balanced growth. Hence, their study reinforces the analysis of Chapter 1 that currency areas need a properly functioning banking union, but not necessarily a fiscal union.

To summarise, the chapters assembled in this book provide an innovative look at competitiveness issues in the Euro Area, with specific focus on Germany and Italy. Beyond the slogans of 'necessary labour market reforms', a much more complex picture emerges when one analyses industrial structures and macroeconomic developments. In this respect, the book could make a contribution towards changing preconceived ideas about Germany and Italy, or about how to lead the Euro Area out of the crisis.

Notes

1 The Presidency Conclusions of the Lisbon European Council said:

> The Union has today set itself a new strategic goal for the next decade: to become the most competitive and dynamic knowledge-based economy in the world, capable of sustainable economic growth with more and better jobs and greater social cohesion.
> See www.consilium.europa.eu/uedocs/cms_data/docs/pressdata/en/ec/00100-r1.en0.htm

2 'The on-going adjustment to imbalances is necessary, but is costly in the short term and has resulted in higher unemployment. Adjustment is taking place, but the way forward for a complete and durable rebalancing is still long. Reforms in wage-setting mechanisms are starting to show their effectiveness in improving cost-competitiveness. High or rising unemployment in several member states, in a context of subdued aggregate demand, points to a labour market adjustment process that is still incomplete' (European Commission, 2012: 5).

References

Belke, A. H. and C. Drager (2011), 'Current account imbalances in the Euro Area: catching up or competitiveness?' *Ruhr Economic Paper* 241.

Blanchard, O. and F. Giavazzi (2002), 'Current account deficits in the Euro Area: the end of the Feldstein Horioka Puzzle'. *Brookings Papers on Economic Activity*, 33(2): 147–186.

Brancaccio, E. (2012), 'Current account imbalances, the Eurozone crisis, and a proposal for a "European wage standard"'. *International Journal of Political Economy*, 41(1): 47–65.

Chen, R., G. M. Milesi-Ferretti and T. Tressel (2013), 'External imbalances in the Eurozone'. *Economic Policy*, 73: 102–142.

Collignon, S. (2008), 'The Lisbon strategy, macroeconomic stability and the dilemma of governance with governments; or why Europe is not becoming the world's most dynamic economy'. *International Journal of Public Policy*, 3(1/2): 72–99.

Collignon, S. (2012a), *Macroeconomic Imbalances and Comparative Advantages in the Euro Area*. Brussels: European Trade Union Institute (ETUI) with Bertelsmann Foundation; Brussels

Collignon, S. (2012b), 'Macroeconomic imbalances and competitiveness in the Euro Area'. *Transfer: European Review of Labour and Research*, 19(1): 63–82.

Collignon, S., P. Esposito and H. Lierse (2013), 'European sovereign bailouts, political risk and the economic consequences of Mrs. Merkel'. *Journal of International Commerce, Economics and Policy*, 4(2): 55–79.

Croci-Agnelini, E. and F. Farina (2012), 'Current account imbalances and systemic risk within a monetary union'. *Journal of Economic Behavior and Organization*, 83: 647–656.

Dullien, S. and U. Fritsche (2009), 'How bad is divergence in the Euro zone? Lessons from the United States and Germany'. *Journal of Post Keynesian Economics*, 31(3): 431–457.

ECB (European Central Bank) (2012), *Euro Area Labour Markets and the Crisis. Structural Issues Report*, October; www.ecb.int/pub/pdf/other/euroarealabourmarketsandthecrisis201210en.pdf.

European Commission, (2012), *Alert Mechanism Report – 2013*; Brussels, 28.11.2012 COM(2012) 751 final; http://ec.europa.eu/europe2020/pdf/amreport2013_en.pdf.

Guerrieri, P. and P. Esposito (2012), 'Intra-European imbalances, adjustment and growth in the Eurozone'. *Oxford Review of Economic Policy*, 28(3): 532–550.

Guerrieri, P. and P. Esposito (2013), 'The determinants of macroeconomic imbalances in the Euro Area: the role of external performance' in L. Paganetto (ed.), *Public Debt, Global Governance and Economic Dynamism*. Milan: Springer Verlag.

Onharan, O. and E. Stockhammer (2013), 'Rethinking wage policy in the face of the Euro crisis. Implications of the wage-led demand regime'. *International Review of Applied Economics*, 26(2): 191–203.

Schnabl, G. and S. Freitag (2012) 'Reverse causality in global and intra-european imbalances'. *Review of International Economics*, 20(4): 674–690.

Part I

European imbalances and competitiveness

1 Taking European integration seriously

Competitiveness, imbalances and economic stability in the Euro Area

Stefan Collignon

Introduction

The euro crisis presents a challenge not only to policy-makers, but to economic theory as well. The explanation of a problem often traces already the path for its remedy. But if the diagnosis is mistaken, the medicine could kill the patient. Economic theory plays, therefore, an important role in overcoming the euro crisis, in preserving stability, and in keeping Europe together. Five years of unabated crisis have eroded the trust of citizens that the euro will improve their prosperity and welfare. The rejection of the euro and of European integration is gaining ground in public opinion. Hence, if Europe has failed to end the crisis, it may have erred in explaining it. It is time to review the theory that has guided policies so far.

In this chapter I will first look at the link between competitiveness and macro-economic imbalances and then discuss the fallacies of this approach. I will propose flow of funds analysis as an alternative to the current account based theories of the euro crisis and then draw some conclusions.

Competitiveness and imbalances in the Euro Area

Economic models explaining financial crises in general and the euro crisis in particular abound. Many deal with money, foreign debt, exchange rates and contagion in global financial markets; some deal with domestic institutions, banks and local debt; but increasingly the focus is on competitiveness, or rather the loss of competitiveness in Europe's south.[1] Unfortunately, most of these explanations mix foreign and domestic aspects from different theories into inconsistent policy advice. This amalgam reflects the complex governance of the Euro Area, where governments act as if they were fully independent nations without considering the external effects of their policies on citizens living in other member states. Competitiveness is a prime example for such interdependence, for the competitive gain of one party is the loss of another. Reforms improving competitiveness in one country will inevitably deteriorate relative conditions in another. Because policy-makers are ignoring the systemic changes and interdependencies caused by monetary integration, they are unable to adopt coherent strategies for overcoming the crisis. The shortcomings in the way governments have handled the crisis throw a shadow on the future of the euro and European integration. This chapter is an invitation to reconsider one important dimension of the crisis explanation: competitiveness.

Macroeconomic imbalances in the Euro Area are related to competitiveness. At first, blame for the euro crisis was put on public debt and fiscal irresponsibility, in particular on the violations of the Stability and Growth Pact. Greece was the paradigmatic case. But soon a new aspect emerged: in some countries, notably in Ireland and Spain, private debt, granted by commercial banks, had been excessive, and when the economy slowed down banks got into trouble. Governments needed to bail out their banks to preserve financial stability and private debt spilled over into public debt. When the sum of public deficits and private investment exceeds national savings, the gap has to be financed by borrowing from non-residents and this is recorded by national current account deficits. Because it was observed that most crisis countries had accumulated large current account deficits, the emergence of excessive imbalances became the prominent explanation of the crisis.

Deficits increase the stock of outstanding debt; current account deficits increase foreign debt. The sustainability of foreign debt requires, therefore, that the discounted value of all future current account positions be equal to the outstanding value of foreign debt today. Hence, according to standard international macroeconomics, countries with large foreign debt must generate current account surpluses in the future, because that is how they earn the foreign currency necessary to service foreign debt. Following this logic, the European Commission has designed a new policy procedure aimed at reducing what it calls *external* imbalances *within* the Euro Area. It argues that 'nominal exchange rate devaluations are not an available policy tool for the correction of external imbalances in EMU', so that various 'internal devaluation' measures must 'mimic the effects of nominal devaluations by reducing domestic prices and encourage expenditure-switching effects' (European Commission, 2011: 21). In practice this means that austerity is the main tool for correcting 'external' imbalances and promoting net exports from southern states.

Austerity means cutting public expenditure, reducing wages or lowering statutory wage costs by tax and welfare reforms. Whether current account imbalances are corrected by cutting aggregate demand or changing relative costs and prices may depend on where one sees the causes of the imbalances, but in any case different policies must be applied in deficit and surplus countries. Eurosceptics have always insisted that with respect to monetary policy 'one size does not fit all', and even the German chancellor Merkel seems to have been convinced by them.[2] The Walters Critique had argued long ago that in high inflation countries the unified nominal interest rate in monetary union would lower real interest rates below the euro average and thereby fuel local demand booms and reinforce relative price distortions. Mongelli and Wyplosz (2008) have rightly objected that this disequilibrium would be corrected by the negative effects on competitiveness, because rising prices will bring the demand boom to an end. A better explanation for diverging booms and busts in the Euro Area is, therefore, the convergence of nominal interest rates that has followed the creation of monetary union. It has made credit cheap in the south which has caused the over-accumulation and waste of capital resources (Sinn, 2013; Giavazzi and Spaventa, 2010) and the excess demand that has pushed inflation over and above the euro average (Wyplosz, 2013). A variant of this argument focuses on the cost side and especially on unit labour costs and wage bargaining. 'Irresponsible' and 'uncoordinated' price- and wage-setting behaviour is then blamed for the crisis (Flassbeck and Spiecker, 2011). The boom was not sustainable because the deteriorating competitiveness and the slow growth during the crisis have widened budget deficits. However, regardless of what kind of explanation one favours, both approaches share the idea that current account deficits are a good indicator for emerging macroeconomic imbalances within the Euro Area.

The recent reconsideration of current account imbalances between member states of the Euro Area represents a significant shift in political thinking. In the early years of monetary union, rising current account deficits were actually seen as beneficial, because they reflected deeper financial integration and the more efficient allocation of resources across the Euro Area (Blanchard and Giavazzi, 2002).[3] Capital markets could allocate savings to where they would yield the highest return within the single currency area, and the Euro Area was seen as an integrated monetary economy. After 2009, this interpretation was abandoned. Member states were again represented as separate jurisdictions, in which local governments had to minimise risk exposure for local taxpayers rather than max-imise the welfare of all citizens. The resulting lack of political coherence is one of the main causes for the continuous deterioration of the crisis.

The European Commission took the lead in this new interpretation by invent-ing the Macroeconomic Imbalance Procedure (MIP), modelled on the Stability and Growth Pact. It aims 'to prevent and correct the harmful macroeconomic imbalances by identifying potential risks early on'.[4] The so-called surveillance mechanism starts with the Alert Mechanism Report, which uses a scoreboard of indicators to identify where and when an 'in-depth review' is necessary. If the situation is deemed unsustainable, the Excessive Imbalance Procedure sets up rules for member states to remedy the situation. The scoreboard indicators combine stock and flow data to capture deteriorations of imbalances, but the main focus is on correcting current account deficits and external debt caused by distortions in relative prices.[5]

In principle, having a tool for avoiding excessive imbalances is progress in the Euro Area's economic governance. If properly used, it could have helped to prevent the overaccumulation crises in the south. In practice, however, the new procedure's focus on current accounts and external debt is harmful and mislead-ing. Today's adjustment policies in the Euro Area stand in the context of optimum currency area (OCA) theory, which has influenced debates on European monetary union for a long time.[6] This theory interprets a currency area as a fixed exchange rate regime and calculates its benefits as the balance between gains from lower transaction costs and the loss of the exchange rate as an adjustment tool (de Grauwe, 2007). It argues that if a country is hit by a negative shock, say a recession or deteriorating competitiveness, and it has its own currency, it can use the exchange rate to adjust the country's relative prices. This depreciates domestic wealth relative to the rest of the world, but at least the economy can maintain domestic demand and add to it additional demand for exports. By contrast, in a fixed exchange rate regime, one cannot use the exchange rate to devalue; with inflexible prices and wages, a prolonged recession with high and persistent unemployment would follow. Furthermore, the higher external debt levels of a country are, the steeper should be the real depreciations in order to 'put the price watch back' (Sinn, 2013). Hence, giving up the possibility of correcting the exchange rate is costly. The negative effects of regional recessions could be mitigated by a transfer union, where the surplus countries subsidise the deficit countries; but this solution is resisted by voters in the prosperous north of Europe. Hence, prices and wages are the main adjustment tool in the Euro Area, and OCA theory has made labour-market flexibility the principal criterion for judging the optimality of currency areas. In this model, the net benefits of monetary union will become negative if labour markets are rigid and shocks are large. However, the role of financial markets and the central bank is rarely discussed in this context. I will show below that the existence of a single lender of last resort makes monetary union much more robust than an ordinary fixed exchange rate regime.

No doubt, macroeconomic imbalances must be corrected. The question is how this can be done with minimal welfare losses. If current accounts are the target, austerity is inevitable because 'excessive' domestic expenditure must be cut back. However, the burden of such welfare losses depends on who is doing the adjustment. Member states with current account surpluses favour asymmetric adjustment, where the brunt of the correction must be borne by 'non-competitive' deficit countries, while they themselves can continue with their 'competitive' performance as before. Of course, the reduction of deficits in the south is incompatible with the maintenance of surpluses in the north, but few policy-makers seem to notice the inconsistency of their demands. By contrast, deficit countries seek more symmetric solutions, where surplus countries increase spending on goods from deficit countries, hoping thereby to soften the adjustment pain. Sinn (2013: 2) has summarised the argument by saying that 'Europe needs austerity in the south and inflationary growth in the north to improve the competitiveness of the south and to structurally improve the current account imbalances'. Similarly, Flassbeck and Spiecker (2011: 186) have argued that

> wages in Germany have to rise for a considerable amount of time by more than is warranted by the traditional wage rule (national productivity growth plus the common inflation target) and the Southern European countries must pursue the opposite strategy.

While leaning towards asymmetry in the official policy documents submitted for approval by the Council, the European Commission has favoured in its analytic studies a more balanced approach.[7] However, whether symmetric or asymmetric and whether based on aggregate demand or relative prices, most policy recommendations end up with proposing the correction of member states' current accounts.

The focus on current accounts implies that national investment must be financed by national savings. There is no good reason for such a proposal in a currency union. It violates the basic principles of a single market and creates financial fragmentation. The prevailing policy consensus has the unintended consequence of unravelling the European edifice. Furthermore, balancing current accounts between member states also means that adjustment must work through the tradable goods sector. A real depreciation shifts the competitive advantage in favour of exports, so that the trade balance improves. When countries have their own currencies, a nominal devaluation can support adjustment at least in the short run, but we know from a long history of adjustments in the global and European economies that such policies often cause substantial welfare losses. Nominal devaluations seem initially less painful, but over time they will import inflation, which will annihilate the competitive cost advantage. By contrast, shifting relative prices in favour of tradable goods without adjusting nominal exchange rates may be initially more painful, but might be more sustainable in the long run. Europe's experience with flexible exchange rates from the 1970s to the 1990s has shown that exchange rate flexibility is not compatible with a fully integrated internal market in Europe (Collignon and Schwarzer, 2003; Padoa-Schioppa, 1987). Furthermore, a nominal devaluation will reduce the value of domestic assets, liabilities and income and that makes residents poorer. Hence, it is not surprising that southern member states resist leaving the euro as this would reduce their welfare.

However, if prices are not flexible and devaluations are ruled out, adjustment seems impossible and monetary union may be doomed. Referring to fixed exchange rate systems like Bretton Woods, Flassbeck and Spiecker (2011: 181) have argued:

> persistent divergences of inflation rates inside the monetary union are fatal because the differences in the cost and price level among the member countries accumulate over time and produce real exchange rate appreciation and depreciation, or, in other words, unsustainable over- and undervaluation for currencies that no longer exist.

Sinn and Wollmershaeuser (2011) also compare the Euro Area with the fixed exchange rate system of Bretton Woods and then talk of nonexistent currencies, namely 'German' and 'Irish euros'. This is odd. Why should anyone bother about ghost currencies that no longer exist? Clearly, there is a theoretical inconsistency in these models.

I will now argue that a currency area is not a fixed exchange rate arrangement and imbalances between members of the same currency union must not be treated like 'external' imbalances in international economics. Shifting incentives in favour of exports is less important in a monetary union than in international economics, because growth in the non-tradable sector can compensate some of the welfare losses. Instead, the primary economic policy objective must be balanced growth as already postulated in the Treaty on the European Union, Article 3.3. Investment is a crucial variable in this context and a better indicator for imbalances is the flow of funds between institutional sectors of the Euro Area.

Fallacies in the debate on macroeconomic imbalances in the Euro Area

It would be a mistake to believe that because it emerged from the European Monetary System where exchange rates were fixed but adjustable, European monetary union is nothing else but a permanent locking of national currencies to a common currency. This view, widespread as it is, does not take into account how a monetary union works. I will therefore first review how a currency area functions and then discuss the role of the often neglected non-tradable sector, before drawing the conclusions for the macroeconomic adjustment programs in the Euro Area.

Monetary union as a payment union

A currency area is a payment union. It is defined as the territory where credit contracts can be enforced and extinguished by paying the legally defined and generally accepted currency.[8] In other words, everyone has to use the same currency for making payments. The Euro Area functions exactly like any other currency area. When European monetary union started on 1 January 1999, the euro became legal tender in the participating member states (Treaty of the European Union (TEU), Art. 3.4). Previously existing monetary laws in member states were abrogated and the European Central Bank (ECB) was set up as the directive organ and head office for the conduct of monetary policy. The existing national central banks (NCB) were merged with the ECB to form the Eurosystem.[9]

The central bank is the bank of banks. Money, i.e. legal tender, is created by the central bank when it is granting credit to the domestic banking system or buying foreign assets. The central bank's assets are therefore claims against domestic and foreign economies. Central bank money is credited to the accounts in which commercial banks hold their reserves with the central bank; money is therefore a *liability* by the central bank, but also a claim (an *asset*) by banks[10] on the central bank. Against their reserve holdings, banks can also draw banknotes which they put into circulation among their clients, but this fact is analytically less interesting and we can concentrate our discussion on central bank money. Thus, in the Euro Area, domestic money, i.e. the currency of the currency area, is the liability of the Eurosystem.[11] Contrary to the assumption of ghost-currencies, there is no 'national' euro. Money proper is central bank money, also called narrow money. *Broad money* is defined as currency and bank deposits held by non-financial agents (corporations and households). It consists essentially of liabilities of commercial banks. Commercial banks hold reserves of central bank money in accordance with legal requirements (minimum reserves) and their own liquidity preferences, and they create broad money when they give credit to other economic sectors. When economic agents make payments in the Euro Area, they transfer these liabilities to each other.[12]

By contrast, payments outside the currency area are made in *foreign* currency. Foreign currency cannot be created by the domestic central bank. The money readily available for making foreign payments consists therefore of *reserve assets* held by the central bank in foreign currency.[13] As the name indicates, these reserves are recorded as assets in the central bank's balance sheet. Thus, there is a clear categorical distinction between domestic money (a *liability*) and international money (an *asset*). It follows that a currency area is defined by the fact that it has a central bank whose liabilities serve for making payments and extinguishing debt. The abrogation of national monetary laws has lifted the distinction of monetary jurisdictions and turned the Euro Area into an 'economic country'. To analyse monetary transactions between residents of different member states in the Euro Area as if they took place between independent 'foreign' countries is therefore no longer appropriate.[14] Within a monetary union, trans-border payments have the same status as payments within a nation-state.

Intra-currency area payments

The distinction between payments within the monetary union and the rest of the world (RoW) can be shown by a stylised example.[15] Let us assume our currency area consists of only two countries, Germany and Italy. It operates through the Eurosystem, in which the European Central Bank (ECB) is integrated with national central banks (the Bundesbank and the Banca d'Italia). The ECB decides on monetary policy and manages the foreign reserve assets for the union. National central banks act as intermediaries that hold the deposit accounts of commercial banks[16] and have a net claim on the ECB's reserve assets.[17] Now imagine someone in Italy imports goods from Germany for an amount of €120.[18] The transaction is settled in domestic currency through the banking system. The importer's local bank makes a transfer to the exporter's bank through the payment system of the Eurosystem: the Italian bank's account with the Banca d'Italia is debited by €120, while the German bank's account with the Bundesbank is credited by the same amount.[19] Hence, the claims of the German economy on the Eurosystem increase by €120 and the net claims of Italy decline as a result of debiting the Banca d'Italia accounts. For Germany, the reserve asset claim on the ECB increases and as a balancing item bank deposits (i.e. the broad money component held in German banks) increase as well; by contrast, in Italy, the claim by Banca d'Italia on the ECB is reduced and so is local money supply.[20] However, the transaction is neutral for the Eurosystem as a whole; the overall amount of foreign reserve assets and money supply does not change. See Table 1.1. This is how payments are made within a currency area.

Table 1.1 Intra-Euro Area payments

Bundesbank opening balance sheet

Assets		Liabilities	
Net claim on ECB (reserve asset)	200	Banknotes	1,000
Domestic assets (claims on German residents)	950	Bank deposits	150
Total	1,150	Total	1,150

Banca d'Italia opening balance sheet

Assets		Liabilities	
Net claim on ECB (reserve asset)	200	Banknotes	600
Domestic assets (claims on Italian residents)	550	Bank deposits	150
Total	750	Total	750

Eurosystem opening balance sheet

Assets		Liabilities	
Net claim by ECB (reserve asset)	400	Banknotes	1,600
Domestic assets (claims on Italian residents)	1,500	Bank deposits	300
Total	1,900	Total	1,900

Balance of payments

Germany

	credit	debit
Current account goods	120	
Financial account reserve asset		120

Italy

	credit	debit
Current account goods		120
Financial account reserve asset	120	

Bundesbank closing balance sheet

Assets		Liabilities	
Net claim on ECB (reserve asset)	320	Banknotes	1,000
Domestic assets (claims on German residents)	950	Bank deposits	270
Total	1,270	Total	1,270

Banca d'Italia closing balance sheet

Assets		Liabilities	
Net claim on ECB (reserve asset)	80	Banknotes	600
Domestic assets (claims on Italian residents)	550	Bank deposits	30
Total	630	Total	630

Eurosystem closing balance sheet

Assets		Liabilities	
Net claim by ECB (reserve asset)	400	Banknotes	1,600
Domestic assets (claims on Italian residents)	1,500	Bank deposits	300
Total	1,900	Total	1,900

Source: Bundesbank, Banca d'Italia, ECB.

Inter-currency area payments

Next, we look at international payments into a different currency area. Assume Germany exports goods worth €150 to the United Kingdom. The transaction is settled in pounds sterling (GBP), which implies that the German exporter sells his foreign exchange receipts to his German bank and his account is credited €150. The bank sells now the foreign currency to the Eurosystem and its account with the Bundesbank is credited by the equivalent amount. Thus, the ECB increases its reserve assets and the account of the Bundesbank with the ECB is credited by €150. Net claims by Germany on the ECB have increased and so has broad money supply in Germany. Nothing has changed in Italy, but for the Euro Area as a whole reserve assets and money supply have increased. See Table 1.2. Of course, a net import from the rest of the world into the Euro Area would have the opposite effect of reducing reserve assets and money supply, assuming that the ECB does not sterilise the variations in reserve assets. However, if the ECB had reasons to be concerned about price stability, it would tighten monetary policy by selling domestic assets equivalent to the foreign assets it bought. In that case, monetary tightening would negatively affect growth in the non-exporting member states. For our argument here we can assume that prices remain stable and the ECB accommodates the growth-induced demand for liquidity. Export-led growth in Germany is then compatible with relative stagnation in Italy.

This analysis throws an interesting light on the role of balance of payments for the Euro Area: if Germany is the export champion into the rest of the world, it earns the foreign currency which other net importers in the Euro Area can spend without running into balance of payment crises. This is clearly a win–win situation, for it allows the efficient allocation of resources (buying cheaply abroad) in deficit economies, while it increases net financial wealth in surplus countries. Hence, by lifting the foreign exchange constraint on deficit countries, European monetary union is trade-creating in the global economy. These benefits are a major reason why small countries have an interest in joining and staying in the monetary union. One may argue, however, that the export strength of Germany is keeping the euro-exchange rate against the rest of the world higher than is advantageous for the deficit countries. However, that raises again the question of how adjustment within the Euro Area affects member states.

This analysis does not imply that member states in the currency area are able to run deficits without constraints. If regional economic growth slows down below the rate at which the debt service can be assured, the risk of debt defaults increases rapidly. Once the solvency of debtors in stagnating regions is in doubt, financial markets will massively shorten their exposure to private and public debtors residing in these states. The resulting financial outflow will aggravate the problems of economic growth and cause a negative feedback loop. Thus, fundamental factors and market expectations may mutually reinforce each other and political conflicts will further enlarge these effects. There is evidence that in the euro crisis financial markets have responded more to political news and

Table 1.2 Outside Euro Area payments

Bundesbank opening balance sheet

Assets		Liabilities	
Net claim on ECB (reserve asset)	200	Banknotes	1,000
Domestic assets	950	Bank deposits	150
(claims on German residents)			
Total	1,150	Total	1,150

Banca d'Italia opening balance sheet

Assets		Liabilities	
Net claim on ECB (reserve asset)	200	Banknotes	600
Domestic assets	550	Bank deposits	150
(claims on Italian residents)			
Total	750	Total	750

Eurosystem opening balance sheet

Assets		Liabilities	
Net claim by ECB (reserve asset)	400	Banknotes	1,600
Domestic assets	1,500	Bank deposits	300
(claims on Italian residents)			
Total	1,900	Total	1,900

Balance of payments

Germany

	credit	debit
Current account goods	150	
Financial account reserve assets		150

Italy

	credit	debit
Current account goods		0
Financial account reserve assets		0

Bundesbank closing balance sheet

Assets		Liabilities	
Net claim on ECB (reserve asset)	350	Banknotes	1,000
Domestic assets	950	Bank deposits	300
(claims on German residents)			
Total	1,300	Total	1,300

Banca d'Italia closing balance sheet

Assets		Liabilities	
Net claim on ECB (reserve asset)	200	Banknotes	600
Domestic assets	550	Bank deposits	150
(claims on Italian residents)			
Total	750	Total	750

Eurosystem closing balance sheet

Assets		Liabilities	
Net claim by ECB (reserve asset)	550	Banknotes	1,600
Domestic assets	1,500	Bank deposits	450
(claims on Italian residents)			
Total	2,050	Total	2,050

Source: Bundesbank, Banca d'Italia, ECB.

uncertainties than to economic fundamentals (Collignon *et al.*, 2013). This fact points at the need to reform the governance of the Euro Area, but it says little about the need for adjustment within a currency area.

The role of the non-tradable sector

The truth is that monetary union provides its own adjustment mechanism, which is robust in economic terms, but likely to create political problems. This mechanism is often overlooked in the literature and in public policy discussions. As we have seen in Table 1.1, the effect of a regional current account deficit without a compensating capital inflow is an outflow of money from the deficit into the surplus area. *Ceteris paribus*, this reduction in money balances will endogenously generate macroeconomic adjustment. The money outflow will depress demand and reduce prices and wages in the deficit economy; the inflow of money into the surplus economy is stimulating growth there.[21] Thus, current account imbalances will not last forever, although the adjustment process may be slow. This built-in adjustment mechanism is at work in all currency areas, whether nation-states or monetary unions, but not in fixed exchange rate systems. This is precisely why multi-currency systems, contrary to monetary unions, need the 'exchange rate instrument' of nominal devaluations, while currency unions do not.

Yet, this built-in adjustment mechanism is not pleasant. It causes what Olivier Blanchard once called 'rotating slumps' (Blanchard, 2006). These slumps may have disruptive social consequences, which, given that member states retain authority for policies, may lead to anti-European backlashes.[22] Furthermore, recessions in member states will raise the probability of the regional cumulation of debt defaults. The conventional policy response is to blame deficit countries and to impose internal adjustment policies on them; but austerity and drastic real exchange rate depreciations through lower wages are unlikely to improve regional growth at least in the short and medium run. Germany, to take a prominent example, has gone through nearly a decade of slow growth when pursuing such adjustment strategy. The European Commission (2012a: 3) has acknowledged that European adjustment policies have weakened economic growth, but it claims that 'progress in re-balancing will open up the way for growth and convergence'. In other words, adjustment is painful, but once the 'external' balance is restored, growth will return.

We now know that this policy view is extremely costly in welfare terms. The medicine could actually kill the patient.[23] The reduction in wages and in private and public spending will in the short run reduce effective demand below the growth potential, and in the long run it will slow down the potential growth rates themselves, because there will be more bankruptcies, less investment and rising unemployment.[24] All this makes servicing debt more difficult. If the response to increasing default risks is more austerity, the economy will collapse in a negative feedback loop, as we have witnessed in Greece. The question is whether other policy options are available. This is where the distinction between domestic and foreign currency becomes crucial. If a currency area runs out of foreign reserves, its external debt will become unsustainable and a real devaluation must shift the incentives toward generating net exports and attracting foreign investment. In monetary union, this is certainly one policy option, but not the only one. What is needed is generating economic growth out of which the debt can be serviced and it does not matter whether it originates in the tradable or non-tradable sector. An alternative to 'internal adjustment' is therefore to stimulate internal demand in the non-tradable sector. I will now show that economic growth in member states can be sustained by investment in the non-tradable sector without risk for price stability.

Because aggregate demand is related to the growth of money supply, the effects of stimulating demand in the non-tradable sector can be shown by including the non-tradable sector into Table 1.1. By definition, this sector does not affect the balance of payments. For simplicity, we assume that the Italian government borrows from commercial banks to finance local services. Commercial banks then need to refinance themselves by obtaining liquidity from Banca d'Italia. Let this demand for increased central bank money be €120. Referring back to Table 1.1, we see that domestic assets in Banca d'Italia's balance sheet will increase from €550 to €670 and bank deposits will grow by the same amount from 30 to 150. *Ceteris paribus*, domestic assets, as shown by the integrated balance sheet of the Eurosystem, increase also by €120 and bank deposits in the Euro Area go up to €420.

So far, this is a standard model of expansionary monetary policy. However, let us assume that monetary policy is committed to price stability. As in the case of a current account surplus with the rest of the world, the central bank has to decide whether it is willing to accommodate the increase in money supply. If it considers this to be incompatible with price stability, it will raise interest rates and credit demand will slow down. Given that public spending is less sensitive to interest rates than private credit demand, we now assume that domestic assets and bank deposits will fall in Germany by the same amount (€120) as they have increased in Italy, so that Euro Area money supply and prices remain constant over the medium term. In this case the combined effect of an Italian trade deficit plus stimulus in the non-tradable sector increases bank deposits in Italy to €150 (see Table 1.3) and leaves Germany with bank deposits of €150, which was exactly the original position in the balance sheets of Banca d'Italia and the Bundesbank shown in Table 1.1. Of course, in reality the adjustment may not be as symmetric as in our example, but the point is to show that, in principle, it is possible to compensate the depressive features of negative regional trade balances by stimulating demand in the non-tradable sector without jeopardising price stability and the sustainability of debt in deficit countries of monetary union.

For economists who believe that Italy and Germany are still separate economies – as they were until 1999 – this may look like voodoo economics. How can a country accumulate foreign debt without paying it back by future surpluses? The miracle is possible because the debt is repaid not in foreign, but in domestic currency available anywhere in the Euro Area. The sustainability is not

Table 1.3 Balance sheet position after non-tradable credit expansion in Italy

1. Ater the initial credit expansion

Bundesbank balance sheet

Assets		Liabilities	
Net claim on ECB (reserve asset)	320	Banknotes	1,000
Domestic assets	950	Bank deposits	270
(claims on German residents)			
Total	1,270	Total	1,270

Banca d'Italia balance sheet

Assets		Liabilities	
Net claim on ECB (reserve asset)	80	Banknotes	600
Domestic assets	670	Bank deposits	150
(claims on Italian residents)			
Total	750	Total	750

Eurosystem closing balance sheet

Assets		Liabilities	
Net claim by ECB (reserve asset)	400	Banknotes	1,600
Domestic assets	1,620	Bank deposits	420
(claims on Italian residents)			
Total	2,020	Total	2,020

2. After tightening money supply

Bundesbank balance sheet

Assets		Liabilities	
Net claim on ECB (reserve asset)	320	Banknotes	1,000
Domestic assets	830	Bank deposits	150
(claims on German residents)			
Total	1,150	Total	1,150

Banca d'Italia balance sheet

Assets		Liabilities	
Net claim on ECB (reserve asset)	80	Banknotes	600
Domestic assets	670	Bank deposits	150
(claims on Italian residents)			
Total	750	Total	750

Eurosystem closing balance sheet

Assets		Liabilities	
Net claim by ECB (reserve asset)	400	Banknotes	1,600
Domestic assets	1,500	Bank deposits	300
(claims on Italian residents)			
Total	1,900	Total	1,900

Source: Bundesbank, Banca d'Italia, ECB.

assured by gaining sufficient foreign currency, but by each debtor fulfilling the solvency constraint whereby future discounted income matches the outstanding debt. In other words, debtors are responsible for their liabilities not as a community but as individual borrowers. This is a fundamental difference between a monetary union and a fixed exchange rate system. If a currency area did not work like an integrated payment union in this way, no nation-state would ever have survived. Italy's north and south would have separated, the United Kingdom would have split into England and Scotland, and Bavaria would have introduced its own currency.

A common objection to this view is that nation-states and federations are sustained by the solidarity of fiscal transfers, which citizens are willing to pay within their nation, but not for others. Yet, the cohesive power of solidarity quickly fades when economic benefits are in doubt, as one can witness in Flanders, Lombardy, Scotland, Catalonia or Bavaria. More importantly, as Fatás (1998) has shown, the stabilising effects of automatic interregional transfers are grossly overvalued. If this is so, the monetary adjustment mechanism explains how the payment union is sustained.

Implications for economic adjustment

We can now sum up how macroeconomic imbalances work out in a monetary union: a current account deficit within the currency area shifts the distribution of wealth and money supply from the net importer to the net exporter, but does not affect macroeconomic aggregates of the area. The distributional effects are not banal: surplus countries increase their financial net wealth, while deficits countries become financially poorer – although they may gain from the more efficient allocation of resources and capital that over time could narrow the gap between high- and low-income countries. Nevertheless, the monetary union is robust, because deficit countries cannot run out of reserves. Foreign reserves are irrelevant for the transactions between member states. For domestic transactions, money balances are needed and they are obtained either by borrowing from commercial banks in the surplus countries, or from the Eurosystem, which guarantees equal access to liquidity for all solvent banks in the Euro Area. As long as this is compatible with the money supply policies, the outcome is Pareto optimal; if the ECB tightens monetary policy in order to preserve price stability, export-oriented economies have a comparative advantage. Hence, the fragility of the Euro Area is not in the economics, but in the politics of monetary union: distributional conflicts may undermine the popular acceptance of the euro and the policies by which it is ruled.

While one may agree that current account deficits are irrelevant for the payment mechanism within the monetary union, one could argue that the accumulation of large 'foreign' debt positions will become problematic. Indeed, a large negative net international investment position, which reflects the accumulation of past current account deficits, may not be sustainable. However, liabilities within the Euro Area are not 'foreign' debt and should not be counted as a component of the international investment position. We have seen that intra-Euro Area deficits do *not* build up *external* indebtedness, because they are domestic borrowings, which are repaid by transferring domestic money. The only international investment position that matters is the foreign debt of the Euro Area. This makes a huge difference for the adjustment mechanisms.

The overall purpose of adjustment within a currency area is to guarantee the stability of the financial system. Intertemporal solvency requires that the discounted value of future income is equal to today's debt. Domestic debt solvency requires income in domestic currency, while liabilities to the rest of the world must be paid in foreign currency. Hence, intra-Euro Area debt is settled by drawing on deposits in local banks and it makes no difference for the sustainability of domestic currency debt *where* the source of future domestic income is located.[25] Domestic income may be generated by exporting to other member states (improving the trade balance) or by economic growth originating in the non-tradable sector. But as long as the domestic solvency constraint is met, there is no need to switch expenditure from the non-tradable to tradable goods sectors. For example, Italy may have a fast growing non-tradable service sector, which imports capital equipment from Germany. If this investment is financed by bank credit, it will at first increase money supply in Italy, while the payments to German suppliers will reduce money holdings in Italy again. Thus, the credit-financed investment in the non-tradable sector can compensate the outflow of money balances from the deficit country. As long as profits in the non-tradable sector are sufficient to service the debt, solvency is assured.

In aggregate, this logic requires that the economic growth rate in the region is larger or equal to the average interest rate in order to fulfil the solvency constraint. But this means also that, contrary to the claims by new mainstream orthodoxy, *one cannot judge competitiveness by developments in the tradable sector alone*. Instead, competitiveness must be measured by the overall profitability of the national capital stock, because that determines whether the region is able to attract new investment, and whether the contracted credit liabilities are sustainable. How to use this criterion for assessing competitiveness empirically will be shown in the next chapter. Here, we need to insist that balance of payment accounting is not the appropriate instrument for detecting imbalances in the Euro Area. The proper tool for analysing payment flows in a monetary union is flow of funds analysis which gives a more differentiated picture of macroeconomic imbalances in the Euro Area. By using flow of funds analysis we will also discover that simply comparing returns to capital is not sufficient for a full picture of competitiveness.

Flow of funds in European monetary union

Flow of funds analysis measures payment flows across the economy and presents the financial assets and liabilities of all institutional sectors in the Euro Area, i.e. households, financial and non-financial corporations (NFCs), government and the rest of the world. Similar to profit and loss, cash flow and balance sheet statements in business accounting, flow of funds accounts provide a coherent and integrated picture of the financial wealth of an economy and its variations. They are tracking funds as they move from sectors that serve as sources of capital, through intermediaries (such as banks, mutual funds and pension funds), to sectors that use the capital to acquire physical and financial assets (Teplin, 2001).Because changes in competitiveness will inevitably affect payments, the flow of funds is a useful tool for analysing imbalances in the Euro Area.

The conceptual framework

One distinguishes between economic and financial accounts. The *economic accounts* record 'real' economy transactions in accordance with the European System of Accounts (ESA)[26] and show how various categories of income (GDP) are first allocated as primary income to labour and property (national income) and then reallocated through the secondary distribution of transfer payments. Disposable income (retained earnings for the corporate sector) is either spent on consumption and investment or saved and lent to other agents, which means savings are used to purchase financial assets. The *financial accounts*, on the other hand, are a picture of the financial wealth and record the balance sheet positions of assets and liabilities in the different sectors and their variations over a period of time. These variations are split into *changes due to transactions* which reflect the balance of the economic accounts, and *other changes* which represent write-offs or changes in values of assets and liabilities. The financial transactions indicate, therefore, how the financial net wealth of institutional sectors and economies change. The link between the economic and financial accounts is the *capital account*.

Because transactions are recorded as net purchases (or net sales) at the current market prices, exchanges *within* a sector – for example, the sale of equities by one corporation and the corresponding purchase by another corporation – cancel each other out and do not show up in the sectoral accounts. Transactions *between* sectors, on the other hand – such as the sale of equities by a household to a mutual fund or the purchase of government bonds by households or banks – are recorded as a negative value for the sector selling the instrument and a positive value for the sector purchasing the instrument (Teplin, 2001: 433). For the same reason, transactions within the same aggregate sector but between different national sectors, say between Italian and German non-financial corporations, may appear as imbalances in national accounts, but they cancel out in the Euro aggregate. Hence, nationally disaggregated flow of funds statistics can reveal macroeconomic imbalances not only with respect to borrowing or lending between different member states (i.e. current account positions), but also between institutional sectors within the currency area. However, most importantly, flow of funds accounts present a fully integrated picture of an economy, because the lending of one sector must have a borrower in another sector as its counterpart. To clarify the principles, we will first concentrate on the Euro Area as a whole.

The transaction balances between institutional sectors are easily derived from the standard national income identity, whereby income reflects expenditure on consumption, investment and net exports:

$$Y = C + I + X - M$$

Amalgamating first for simplicity the financial and non-financial corporate sector, we show in Table 1.4 how the four institutional sectors of the economy interact.[27] The bottom line is the sum of all sectors of the economy. Y_1 is the factor income earned by households (wages, rents, etc.). Y_2 stands for corporate profits plus rent, Y_3 for the same by government enterprises. After the generation of primary income by the factors of production, income is redistributed between sectors by the payment of transfers (T), which increases or reduces disposable income in the sectors. For example, the corporate sector pays social security contributions, which benefit households. Obviously, the sum of all transfers is zero. C_1 and C_3 are consumer expenditure by households and government and the difference between income and consumption is gross savings. The Is reflect investment in the different sectors, but usually the corporate sector is driving investment.

Reading across the rows of Table 1.4, it is apparent that individual sectors may have a surplus or deficit of savings over investment. In the flow of funds statistics of the European Union the financial surplus/deficit is called net lending (+) or net borrowing (−) of the different sectors. Because saving is income minus consumption, the financial balance of a sector is in surplus if its savings exceed investment. Wealth owners will then acquire financial assets (claims on other sectors or cash) instead of real resources for productive purposes.[28] The mirror image is net borrowing (incurring net financial liabilities) by a sector where investment exceeds savings. However, for the economy as a whole, domestic and foreign savings must be equal to total investment.

The transactions in the fourth sector are entered from the point of view of the rest of the world, and not from the point of view of the domestic economy. $(Y_4 + T_4)$ is income and transfers claimed by the rest of the world, while $(X - M)$ is net exports. Thus, if the foreign sector is in surplus $(F_4 > 0)$, the domestic economy must make payments to the rest of the world that are larger than the earnings from net exports; thus, the rest of the world is lending and the economy's current account balance is in deficit. In that case, part of GDP will be owned by non-residents. On the other hand, if the trade balance is positive and few external liabilities exist $(F_4 < 0)$, the domestic economy is lending to the rest of the world and building up financial claims against non-residents. This is why current accounts in surplus are often associated with high competitiveness.

Financial flows in the Euro Area

Standard textbooks assume that households' revenue exceeds their expenditure, so that they are net lenders to the rest of the economy. Non-financial corporations are

Table 1.4 Basic accounting identities of national income

	Income	Transfers (net)	Consumption	Investment	Trade balance	= Financial surplus/deficit
Households	Y_1	$+T_1$	$-C_1$	$-I_1$		$= F_1$
Corporate sector	Y_2	$+T_2$		$-I_2$		$= F_2$
Government	Y_3	$+T_3$	$-C_3$	$-I_3$		$= F_3$
Rest of the world	Y_4	$+T_4$		$-I_4$	$-X+M$	$= F_4$
Total	Y	0	$-C$	$-I$	$-X+M$	0

supposed to be borrowers because they do not cover their investment out of cash flow. They must therefore finance at least part of their investment by borrowing from other sectors. Financial corporations are intermediaries which lend out the resources they borrow. Ideally, the government and the external sector are in balance. However this is rarely the case. In Europe, governments usually borrow (i.e. run deficits), and the Euro Area in aggregate has at times been a lender and at others a borrower vis-à-vis the rest of the world.

Figure 1.1 shows the evolution of the financial surplus/deficit for the four domestic sectors of the Euro Area and for the rest of the world.[29] Before the crisis, balances were relatively stable. When the so-called dot.com bubble in the IT sector burst and the attacks of September 11, 2001 destabilised financial markets worldwide, monetary policy became very accommodating. However, the excess liquidity then generated the next credit boom which crashed in 2007–2008. During that early easy money period, euro households were saving less and many borrowed to invest in the real estate boom, especially in the south. Non-financial corporations, which had previously cut down on their investment, now started to borrow again. By contrast, governments reduced their deficits, although arguably not enough to bring their debt levels significantly down.

The global financial crisis started with liquidity problems at Bear Sterns in August 2007 and fully erupted with the Lehman bankruptcy in September 2008. After this event, all economic agents changed their behaviour. In Europe, house-holds' savings increased strongly, reflecting their risk-averse behaviour in a climate of general uncertainty. Companies stopped borrowing instead of invest-ing their retained earnings. In 2010, non-financial corporations even became net lenders, which means they used their profits to repay debt and deleverage their balance sheets. Governments were negatively affected by the sudden drop of GDP in the crisis; the associated loss of revenue increased budget deficits, but this fact also stabilised the euro economy because governments borrowed the excess savings from households and NFCs. After the election of a new govern-ment in Greece in late 2009, the sovereign debt crisis pushed policy-makers in the Euro Area into precipitated fiscal consolidation. With all the main domestic sectors – households, corporations, governments – increasing their savings and no one borrowing, the Euro Area fell into its second recession which translated into a prolonged depression in the southern member states. The external accounts of the Euro Area with the rest of the world (RoW) had remained largely in balance before the euro crisis, but now they turned into surplus. Given the diffi-cult international environment, borrowing by non-residents also remained slug-gish so that foreign investment presented few alternative outlets for domestic euro savings. Instead, the combined excess savings of households, corporations and governments were used to reduce outstanding domestic and foreign liabil-ities. This fact may have helped to improve the net international investment position of the Euro Area, but when the corporate sector does not invest in the formation of domestic capital, economic growth will come to a halt (Ahearne and Wolff, 2012). The question is then why did the non-financial corporations in the Euro Area stop investing and borrowing from the other sectors?

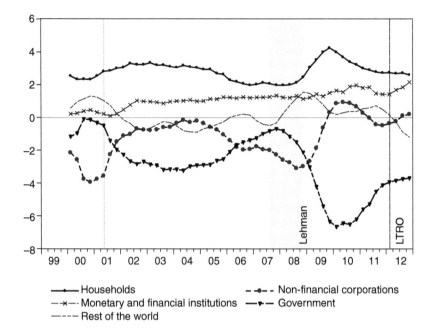

Figure 1.1 Gross lending (+)/net borrowing (−) by institutional sector, four quarters cumulated sum (% of GDP) (source: Eurostat).

Competitiveness and investment

The classic argument for explaining investment is that companies invest in order to make a profit. They allocate funds to those projects which yield the highest return. Thus, the capacity to earn high returns to capital reflects high competitiveness. However, at the time a firm makes the decision to invest, the future returns are uncertain. The larger the chance that the future returns will be different from what is expected, the larger the risk. If firms are risk averse, higher returns may not automatically guarantee higher investment, employment and growth. Additional funds will only be invested, if the return to capital exceeds the cost of capital plus the risk premium. Companies have the choice of borrowing and buying real resources for productive purposes or of using their cash flow for redeeming liabilities or acquiring financial assets (including cash holdings). A comprehensive concept of competitiveness must take the effects of risk on corporate decisions into account.[30]

Figure 1.2 shows the risk–return trade-off in a simple stylised form.[31] The steepness of the trade-off curve indicates the degree of risk averseness. The return for riskless assets at the intercept of the required return axis reflects liquidity preference, because by definition liquid assets (money) are the least risky assets. The risk premium is the difference between this risk-free required

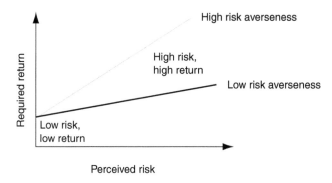

Figure 1.2 The risk–return dilemma.

return and point on the trade-off curve. If the expected return on capital is below the trade-off curve, no investment will be forthcoming. Thus, if the perceived risk in the firm's environment increases, or if risk averseness or liquidity preference increases, higher returns to capital are required in order to cover the higher risk premium. If the firm wants to remain competitive, i.e. maintain the firm's share in the economy's long-term growth, it must increase the return to capital. The degree of uncertainty, in the environment within which firms are operating, is then an essential part of competitiveness.

In a financial crisis, the sudden drop in aggregate demand and the increased perception of risk are raising the preference for holding wealth in liquid form rather than investing it in resources. The crisis is therefore a cause and not only the effect of lower competitiveness. With persistent uncertainty, risk-averse entrepreneurs will also seek to reduce outstanding liabilities. This deleveraging process will become the dominant corporate strategy in financial crises, because the value of assets is deteriorating while liabilities are nominally fixed, so that corporate equity will be reduced (Koo, 2002). Paying back debt will then help to restore shareholders' wealth, but it may have the unintended aggregate consequence of lower output and employment.

This places the competitiveness issue into a new context: firms may not invest because their costs are too high and profits too low (see Chapter 2), but also because they operate in an environment that is too uncertain to justify spending money on capital accumulation. Of course, higher risks require higher returns on capital in order to compensate for the potential losses, but at these high returns there are usually fewer investment opportunities available. Furthermore, if uncertainty is very high, it may practically be impossible to compensate the risk premium for investment by raising profits in the corporate sector.[32]

How can an economy become more competitive? Our analysis says that firms should increase their returns and policies should reduce uncertainty. In order to improve profits, firms could increase their gross operating surplus by cutting wages, but from Table 1.4 it is clear that this would be counterproductive when the reduction in Y_1 is not fully compensated by an increase in Y_2, which may result from the fact that households have less income to spend and do not reduce savings sufficiently to keep consumption stable. In that case, compensating public policies could substitute for the wage reduction by increasing public consumption and a fiscal stimulus would increase corporate profitability. Aggregate income would be stabilised as private consumption would be shifted to public consumption. However, this raises distributional issues for the tax burden and its consequences for investment.

Other than cutting wages, paying lower transfers could also increase profits in the corporate sector. Structural reforms in the system of secondary income transfers can shift net benefits from households to corporations and thereby improve competitiveness. Such reforms are typically associated with the Hartz IV reforms in Germany (see Dullien in Chapter 8 of this book). However, while wages and gross operating surplus are key variables for the primary distribution of income, one should not forget that the cost of capital, and in particular interest liabilities, needs to be serviced out of current cash flow. The balance of primary income, which takes into account the rental cost of capital, or retained earnings, which are a measure corporate income after the secondary redistribution, are therefore better indicators for corporate profitability.

Which of these two dimensions, low profits or high uncertainty, provides a better explanation for Europe's lack of competitiveness and anaemic corporate investment performance? Flow of fund analysis allows us to detect the effects of corporate strategies and their consequences for other sectors. Figure 1.3 shows corporate incomes and savings in the Euro Area as a percentage of GDP. The gross operating surplus has risen during the pre-crisis boom, but it fell in the crisis. In 2010 it improved, reaching levels of the early 2000s, but the austerity policy since 2011 has again reduced net income for Europe's non-financial corporations. Nevertheless, these developments were in part corrected by the strong reduction in the cost of capital and especially the reduction in interest payable, although the euro crisis has pushed the cost of capital up again. As a result, corporate primary income is now back to the level, where it was before the crisis. Furthermore, tax and social transfer payments have also come down during the crisis, so that retained earnings of NFCs, which are a good measure of corporate cash flow, are now higher than they were before the Lehman shock. Yet, despite this improved financial situation, companies are not investing. Even the unconventional monetary policies (long-term refinancing operation: LTRO) at the end of 2011/early 2012, which have responded to the high liquidity preference of banks and other economic agents, did not stimulate demand for investment. The investment ratio has fallen after Lehman by three percentage points of GDP and although it has regained one point, it is still well below pre-crisis levels. Hence, net borrowing in the corporate sector has not stopped because of insufficient profits or lack of competitiveness, but because in the prevailing environment of crisis and uncertainty firms have deliberately used their cash flow to pay back debt. The Euro Area is caught in a balance sheet recession.[33] Hence, Europe's crisis is less a consequence of structural weaknesses than of uncertain expectations

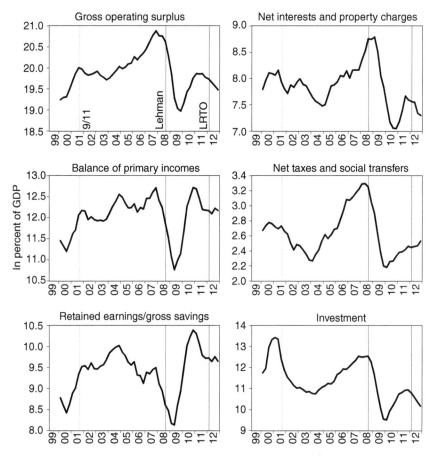

Figure 1.3 Corporate income and investment in the Euro Area (source: ECB).

by investors. Restoring trust and confidence is, however, the task of governments and in this they have failed miserably.[34]

The reluctance to invest in real capital and the massive use of cash flow to reduce debt can be explained by liquidity preference in an environment of great uncertainty. Holding cash and deposits reduces the risk of running into liquidity problems when clients default on their obligations or banks ration credit to their clients and refuse to roll over credit. Figure 1.4 presents the ratio of currency and deposits held by NFCs relative to loan liabilities, a measure of liquidity preferences. Since the Lehman crisis, the ratio has risen by nearly 25 per cent. A closer inspection reveals that in the early 2000s and again after 2004 cash and deposits grew at a stable rate, but corporations increased their borrowings more than cash. Hence, the ratio came down in those years. By contrast, after the Lehman shock the volume of loan liabilities either stagnated or fell, while liquid assets still continued to increase at a steady rate, so that the cash/loan liability ratio rose up.

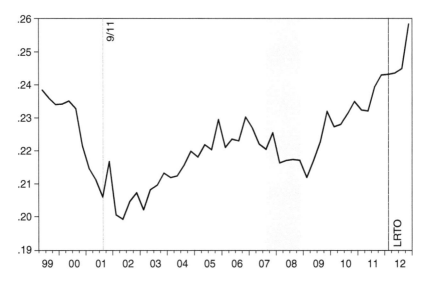

Figure 1.4 Liquidity preference in the NFC sector (currency and deposits/loan liabilities) (source: ECB).

The European Commission (2013) has assessed the impact of uncertainty on consumption and investment in the Euro Area. It found that uncertainty has increased not only in financial markets but also for enterprises and consumers. Furthermore, the significant negative effect of uncertainty has become stronger during the crisis. The study also found that this uncertainty is now at record high levels in the southern periphery (including Ireland), but remains much lower in the core countries. These observations explain why liquidity preference and debt deleveraging have become such an important factor in the slowdown of investment and economic growth in the southern crisis states.

Figure 1.5 presents evidence for individual member states. We are using here the disaggregated flow of funds data provided by Eurostat, which aggregate to the Euro Area data for all 17 member states. Remarkably, the German corporate sector has been a net lender since the early days of monetary union, although in small proportions. In France, NFCs have been net borrowing except during the crisis years 2009–2010. Spain and Portugal have been the largest corporate net borrowers during the boom years; Italy borrowed before the crisis, too. But after Lehman and especially since the Greek debt crisis, NFCs in all six member states have reduced their external borrowing and even started to repay their debt. Greece is a particular case, as retained earnings have always exceeded investment to a very large degree. Since the start of the Greek crisis, however, companies have dramatically increased their profitability; retained earnings in NFCs are now nearly 20 per cent of GDP compared to 10 per cent in Germany. However, investment has fallen to zero,

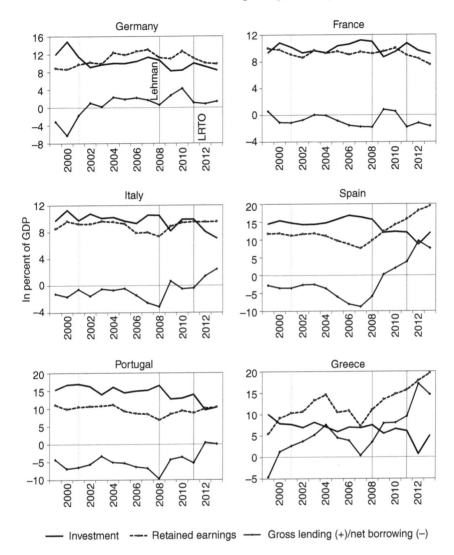

Figure 1.5 Retained earnings, investment and borrowing in some member states (source: AMECO and own calculations).

so that the cash flow of Greek companies is now nearly exclusively used to repay debt.

The broad picture is very similar in all member states: corporate retained earnings have improved, but investment ratios have come down. The higher cash flow is used to repay corporate liabilities. Hence, the Euro Area suffers primarily from insufficient investment and less from supply-side factors like rigid labour markets which prevent higher profits.

Maybe the biggest surprise is Germany's lack of investment. The industrial hub of the Euro Area has not invested in domestic production facilities, but lent its retained earnings to the rest of the world, of which two thirds went to Europe's south. Why? An obvious explanation is that structural reforms and wage restraint have improved the competitiveness and cash flow of German companies, but local demand was insufficient to justify the expansion of local facilities, so that lending money to the booming south seemed more attractive than real investment at home. Another explanation may be that financial innovation in the deeper and more integrated euro market has promised higher returns for financial assets than for real investment. Chapter 2 looks at the returns on capital in the Euro Area. The facts reported there confirm this analysis for the early years of European monetary union, but not for the years after the Hartz IV reforms. By contrast, before the financial crisis, NFCs in the south had been borrowing as economic textbooks would lead us to expect. However, the rapid accumulation of capital generated diminishing returns, which has increased the pressures to deleverage once the crisis had erupted and – unintentionally – pushed Europe into a balance sheet recession.

Conclusions

The euro crisis is a challenge on many fronts. Mistaken analysis causes bad policies and bad policies make the economy worse. By putting competitiveness at the centre of the euro crisis explanation, the mainstream was not wrong. Competitiveness matters. But interpreting competitiveness exclusively through the lenses of macroeconomic imbalances or relative cost distortions does not go far enough. Because the European Commission largely identifies macroeconomic imbalances with current account deficits it neglects the imbalances between other institutional sectors in the Euro Area. This leads them to recommend excessive austerity policies, which have made the crisis worse. Fringe economists on the left and the right, by contrast, focus on relative price and cost indicators, which are arbitrary in their construction and devoid of an equilibrium theory as benchmark (for further evidence, see Chapter 2). They therefore do not shy away from recommending a break-up of the Euro Area. Both these approaches are not sustainable and risk destroying 50 years of European integration.

The idea that current account positions of member states of a currency area need to be balanced violates the logic and undermines the functioning of an integrated European internal market for goods and capital. It ignores that deficits within a currency area may reflect efficient resource allocation; it also leads to the imposition of austerity policies, which not only undermine the cohesion and support for European integration, but also threaten the stability of the financial system. Amalgamating intra- and extra-European current account balances in the Euro Area is sloppy accounting, bad economics and dangerous politics.

Similarly, structural reforms of the welfare system and massive wage cuts to restore supposedly unsustainable cost divergence, as has been advocated by some, are also counterproductive in today's European environment. Lower wage cost may improve the return to capital, but if economic and political uncertainty is high, higher profitability will not necessarily translate into higher investment. In fact, the mismanagement of the euro crisis by national governments, which only considered their narrow taxpayers' constituency instead of the common welfare, has pushed the risk premium up to levels at which the volume of profitable investment has shrunk considerably. Cutting wages and transfers to bring actual rates of return to the point where they would compensate entrepreneurs' risk premiums would reduce aggregate demand to levels of unbearable unemployment. These policies make the crisis worse. They are the kind of policies, which have thrown Europe into turmoil before. As Feldman (1997: 854) concluded in his thorough study of the German economy in the 1920s:

> Germany's leaders between 1930 and 1933 obviously miscalculated what massive unemployment, a rollback of the social welfare system, and measures creating even more extreme misery than 1923 and 1924 would bring. They also failed to realize that the undermining of parliamentary democracy would create an unprecedented social and political crisis and unleash forces and tendencies in the political culture quite beyond their control.

Germany's leaders seem to miscalculate again the damage austerity and disrespect for European democracy could cause.

As an alternative to such misdirected policies, this chapter has suggested the necessity to take European monetary union seriously and to analyse it for what it is: an integrated economic area with a payment union. It was always clear that the single market would not survive without monetary stability in space and time and the creation of the euro was the only feasible response to the desire to fully integrate the European economy.

If this is properly understood, the policy discourse must change. It does not make sense to ponder whether member states with severe debt and growth problems should leave the Euro Area, not even temporarily. Private and public debt sustainability is to a large degree dependent on economic growth and large growth differentials threaten the solvency of financial and non-financial corporations. The primary objective for economic policy in monetary union must, therefore, focus on maintaining balanced growth. Competitiveness in terms of cost and price differentials has a role to play in maintaining stability, but it is not the only one. A number of important consequences follow.

First of all, stimulating growth in the euro economy, especially in the peripheral regions, requires that NFCs start to borrow again in order to invest in real resources rather than repay their outstanding debt. No doubt, the expectation of higher returns to capital would be an incentive to invest, provided everything else remains unchanged. However, during the crisis, everything else has changed. Uncertainty has lowered the propensity to invest and increased liquidity preference. Improving the competitiveness of the European economy would, therefore, require restoring financial stability as well and not only focusing on profitability and related structural reforms. The European Union has privileged austerity as a tool for restoring confidence, but it has underestimated the damage this has created in peripheral member states, where the slowdown of growth has threatened the sustainability of private and public debt. By contrast, member states have been dragging their feet with respect to the banking union, which could strengthen trust and confidence in the European economy. The hesitations and the back and forth in negotiating positions are prolonging uncertainty and block the way to recovery.

Second, the euro crisis is not a balance of payment crisis because member states cannot run out of foreign currency. Nor is there a problem of 'sudden stops' (Calvo, 1998) of capital inflows into southern member states, although there is a problem with money outflows. True, during the first decade of the euro, the corporate sector in the north lent to the south directly or through the banking system, and these transfers have financed investment and consumer demand and enabled huge current account deficits. It is also true that this large volume of lending has come to a halt during the crisis (Merler and Pisani-Ferry, 2012). However, in a monetary union, the reduction in lending from other member states could be compensated by lending from domestic banks which refinance themselves through the Eurosystem – provided there is sufficient demand for borrowing in the corporate sector. This is the quintessential difference that separates currency regimes, where the expansion of domestic credit and the 'printing of money' are causing the immediate depreciation of exchange rates.[35] The main problem of the euro crisis has been the credit crunch and balance sheet deleveraging. The crisis was, therefore, not caused by national balance of payments problems, but by the fragility of the European banking system combined with excessive austerity, which has killed the appetite for investment.

Third, macroeconomic imbalances in the Euro Area are not correctly represented by current account positions, but by growth differentials. These divergences point at significant structural distortions, which certainly need to be addressed. However, the harsh austerity policies imposed on deficit countries have compounded the supply-side problems, because the lack of demand has lowered the willingness to invest (Collignon, 2013). Economic policies for the Euro Area must therefore concentrate on *balanced* economic growth. Balanced growth is also a necessary condition to restore a sense of social justice and fairness among European citizens. It would therefore sustain the politics of monetary union.

Fourth, balanced growth implies balanced demand, even when lending from other member states ceases. The automatic adjustment mechanism in the Euro Area is the outflow of money, unless new credit is generated in the non-tradable sector. This reduction in money balances can cause 'rotating slumps'. Because monetary policy aims at maintaining price stability for the Euro Area as a whole, the distribution of money balances becomes a zero-sum game. If Germany pursues an aggressive export-led growth strategy toward the rest of the world, the burden of adjustment falls on the other economies. On the other hand, if member states suffer from negative money flows and seek to stimulate domestic demand by fiscal policy, they are constrained by Europe's fiscal rules. The Euro Area's present fiscal policy framework is not sufficiently developed to deal with these issues. Instead of imposing identical debt and deficit ratios on each member state, as stipulated by the Stability and Growth Pact, a more diversified approach is recommendable that would take into account the developments in the individual member states as well as the aggregate situation in the Euro Area (Collignon, 2004). Yet, reform of the fiscal framework would need accrued powers at the European level, which can only happen if European citizens could also exercise their democratic rights at the European level (Collignon, 2002; Collignon and Paul, 2008).

Fifth, taking European integration seriously also has a political and cultural dimension. Because people feel emotionally attached to 'their' countries, governments use this emotional bond to preserve their power, but the resulting collective action problems prevent the design and implementation of policies consistent with the functioning of a currency area.[36]

We have analysed the mechanisms which turn a currency area into an integrated economy as if it were one economic nation. But, of course, Europe is not one nation. Polities and civil societies are fractioned. Policies diverge because there is no epistemic consensus. This is the Achilles heel of the euro. Protecting the economic interests of European citizens from the disturbing interferences of national governments is the real challenge revealed by the euro crisis. It will require a genuine European government, but that will be the subject of another chapter in Europe's history.

Notes

1 The 'south' covers Italy, Spain, Greece, Cyprus, Portugal and when data available Ireland.

2 www.faz.net/aktuell/wirtschaft/europas-schuldenkrise/vor-ezb-zinsentscheid-merkel-fuer-deutschland-muessten-zinsen-hoeher-sein-12161702.html.

3 Of course, markets are not perfect; as monopolies, politics and institutions may also generate waste and misallocated resources. The point is that lifting the foreign exchange constraint *opens the possibility* to more efficient allocation of resources and, as the European Commission (2012b: 11) recognises: 'Current account deficits and surpluses are not necessarily macroeconomic imbalances in the sense of developments which are adversely affecting, or have the potential to affect the proper functioning of economies, of the monetary union, or on a wider scale.'

4 See: http://ec.europa.eu/economy_finance/economic_governance/macroeconomic_imbalance_procedure/index_en.htm.

5 See: http://ec.europa.eu/economy_finance/economic_governance/macroeconomic_imbalance_procedure/mip_scoreboard/index_en.htm.

6 Collignon and Schwarzer (2003) have shown how OCA theory became influential among academics, and politicians who used it to keep member states out of the euro, but less so among policy-makers and the business community, who were interested in solidifying the single market.

7 For the first see European Commission, 2012a, for the second European Commission, 2012b.

8 The IMF (2009: 44) defines:

> For an economy, a domestic currency is distinguished from foreign currency. Domestic currency is that which is legal tender in the economy and issued by the monetary authority for that economy; that is, either that of an individual economy or, in a currency union, that of the common currency area to which the economy belongs. All other currencies are foreign currencies.

9 See Collignon, 2012. The IMF (2009: 261) distinguishes between centralised (African and Caribbean currency unions) and decentralised currency unions (Euro Area). Their main variance consists in whether the central bank has a single balance sheet or a consolidated balance sheet with national monetary agencies, but from an economic point of view there is little difference between the two.

10 The official denomination is monetary and financial institutions (MFI), but the name 'banks' or 'commercial banks' conveys the underlying function more intuitively.

11

> The effects of the Eurosystem's monetary policy operations appear on the balance sheets of a number of central banks. Given that the Eurosystem conducts a single monetary policy, its financial statements should reflect the financial impact of, and describe, the operations conducted by all Euro Area central banks as though they were one single entity. Consequently, the preparation of the Eurosystem's financial statements requires the consolidation of all NCB and ECB data.
>
> (ECB *Monthly Bulletin* April 2012: 88)

12

> The currency issued in a CU [currency union] is the domestic currency of the CU. It should always be considered a domestic currency from the viewpoint of each member economy, even though this currency can be issued by a nonresident institution (either another CUNCB [CU national central bank] or the CUCB [central bank]). One consequence is that, in a CU, from a national perspective, holdings of domestic currency can be a claim on a nonresident.
>
> (IMF, 2009: 257)

13 Foreign exchange reserves are the equivalent of narrow money in the international context. Of course, economic agents can also draw on foreign assets they own, which is a form of 'broad international money'.

14 The wide-spread confusion of economic countries and member states of the Euro Area results probably from the fact that as juridical entities member states still record national balance of payment statistics which summarise the economic relationships between residents and non-residents of an economy, while currency areas with a centralised government do not do so. However, even this convention has some arbitrariness. The System of National Accounts (SNA: United Nations, 2008: 17) defines residency in non-jurisdictional terms:

> The concept of residence in the SNA is not based on nationality or legal criteria. An institutional unit is said to be a resident unit of a country when it has a center of predominant economic interest in the economic territory of that country; that is, when it engages for an extended period (one year or more being taken as a practical guideline) in economic activities on this territory.

The difficulties of allocating all payments to regional residents within the currency area are substantial, and while they can possibly be solved for trade flows (IMF, 2009), they are literally impossible for movements of cash (Jobst, 2011). Balance of payment statistics are much more reliable for international payments between territories with different currencies, because commercial banks acquire foreign currency for their clients from the central bank and these transactions are well documented.

15 The following is based on IMF, 2009: 265–268.
16 According to the ECB, there are three main reasons for having a 'system of central banks' in Europe instead of a single central bank: (1) The Eurosystem approach builds on the existing competencies of the NCBs, their institutional set-up, infrastructure, expertise and operational capabilities. Several central banks also perform additional tasks beside those of the Eurosystem. (2) Given the geographically large Euro Area and the long-established relationships between the national banking communities and their NCBs, the credit institutions should have an access point to central banking in each participating member state. (3) NCBs are better suited to deal with the multitude of nations, languages and cultures in the Euro Area instead of the supranational ECB. See: www.ecb.int/ecb/educational/facts/orga/html/or_002.en.html.
17 National central banks are remunerated for these claims.
18 The same logic would apply if we consider the net purchase of German securities by Italian investors.
19 These claims show up in the ECB balance sheet as 'intra-Eurosystem claims' which are netted out in the consolidation of the Eurosystem balance sheet. Sinn and Wollmershaeuser (2011) have interpreted the claims by national central banks on the TARGET2 payment system as reflecting current account payments. In our simplified example here, where no autonomous financial transactions are taking place, this would be valid, but when one takes cash payments (Jobst, 2011) and autonomous credit and payment flows between banks (Collignon, 2012) into consideration this is no longer correct. It is also worth noting that intra Eurosystem claims can only be interpreted as potentially risky if the commitment by political authorities to sustain monetary union is put into question. Economically, they have no significance.
20 It is useful to recall that all transactions are made by individual actors; *Germany* or *Italy* do not exist as actors. These are simply names for a group of actors who happen to live in the jurisdiction of a state.
21 This mechanism resembles the classical specie flow mechanism of the pure gold standard.
23 For the destabilising effects of the crisis see Mongelli, 2013.
24 Interestingly, Dawson (2004: 246) has noted similar mistakes during the Asian crisis: 'tight monetary and fiscal policies and immediate, radical restructuring of financial markets turned out to be the wrong medicine. Fund programs did not quickly restore confidence, and exchange rates continued their decline.' What seems to have helped to restore growth was 'expanded flow of bank credit' and 'the policy of credit ease pursued by the monetary Authorities' (p. 251). In Europe, political authorities under German leadership are killing the patient, while the ECB keeps him alive.
25 For econometric evidence that negative output gaps reduce long-run growth, see Collignon, 2013.
26 However, the loss of deposits may destabilise banks in the region, as they become more dependent on liquidity borrowed in the interbank market or from the Eurosystem. We cannot pursue this logic here, but is a powerful argument for a banking union in Europe.
27 See United Nations, 2008 and also any of the General Notes in the ECB's *Monthly Bulletin*.
28 This exposition is based on Fleming and Giugale, 2000. Later we will separate financial and non-financial corporations.
29 When firms are repaying debt, this can be interpreted as acquiring a debt claim from creditors against themselves.
30 As pointed out above, the rest of the world (RoW) is the mirror image of the aggregate balances of the Euro Area. A positive value for RoW indicates lending by non-residents, which is equivalent to a current account deficit.
31 See also Stiglitz and Greenwald, 2003: 175–182.
32 For a formal model of this argument see Collignon, 2002b.

33 In most risk–return models, the trade-off curve is not linearly but exponentially upward sloping. See Collignon, 2002b.
34 For the theory of balance sheet recessions, see Koo, 2002.
35 See for example Collignon *et al.*, 2013 for evidence how statements by the German chancellor Merkel have pushed up the risk premiums in bond markets.
36 For example during the Asian crisis, the 'sudden stop' of foreign capital inflows led to domestic credit expansions in Thailand and Korea and drastic depreciations.
37 See also Collignon, 2002a.

References

Ahearne, A. and G. B. Wolff (2012), 'The debt challenge in Europe'. *Bruegel Working Paper* 2012/2.

Blanchard, O. (2006), 'Is there a viable European social and economic model?' *MIT Department of Economics Working Paper* 06-21. Massachusetts Institute of Technology.

Blanchard, O. and F. Giavazzi (2002), 'Current account deficits in the Euro Area: the end of the Feldstein Horioka puzzle'. *Brookings Papers on Economic Activity*, 33(2): 147–186.

Calvo, G. (1998), 'Capital flows and capital-market crises: the simple economics of sudden stops'. *Journal of Applied Economics*, 1 (November): 35–54.

Collignon, S. (2002a), *The European Republic; Reflections on the Political Economy of a European Constitution*. London: The Federal Trust. Downloadable from www.stefan-collignon.eu.

Collignon, S. (2002b), *Monetary Stability in Europe*. London: Routledge.

Collignon, S. (2004), *Fiscal Policy and Democracy in Europe*. Paper presented at Monetary Workshop, Österreichische Nationalbank, Vienna, 2004; published as *ÖNB Discussion Paper* 4, 'A constitutional treaty for an enlarged Europe: institutional and economic implications for economic and monetary union' (November). Download: www.stefancollignon.de/PDF/OENBank.pdf.

Collignon, S. (2012), *Macroeconomic Imbalances and Comparative Advantages in the Euro Area*. Brussels: European Trade Union Institute (ETUI) with Bertelsmann Foundation.

Collignon, S. (2013), 'Economic growth versus austerity'. Note for the European Parliament's Commitee on Economic and Monetary Affairs, January. Downloadable from www.stefancollignon.eu.

Collignon, S. and C. Paul (2008), *Pour la république européenne*. Paris: Odile Jacob.

Collignon, S. and D. Schwarzer (2003), *Private Sector Involvement in the Euro: The Power of Ideas*. London: Routledge.

Collignon, S., P. Esposito and H. Lierse (2013) 'European sovereign bailouts, political risk and the economic consequences of Mrs Merkel'. *Journal of International Commerce, Economics and Policy*, 4(2): 55–79.

Dawson, J. C. (2004), 'The Asian crisis and flow-of-funds analysis'. *Review of Income and Wealth*, 50(2): 243–260.

De Grauwe, P. (2007), *Economics of Monetary Union*. Oxford: Oxford University Press.

European Commission (2011), *Quarterly Report on the Euro Area* 3/2011; Brussels.

European Commission (2012a), *Alert Mechanism Report – 2013*; Brussels, 28.11.2012 COM(2012) 751 final. http://eur-lex.europa.eu/LexUriServ/LexUriServ.do?uri=COM: 2012:0751:FIN:EN:PDF.

European Commission (2012b), 'Current account surpluses in the EU'. *European Economy* 9/2012.

European Commission (2013), *Quarterly Report on the Euro Area*, 2/2013; Brussels.

Fatás, A. (1998), 'Does EMU need a fiscal federation?' *Economic Policy*, April: 165–203.

Feldman, G. D. (1997), *The Great Disorder: Politics, Economics, and Society in the German Inflation, 1914–1924*. Oxford: Oxford University Press (originally published 1993).

Flassbeck, H. and F. Spiecker (2011), 'The euro – a story of misunderstanding'. *Intereconomics – Review of European Economic Policy*, 4: 180–187.

Fleming, A. E. and M. Giugale (2000), *Financial Systems in Transaction. A Flow of Funds Analysis of Financial Evolution in Eastern Europe and Central Asia*. Singapore: World Scientific.

Giavazzi, F. and L. Spaventa (2010) 'Why the current account may matter in a monetary union: lessons from the financial crisis in the Euro Area'. *CEPR Discussion Paper* DP8008.

IMF (2009), *Balance of Payment Manual*, 6th edn. Washington, DC: IMF.

Jobst, C. (2011), 'A balance sheet view on TARGET – and why restrictions on TARGET would have hit Germany first'. *Voxeu.org*: 19 July 2011, available at: http://voxeu.org/index.php?q=node/6768.

Koo, R. (2002), *The Holy Grail of Macroeconomics: Lesson's from Japan's Great Recession*. Singapore: John Wiley and Sons.

Merler, S. and J. Pisani-Ferry (2012), 'Sudden stops in the Euro Area'. *Bruegel Policy Contribution* 2012/06, March 2012.

Mongelli, F. P. (2013), 'The mutating Euro Area crisis. Is the balance between "sceptics" and "advocates" shifting?' *ECB, Occasional Paper Series* No. 144.

Mongelli, F. P. and C. Wyplosz (2008), 'The Euro at ten: unfulfilled threats and unexpected challenges.' Paper presented at Fifth ECB Central Banking Conference 'The Euro at ten: lessons and challenges', available at: www.ecb.int/events/pdf/conferences/cbc5/Mongelli_Wyplosz.pdf?6eaad582d8c07415c9ca0fce2ed11750.

Padoa-Schioppa, T (1987) *Efficiency, Stability and Equity: A Strategy for the Evolution of the Economic System of the European Community.*' Brussels: European Commission, II/49/87.

Sinn, H. W. (2013), 'Austerity, growth and inflation: remarks on the Eurozone's unresolved competitiveness problem'. *Cesifo Working Paper* No. 4086, January.

Sinn, H. W. and T. Wollmershaeuser, ((2011), 'TARGET loans, current account balances and capital flows: the ECB's rescue facility'. *NBER Working Paper Series* 17626. www.nber.org/papers/w17626.

Stiglitz, J. E. and B. Greenwald (2003), *Towards a New Paradigm in Monetary Economics*. Cambridge: Cambridge University Press.

Teplin, A. M. (2001), 'The US flow of funds accounts and their uses.' *Federal Reserve Bulletin*, July: 431–441.

United Nations (2008), 'The System of National Accounts', available at: http://unstats.un.org/unsd/nationalaccount/docs/SNA2008.pdf.

Wyplosz, C. (2013), ''Eurozone crisis and the competitiveness legend'. *Asian Economic Papers*, 12(3): 63–81.

2 Unit labour costs and capital efficiency in the Euro Area

A new competitiveness indicator

Stefan Collignon and Piero Esposito

Introduction

Competitiveness is a controversial concept. Although Paul Krugman (1994; 1996) has called policy-makers' concern with competitiveness 'a dangerous obsession', the compulsion to blame Europe's crisis on competitiveness continues. The Euro Group has discussed the issue of competitiveness divergences repeatedly, and the European Commission has argued that 'over the first decade of the century, the EU has registered serious gaps in competitiveness and major macroeconomic imbalances'.[1] A new surveillance and enforcement mechanism, the Macroeconomic Imbalance Procedure, was set up in December 2011 in order 'to prevent the emergence of harmful macroeconomic imbalances and correct the imbalances that are already in place' (European Commission, 2012). The European Commission now also produces regularly a number of competitiveness reports. In the 2010 report it argues that 'a smooth adjustment of intra-Euro Area competitiveness divergences and macroeconomic imbalances is key for the recovery and, more generally, for the successful and sustainable functioning of EMU in the long term' (European Commission, 2010). Thus, the question of how to measure competitiveness is an important issue for the design of macro-economic policies in the Euro Area.

The literature reveals a wide variety of competitiveness notions, measures and applications (Buckley *et al.*, 1988). Some studies concentrate on firms, some on economic sectors, many on countries. The complexities of phenomena contributing to the evaluation of competitiveness are often combined into a single index that assesses improvements or deteriorations in competitive positions. The European Commission uses a scoreboard that combines different indicators and observes their evolution over time. In the present work we add another indicator to the already long list, because we think it is particularly appropriate for assessing national economies within the European monetary union, although it can also be used even beyond this limited field.

A broad definition of international competitiveness frequently used in the literature is: 'the degree to which [a country] can, under free and fair market conditions, produce goods and services which meet the test of international markets, while simultaneously maintaining and expanding the real incomes of its people over time' (OECD, 1992 cited in Boltho, 1996: 3; Keyder *et al.*, 2004). The British Aldington Report (1985: 13) wrote 'the definition of competitiveness for a nation must ... be tied to its ability to generate the resources required to meet its national needs'. Bennett *et al.* (2008: 6) take 'Competitiveness to mean the success of an economy in seizing the opportunities afforded by an increasingly integrated international economic environment to deliver sustained growth in living standards'. This definition allows them to interpret competitiveness as a 'production technology', where the conditions determining exports are the 'input' into improving living standards.

In this chapter we take a different, narrower approach, but we also interpret competitiveness as a production function because we see competitiveness as a process in which input variables, such as the relative costs of labour and capital, relative prices, productivities and profits generate macroeconomic output data like exports, imports, trade balances, current accounts and foreign direct investment, all of which are relevant for sustained growth of living standards. We develop a new competitiveness indicator which includes the role of capital efficiency and profit rates together with labour costs: the CER Competitiveness Index (CCI). It includes production factors, labour and capital, and it measures competitiveness as the ratio between unit labour costs and their equilibrium level, with the latter determined by the equality between a country's profit rate and the average one. We then test the performance of our compound index against the standard measures.

The structure of the chapter is as follows: in the next section, we will review the main input and output measures and highlight their characteristics and shortcomings. In the third section we introduce the role of capital efficiency and formally develop the CCI. In the fourth section we will test econometrically the performance of the CCI while the final section presents our conclusions.

'Input' and 'output' measures of competitiveness

Input measures

The most commonly used input measures for competitiveness are indices of relative prices or costs, either in levels or rates of change. These indices imply certain assumptions of equilibrium. For example, the *Law of One Price* states that, abstracting from transport and transaction costs, freely traded identical commodities should have the same price in a common currency denomination. *Purchasing power parity* (ppp) applies this law to similar baskets of goods. *Dynamic ppp* says that nominal exchange rate variations should reflect inflation differential between two economies. The *real effective exchange rate* (REER) broadens this idea to a trade-weighted index of relative prices. Deviations from these equilibria may be caused by market imperfections, oligopolistic competition, pricing to market or by using inconsistent price indices, such as consumer prices, wholesale price indices or GDP deflators (Keyder *et al.*, 2004). All major international economic organisations like the IMF, OECD, Bank for

International Settlements, central banks, etc. publish indices for trade-weighted relative prices and costs. The European Commission calculates REER for a broad group of 41 countries, two smaller groups of 36 and 24 industrial countries, the 27 member states of the European Union (EU) and the Euro Area countries (EA) (see ECFIN, 2012). In international economics, real effective exchange rates convert prices in the currency of trade partners into local currency. Given that the exchange rate is an asset price with high volatility, distortions in REERs from ppp are frequent, normal and disturbing. Nevertheless, in a single currency area, this noise factor has been eliminated, so that relative prices between sectors or regions reflect demand and supply conditions.

Because price indices often amalgamate tradable and non-tradable goods, while for the latter trade arbitrage will not ensure convergence to equilibrium, unit labour cost (ULC) indices are often preferred. Unit labour costs are defined as total wage remuneration per unit of output produced. Focusing on ULC in the manufacturing sector is considered a good proxy for relative labour costs in the tradable sector. Figure 2.1 shows the ULC-based REER indices for some countries. The huge fluctuations of over 50 per cent over a decade under flexible exchange rate regimes contrast clearly with the stability after the introduction of the single currency in the European Union, even after the 2008 financial crisis.

Table 2.1 confirms that euro member states experienced a small real appreciation against the most important trade partners within the European Union, and that this was mainly due to the weakening of the British pound and in the first decade, of the euro against the Swedish crown. Greece also depreciated before it

Table 2.1 Changes in REER (in %)

	Relative to EU 15		Relative to 34 industrial countries	
	1999–2007	*2007–2014*	*1999–2007*	*2007–2014*
Austria	0.6	1.5	4.8	−0.4
Belgium	0.8	2.5	6.1	0.4
Denmark	1.1	1.6	5.7	−1.2
Finland	1.2	1.4	8.1	−1.4
France	0.9	2.9	7.5	−0.1
Germany	1.0	2.9	7.9	−0.7
Greece	−3.6	2.0	7.4	2.3
Ireland	1.4	5.0	10.2	0.5
Italy	0.8	2.4	9.1	−0.3
Luxembourg	0.7	2.1	3.0	0.9
Netherlands	0.8	2.8	5.1	0.9
Portugal	0.6	2.0	4.5	0.4
Spain	0.8	2.6	6.8	1.0
Sweden	−4.2	13.3	2.5	9.5
United Kingdom	−3.4	−20.2	4.9	−22.5
Euro Area			17.0	−0.0

Source: AMECO.

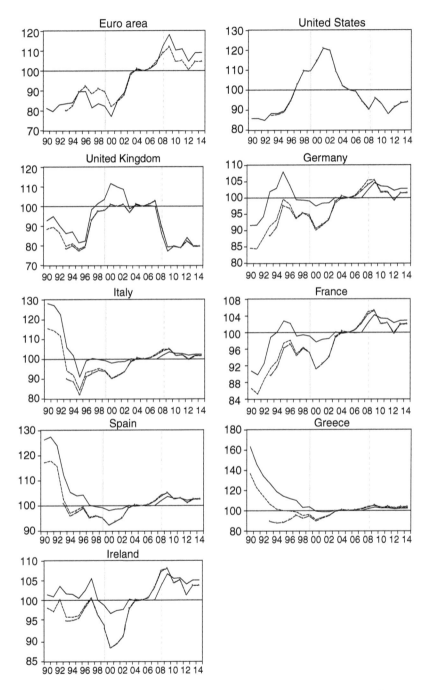

Figure 2.1 Real effective exchange rates based on ULC (base year = 100) (source: AMECO).

joined the Euro Area in 2001. However, against 34 industrial trade partners (including the 15 EU countries), the variations are much bigger, because they reflect trade partners with different currencies and different inflation rates. The Euro Area as a whole has appreciated against its main non-Euro partners by 17 per cent before 2007, and has on average kept its real exchange rate stable since then. Thus, Europe's competitive environment has become much more stable in monetary union. Instead of wasting resources on arbitrage trade caused by relative cost distortions, European firms could concentrate on competing for more efficient production processes and better output of goods and services.

Given this plethora of competitiveness measures, why invent a new one? Unfortunately, none of the above-mentioned indicators is able to provide a full view of the causes and effects of competitiveness. Maybe the most complete picture is given by the *World Economic Forum Competitiveness Report* and the IMD World Competitiveness Center (WCC), which compare the competitiveness of 60 nations on the basis of over 300 criteria. However, while these surveys allow interesting overall rankings between countries, it is desirable to focus on variables which can be affected by policies in a more direct way.

From this perspective, nominal unit labour costs often serve as a privileged variable, as they have the advantage of reflecting wage settlements relative to labour productivity, so that wage policy recommendations can be derived from their developments. In fact, unit labour costs fulfil a double role. On the one hand, they anchor the price level, so that following the rule of keeping average wage increases equal to the sum of increases in labour productivity and the central bank's inflation target will maintain price stability and support monetary policy. On the other hand, if the inflation target is actually achieved, such rule will also stabilise the distribution of income between labour and all other claims. The operating surplus of the economy, i.e. the aggregate profit margin, which is the complement of the wage share in GDP, would remain constant.

However, despite these useful functions, unit labour costs have some shortcomings as an indicator for competitiveness. First, they take account of labour but not of capital productivity. This can cause distortions in comparing overall costs and in the incentives for the accumulation of capital and labour when capital productivity is not constant. Second, given that unit labour cost indices are constructed by GDP deflator indices with arbitrary base years, it is impossible to judge what is the equilibrium *level* of relative costs; only movements can be traced by these indices.

A typical example of such nominal ULC indicators is Figure 3.1 in Chapter 3 and not surprisingly it yields whopping cost gaps of 25 per cent between Italy and Germany, which would indicate a serious competitive disadvantage for Italy. No doubt the evolution of these indicators is interesting information, but it would be wrong to argue that in 1999 labour costs in Germany and Italy were in equilibrium, say reflecting the law of one price in the labour market, and since then Italy has become hopelessly uncompetitive. Taking account of this criticism, de Grauwe (2011) has proposed to take the average for a long period 1970–2010 as the index base. However, this ad hoc methodology yields just as arbitrary results as any other index and it has no theoretical foundation. We therefore need a different approach.

Output measures

In our production function approach, the output measures of competitiveness are aggregates reflecting the economic performance of a country. This output of competitiveness is usually measured in terms of exports, imports, trade balances or current account balances and their rates of change. Here trade balances and current accounts are a popular measure for competitiveness. Exports are a source of foreign exchange earnings, while imports may improve the quality and productivity of local production technologies.[2] If exports perform well, it is easier to finance the upgrading of domestic production facilities through imports. For this reason the trade balance is considered to be the direct outcome of a country's competitiveness. With these assumptions, recent papers have investigated the determinants of trade flows and their balances in European economies (Guerrieri and Esposito, 2012, 2013; Chen *et al.*, 2013).

Current accounts balances are often used as what we call 'output competitiveness indicators' as they closely reflect the balance of goods and services on the one hand and net transfers on the other. Between countries *with different currencies* the importance of current accounts to measure a country's competitiveness is beyond dispute as they add to foreign assets/liabilities and affect foreign exchange reserves with the possibility of causing currency crises as experienced in Europe in 1992–1993 or in Asia in 1998, but within a monetary union current accounts partly lose their original meaning as the problem of foreign exchange reserves is no longer present (Ingram, 1973; Collignon, 2013, see also Chapter 1). In addition, net transfers include net earnings from rents, interest, profits and dividends, and net transfer payments (such as pension funds and worker remittances) both with other EMU countries and with the rest of the world. These flows are not necessarily related to competitiveness although important studies have shown their relation to investment bubbles in Spain and Ireland (Giavazzi and Spaventa, 2010).

As pointed out by the structural current account approach (Buiter, 1981; Sachs, 1981, Obstfeld and Rogoff, 1995), current accounts depend also on the interest rate, the age structure of the population, the relation between saving and investment and so on. On the latter, Blanchard and Giavazzi (2002) have used the saving–investment balance approach to explain the disappearance of the Feldstein and Horioka (1980) puzzle, noting that national saving and investment in the countries belonging to monetary union were increasingly disconnected. The authors conclude that this result was the outcome of the proper functioning of the monetary union as capital has flown from rich to poor countries, but the emergence of huge imbalances during the last decade and their reduction during the recession in southern Europe has generated a growing literature criticising this assumption.[3]

Both trade and current account balances depend on relative prices, but also on aggregate demand in the importing countries and this fact may distort the

competitiveness measure. A better measure for competitiveness output is therefore the export market share of an economy in world or regional trade. A gain of
market share implies a better trade performance than the rest of the world and
this may reflect an improvement in competitiveness for a given country – but of
course also a loss for the rest of the world as market share is a zero-sum game.

While being unrelated to the exporting country's domestic demand, market
shares are still influenced by foreign demand factors as they can increase if
exports are concentrated on rapidly expanding markets, in terms of either products or regions. This means that the geographical and sectoral specialisation as
well as their interactions influence the levels and dynamics of market shares. For
example in recent years, Germany has benefited from high demand for cars
(product effect) in the Chinese market (market effect). These demand effects can
be separated from supply-side conditions by the methodology of the constant
market share analysis (CMS) (Richardson, 1971a, 1971b; Fagerberg and Sollie,
1987; Milana, 1988, ECB, 2005). The residual of the total market share variation
after deducting product and market effects yields the pure competitive supply-
side-effect. This measure, although not directly observed is a tight measure of
changes in a country's competitive position.

Another output variable of our competitiveness function is foreign direct
investment (FDI): if a specific region is competitive it is likely to attract investment funds, which will increase economic and export growth. These capital
inflows shift the foreign exchange constraint and may, in accordance with comparative advantages, improve the efficiency and productivity of the economy. In
this sense, competitiveness would deliver sustained growth in living standards.

The output measures of competitiveness will be used in the final section of
this chapter in order to test the explanatory power of traditional input measures
in comparison with the index we develop in the next section.

The CER Competitiveness Index

Competitiveness and returns to capital

When setting an equilibrium benchmark for competitiveness, it is the *level* in relative costs that matters. Deviations from this benchmark generate incentives for
profitable exports, imports, investment, capital flows, etc. Nominal unit labour
costs indicating total wage compensation per unit of output, are important, because
wages are the largest cost factor for the economy as a whole. Equality of ULCs in
two different economies indicates, therefore, that no savings in labour costs can be
made by relocating production. Nevertheless, focusing on wages alone is not
appropriate, as they are only one element in the total cost structure of an economy.

The second most important production factor is capital. In a single market
with a single currency, the efficient allocation of capital requires that investors
put their money wherever it yields the highest return. There is absolutely no
reason why, say, Italian companies should only borrow from Italian households.
The whole purpose of economic and monetary union is precisely to create a

more efficient framework for the European economy that integrates goods and financial markets. If capital can circulate freely, relative profitability of capital will determine where investment is located. Thus, the proper measure of competitiveness within a currency area is the relative return of a sector or region compared to another and not relative unit labour costs. In the Euro Area, where all returns are denominated by the same currency, we can use the return to the aggregate euro-capital stock as the benchmark, so that the above average return on capital is an indicator of favourable competitiveness conditions, and below average returns for competitive disadvantages.

Differences in profitability have consequences for macroeconomic aggregates. The creation of the euro has improved the efficiency of European financial markets and removed the external budget constraint for member states and as a consequence, investors have reallocated their capital, firms have shifted their supply chain to more efficient sources and exporters have exploited new market opportunities. In other words, the structure of economic incentives has been profoundly transformed, especially in small member states in the European south, where firms used to be handicapped by high interest rates before they joined the euro. Hence, European monetary union has changed not only the relative returns to national capital stocks, but also the output variables of competitiveness such as exports, imports, current account positions and FDI.

Figure 2.2 shows the aggregate rates of return on national capital stocks in some selected member states. The Euro Area average has hardly moved in the

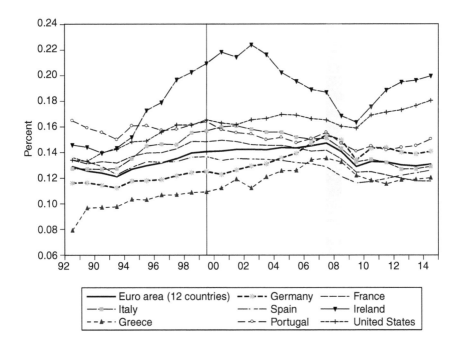

Figure 2.2 Returns to capital (source: own elaboration on AMECO).

first decade, but it dropped notably during the crisis and has now stabilised at a lower level. Ireland, Italy and Portugal, and also to some extent France, have had above average returns before the crisis although with a tendency to deteriorate during monetary union. In Ireland this fall in profits was drastic after 2002, but the situation has turned again in 2010. While Germany and Greece used to have below average returns all through the 1990s and 2000s, they have nevertheless steadily closed the gap relative to the euro average during monetary union. After the labour market reforms in 2005, the German return on capital started to exceed the Euro Area rate and it has further improved in recent years. By contrast, Greece and France have suffered most from the crisis. In Spain, the return on capital has deteriorated significantly in monetary union until it has started to improve after 2010. This may indicate that the heavy net borrowing by Spanish corporations and households before the crisis was not driven by actual returns on capital, but by the irrational exuberance of the Spanish housing bubble (Croci-Angelini and Farina, 2012; Giavazzi and Spaventa, 2010). In the USA, rates of return have consistently been higher than in Europe and the gap has become larger since the crisis. Hence, for many investors, lending to the rest of the world must have been more attractive than placing their funds in the Euro Area.

Our definition of competitiveness as the ability to generate or attract sustained investment assigns a critical role to wages and wage bargaining, but also to productivity of labour and capital. The macroeconomic rate of return on capital can be written as the product of the profit margin times capital productivity:

$$RoC = \frac{PY - wL}{PY} \frac{PY}{P_k K} \tag{1}$$

Where PY is nominal GDP, wL is the nominal compensation of labour and $P_k K$ is the nominal value of the capital stock. We call the second term on the right-hand side the average capital efficiency (ACE), which is equal to capital productivity when the price index for capital goods P_k evolves at the same rate as the GDP deflator P. The expression $^{wL}/_{PY}$ is either called the wage share or real unit labour costs, because nominal unit labour costs are $^{wL}/_Y = ^w/_\lambda$, i.e. the ratio between nominal wages and labour productivity (λ). The profit margin is the complement of the wage share. The return on capital will then increase when the profit margin increases, because unit labour costs are reduced and/or the capital efficiency is improved.

Figure 2.3 shows varied performances for profit margins and rates of return over half a century. Profit margins are shown on the left, returns to capital on the right-hand scale. When the gap between the two curves increases, capital productivity is rising; when it shrinks, the average efficiency of capital diminishes. Under the Bretton Woods regime, profit rates improved in many European countries or remained stable, as in the USA. However, with the collapse of Bretton Woods, profits also collapsed nearly everywhere. Flexible exchange rates were bad for European competitiveness.

After 1980 monetary policies became tight to bring inflation down, and neo-liberal policies of liberalising financial and product markets drove up profit

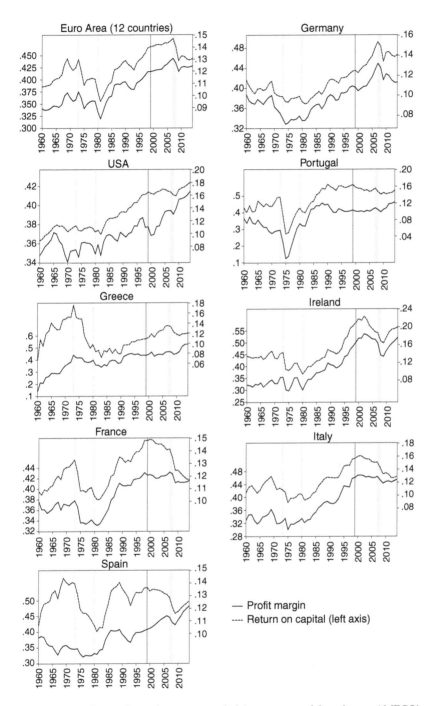

Figure 2.3 Profit margins and return on capital (source: own elaboration on AMECO).

margins and the returns to capital all over the world. Since then, performances have diverged. In Germany, the improvement of rates of return is usually driven by increases in profit margins, while capital productivity does not seem to change much. The labour market reforms by the Schröder government have given a major boost to profit margins. In Ireland, the return to capital is also driven by wages and not by capital efficiency. Irish profit margins have increased in the booming 1980s and 1990s, but then the advantage was lost after EMU began. Profits only finally picked up again during the crisis years. In Greece, profit margins rose only marginally before the crisis, but there was a long-run trend of improved capital efficiency. In Portugal, capital efficiency also did not change, at least not until the recent crisis started to diminish capital productivity, but profit margins have remained flat.

In all the other countries shown in Figure 2.3, the trends for profit margins and rates of return go in opposite directions because capital productivity has diminished. In France, Italy and Spain this loss of profitability is dramatic. Profit margins have remained stable in the first two economies, but in Spain even an increase in margins could not prevent diminishing returns, because capital productivity deteriorated so much. The general picture is that in countries where interest rates have come down after the start of the euro, rapid accumulation of capital has caused diminishing returns on capital, and variations in wage setting have not compensated for this competitive deterioration. In the north, interest rates have not changed much, so that lower wages and higher profit margins have increased the return to capital. In the US, by comparison, wage reductions have pushed profit margins up so that, by and large, the diminishing capital productivity has been compensated and the return on capital has remained stable or even improved after the crisis.

The distinction between profit margins and returns to capital throws a new light on competitiveness. Labour market reforms usually aim at reducing wages, either by increasing labour supply or by lowering social contributions. This has certainly been the effect of the German Hartz IV reforms (see Chapters 4 and 5). Margins also have gone up in the southern countries after the financial crisis. Yet, the main cause for the deteriorating competitiveness in the south during the first euro-decade has been the rapid accumulation of capital. Diminishing returns on investment have lowered the average efficiency of capital. Figure 2.4 shows that before the financial crisis, the average efficiency of the capital stock had fallen in all southern member states except Greece. With the exception of Ireland, this trend has continued even through the crisis, although the negative trend seems to have stopped in Italy, Spain and Portugal; in Greece the adjustment policies imposed have destroyed and reversed the earlier positive trends of capital productivity, but here, too, the downward trend may finally have come to an end in 2013.

Theoretical foundation of the CER Competitiveness Index

If our benchmark for measuring competitiveness is the rate of return to capital, we can derive the equilibrium *level* of unit labour costs (see Collignon, 2013) as

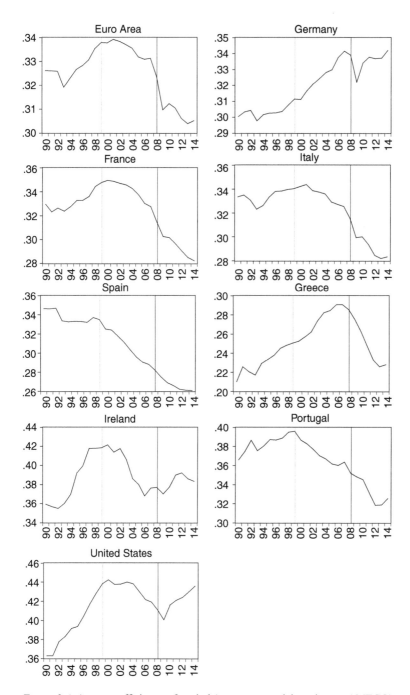

Figure 2.4 Average efficiency of capital (source: own elaboration on AMECO).

the level where, given productivity conditions, wages are just equalising the regional return to capital with the aggregate of the currency area. This does not mean that market dynamics will necessarily and always equalise the returns on capital, but that the equilibrium defines the standard of measurement against which deviations from efficiency can be assessed. Taking the Euro Area as our reference, the relative return on capital in different member states would indicate whether unit labour costs are overvalued when actual costs are above the equilibrium level or undervalued in the opposite case. What follows is a theoretical derivation of the competitiveness index based on these assumptions.

Referring back to equation (1), we get the rate of return as the product of the profit share and ACE

$$R = k\sigma_k = k(1-\sigma_w) = \frac{Py - wL}{Py} \frac{Py}{P_k K} = \left(1 - \frac{w}{P}\frac{1}{\lambda}\right)k = \left(1 - \frac{ULC}{P}\right)k \qquad (2)$$

where $\lambda = y/L$ is labour productivity and the profit share σ_k is the complement of the wage share σ_w

$$\sigma_k = \frac{Py - wL}{Py} = 1 - \sigma_w \qquad (3)$$

k is the average capital efficiency.

Because of (2), the return on capital R improves when the average capital efficiency and/or the profit share improve. The average efficiency of capital rises with the technological productivity of capital (y/K) or when prices for capital goods are less than the GDP deflator $(P/P_K < 1)$. The profit share rises when the wage share falls, which implies that real wages rise less than labour productivity.

Assuming efficient markets, R should converge to the Euro Area average. Thus, for country A and Euroland B we have the two equilibrium returns

$$R_A^* = R_B^* \Leftrightarrow \left(1 - \frac{ULC_A^*}{P_A}\right)k_A = \left(1 - \frac{ULC_B^*}{P_B}\right)k_B \qquad (4)$$

or

$$\sigma_{KA}^* = \sigma_{KB}^* \frac{k_B}{k_A}$$

Hence, in equilibrium the differences in wage shares must reflect the relative productivities of capital and the equilibrium for relative ULC is

$$ULC_A^* = \frac{k_B}{k_A}\frac{P_A}{P_B}ULC_B^* - \left(\frac{k_B}{k_A} - 1\right)P_A \qquad (5)$$

If actual unit labour costs are higher or lower than this theoretical equilibrium level, we will say that a country is over- or undervalued relative to the so-defined competitiveness standard, where the Euro Area is our reference country. The CER Competitive Index (CCI) for country A is then simply defined as the ratio of actual to equilibrium unit labour costs:

$$CCI_A = \frac{ULC_A}{ULC_A^*} \tag{6}$$

Combining equations (5) and (6) we can now define the CCI as function of ACEs, prices and ULCs for a given country and Euro Area as whole:

$$CCI_A = \frac{ULC_A}{\dfrac{k_{EA}}{k_A}\dfrac{P_A}{P_{EA}}ULC_{EA} - \left(\dfrac{k_{EA}}{k_A} - 1\right)P_A} \tag{7}$$

The index is equal to 1 plus the percentage of overvaluation/undervaluation relatively to the Euro Area average, and an increase indicates deteriorating competitiveness. The CCI for a given country depends positively on its ULC and negatively on the Euro Area cost levels (see the appendix for a detailed proof). The additional feature is its negative relation with the domestic ACE while an increase in the Euro Area ACE diminishes the index as the latter causes the equilibrium ULC to fall.

Descriptive evidence

Figure 2.5 describes the evolution of the CER Competitiveness Index. The horizontal line at value 1 indicates that the unit labour cost levels of a given country are at a level where the return to capital is equal to the Euro Area. The position of the index above the horizontal line indicates an overvalued position; below this line is an undervalued indication. Based on these data, not all of which are shown, northern member states are generally undervalued. In Finland this undervaluation goes back to the crisis years in the early 1990s, in the Netherlands it started around the time of monetary union in 1999, and in Germany it occurred with the Schröder labour market reforms. France has moved from undervaluation to overvaluation, Italy has persistently lost competitive advantages over the last two decades, but having started from a much undervalued position it is now close to equilibrium. In the crisis countries, Spain has become more and more overvalued during its property boom; Portugal and Ireland have also lost competitiveness, but they are still undervalued. Cyprus has oscillated in a range below equilibrium. Most surprisingly, Greece had reduced its overvaluation disadvantage before the crisis, but had not yet reached equilibrium. Despite a draconian austerity regime, the country has experienced a slight deterioration in competitiveness since the crisis erupted. The movements reveal very different behaviour in unit labour costs among member states. Although the crisis in 2008 has had an impact on cost levels in most countries, a durable adjustment toward equilibrium levels can hardly be observed anywhere.

Testing the performance of the CER Competitiveness Index

Econometric strategy

In this section we test the performance of the CCI against alternative measures of competitiveness. We wish to know how well input variables of competitiveness,

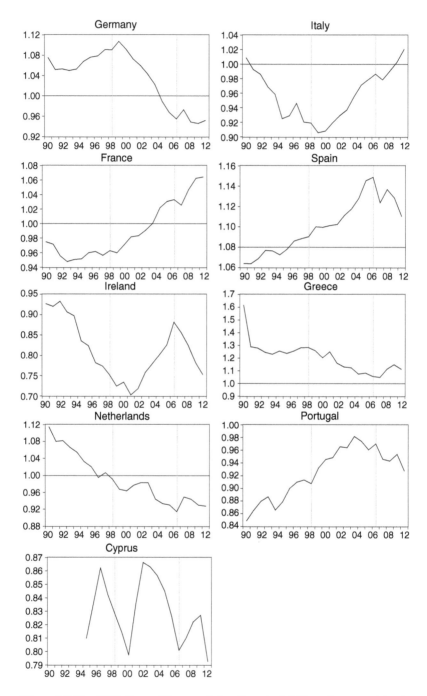

Figure 2.5 The CER Competitiveness Index for selected Euro Area countries (source: CER elaborations on AMECO data).

i.e. relative cost indicators, are able to explain the output of changes in the international position of Euro Area countries in terms of net exports and market penetration. The latter is usually measured in terms of market shares (*MKTsh*), although in order to get a clearer measure of competitiveness we also use variables derived from constant market share analysis (CMS). This analysis has the advantage of distinguishing between demand effects due to trade specialisation in products or markets that expand rapidly and supply effects due to improvements in productivity and cost competitiveness. We apply the CMS methodology as developed by the ECB (2005) and calculate demand and supply effects for total export and for intra-European exports only. We then test the ability of competitiveness indicators to explain these components. The details of the CMS are described in Appendix 1.

Another output indicator of a country's international competitiveness position is given by the trade balance (*TB*), which is the main component of the current account balance, a measure used by the European Commission in the scoreboard for identifying macroeconomic imbalances (EC, 2011). However in our view, the use of current accounts can be misleading as they reflect also other components not necessarily related to the competitiveness of a country's industry (see Chapter 1). We use, therefore, data for net exports and distinguish again for total trade and intra-EU trade.

Hence, we estimate a model with three output or 'revealed' competitiveness indicators, calculated for total and intra-EU trade: the market share (*MKTshT*, *MKTshEU*), the competitiveness effect calculated from the CMS analysis (*CT*, *CEU*) and the trade balance (*TBT*, *TBEU*). The indicators which will be tested against the CCI are conventional nominal and real unit labour costs (*ULCrel* and *RULCrel*) as well as the real effective exchange rate (*REERrel*). All these indicators are expressed in relative terms with the Euro Area level as the common denominator.

The econometric specification includes domestic as well as world GDP in order to account for internal and external demand and a set of country specific fixed effects as in equation (11):

$$Y_{i,t} = \alpha + \beta_1 \log GDPw_{i,t} + \beta_2 \log GDP_{i,t} + \beta_3 COMP_{i,t} + U_i + \varepsilon_{i,t} \qquad (11)$$

where *Y*=*MKTshT*, *MKTshEU*, *CT*, *CEU*, *TBT*, *TBEU* and *COMP*=log(*CCIb*), log(*ULCrel*), log(*RULCrel*), log(*REERrel*).The sample includes the original 12 Euro Area countries over the period 1999–2010.

As to the estimation technique, we first have to test for the stationarity of data as well as for the presence of cross-sectional dependency (CSD). Table 2.A1 in the appendix shows the Pesaran (2004) test for CSD as well as the unit root test developed by Pesaran (2007), which is robust to the presence of CSD. The results indicate that all variables are non-stationary at 10 per cent level while CSD is present in all series except for the two trade balances and *CT*, and is particularly high for *MKTshT* and *REERrel* as well as GDP. This is because global market shares and GDP are affected by common shocks such as the global crisis or the competition of extra-Euro Area countries, while real exchange rates reflect, as we argued in the second section, the exchange rate dynamics between the euro and the other main currencies, especially the US dollar.

Given the non-stationarity and the presence of CSD, the common correlated coefficients (CCE) estimator developed by Pesaran (2006) is the most suitable tool. This estimator builds upon the mean group estimator proposed by Pesaran *et al.* (1999), which returns consistent estimates of a long-run relation even in presence of non-stationary variables and endogenous regressors. Endogeneity is addressed by using an auto-regressive distributed lags (ARDL) model while the improvement of the CCE is the addition of cross-sectional averages of all variables in order to control for CSD. As shown by Kapetanios *et al.* (2011), this estimator controls for a variety of structures of the common factor causing CSD, from a simple symmetric one to more complicate multifactor error structures.

Results

Estimation results of equation (1) for the competitiveness effect, the total market share change and the trade balance are reported respectively in Tables 2.2 to 2.4. At the bottom of each table we report the root mean square error (RMSE) as measure of model fitting and the Pesaran (2007) test for CSD on the estimation residuals. As to the latter, in the market share estimates some specifications still suffer from a weak CSD, but they are acceptable as the 5 per cent threshold for the CSD is never reached. The RMSE indicates that estimates in Tables 2.2 and 2.4 fit the data better. This is an interesting result as it confirms the above-mentioned problems with the use of market shares *tout court*, which amalgamate foreign demand and domestic supply factors. By contrast, our estimates for trade balances measure how much net exports improve in response to our input variables, given the importance of external and domestic demand components.

Our results confirm the better performance of the CCI compared with ULC and REER indices. As we can see in Table 2.2, the CCI is the only significant competitiveness indicator in explaining competitive changes of market shares. In addition, its coefficient is higher when considering intra-European export only (column 5), proving its better ability to reflect the dynamics of intra-European competitiveness. In the latter case, other things equal, a 10 per cent reduction of the CCI (i.e. a competitive gain due to lower ULCs relative to equilibrium) increases the competitiveness effect from the CMS by 8.3 per cent. Although the explanatory power for total market share changes is lower, the results in table 2.3 confirm the ability of the CCI to explain the intra-European dynamics. According to column 5, a 1 per cent increase in the CCI decreases the intra-European market share by 1.2 per cent. Finally, trade balance estimates (Table 2.4) also indicate that the CCI explains intra-European flows better. Yet, while the CCI is statistically significant for the world trade balance, the REER is statistically more significant in spite of its lower coefficient. This is an expected result as REER incorporate also exchange rate dynamics between the Euro Area and the rest of the world.

Summing up, we found a clear confirmation that the CCI is better suited to explain changes in the competitive position of European countries. The comparison

Table 2.2 Estimation results. Dependent variable: supply-side competitiveness effect from CMS

	Total				Intra-EU			
	1	2	3	4	5	6	7	8
Log(GDPw)	-0.224	0.039	-0.753	-0.123	0.183	-0.32	-0.397	1.627*
	[0.471]	[0.611]	[1.000]	[1.504]	[0.354]	[0.441]	[0.352]	[0.951]
Log(GDP)	0.262	0.198	0.425	0.422**	-0.113	0.292	0.27	0.238
	[0.423]	[0.487]	[0.415]	[0.178]	[0.419]	[0.499]	[0.416]	[0.502]
Log(CCI)	-0.659**				-0.832**			
	[0.215]				[0.354]			
Log(ULCrel)		-0.103				-0.492		
		[0.324]				[0.437]		
Log(RULCrel)			-0.263				-0.557	
			[0.263]				[0.541]	
Log(REERrel)				0.130				-0.217
				[0.157]				[0.280]
N	203	203	203	192	203	203	203	192
RMSE	0.023	0.022	0.025	0.019	0.027	0.027	0.029	0.026
CSD	-1.80*	-1.41	-1.94*	-1.73*	-1.66*	-1.15	-0.44	-1.96*

Notes
Standard errors in brackets; *significant at 10% level, **significant at 5% level; ***significant at 1% level.

Table 2.3 Estimation results. Dependent variable: market share change

	Total				Intra-EU			
	1	2	3	4	5	6	7	8
Log(GDPw)	-1.664 [1.475]	0.943 [0.749]	1.361 [0.853]	0.000 [0.001.]	0.161 [0.391]	-0.963 [0.644]	-0.868 [0.565]	0.278 [0.261]
Log(GDP)	0.686 [0.836]	1.68 [1.878]	2.159 [1.967]	2.067 [2.134]	-0.058 [0.493]	0.799 [0.604]	0.619 [0.533]	0.829 [0.679]
Log(CCI)	-0.539 [1.375]				-1.129** [0.397]			
Log(ULCrel)		-0.802 [0.869]				-0.383 [0.571]		
Log(RULCrel)			-0.024 [1.044]				-0.562 [0.673]	
Log(REERrel)				-0.888 [0.774]				-0.183 [0.299]
N	204	203	203	192	203	203	203	192
RMSE	0.54	0.48	0.5	0.43	0.29	0.31	0.33	0.27
CSD	-1.95*	-1.97*	-1.88*	-0.96	-1.92*	-1.95*	-1.55	-1.94*

Notes
Standard errors in brackets; *significant at 10% level, **significant at 5% level; ***significant at 1% level.

Table 2.4 Estimation results. Dependent variable: trade balance

	Total				Intra-EU			
	1	2	3	4	1	2	3	4
Log(GDPw)	0.083 [0.121]	0.029 [0.113]	-0.019 [0.093]	0.059 [0.108]	0.08 [0.085]	0.015 [0.085]	0.07 [0.088]	0.034 [0.103]
Log(GDP)	-0.103* [0.062]	-0.029 [0.043]	-0.073** [0.034]	-0.072 [0.081]	-0.143** [0.063]	-0.063 [0.064]	-0.115* [0.066]	-0.038 [0.081]
Log(CCI)	-0.093* [0.054]				-0.144** [0.060]			
Log(ULCrel)		-0.068 [0.053]				-0.153 [0.099]		
Log(RULCrel)			-0.065 [0.055]				-0.153 [0.111]	
Log(REERrel)				-0.056** [0.012]				-0.077 [0.062]
N	204	203	203	192	200	199	199	188
RMSE	0.003	0.004	0.003	0.002	0.02	0.04	0.03	0.03
CSD	-0.2	0.02	0.33	-0.07	0.64	0.42	-1.04	-0.11

Notes
Standard errors in brackets; *significant at 10% level; **significant at 5% level; ***significant at 1% level.

has shown that standard ULC and REER indices are not able to explain external competitiveness among European countries and the latter in particular tends to capture changes in the nominal exchange rate between the euro and the US$.

Conclusions

This chapter has defined competitiveness as the relative profitability of a country's capital stock relative to the average of the Euro Area. It has derived unit labour cost level indicators, which indicate how much individual member states are over- or undervalued relatively to the average benchmark. We have then confirmed that this measure yields better results for explaining how input variables in the competitiveness process, such as unit labour costs, generate the outcome of traditional competitiveness dynamics, which are reflected in exports or market shares. Using the CER Competitive Index would therefore be a superior tool for policy assessments than the conventional indices used by European and international organisations. It could become particularly useful as a guide for wage-bargaining in the Euro Area.

Appendix 1: Methodological note on the CMS

In calculating the competitiveness effect used in the fourth section we use the CMS methodology developed by the ECB (2005). The basic idea of the CMS is to decompose the growth rate of exports (g) of a country in a given destination market (or in a given region) in a component obtained by applying the growth rate of world exports (g^*) to the initial export flows and a residual component. The residual component represents what causes the market share change and we call it total effect (TE):

$$TE = g - g^* \tag{A1}$$

The total effect is than broken down into two components: a combined structural effect (CSE) and a competitiveness effect (COMP). The CSE is obtained by applying to each export flow the difference between the world export growth rate and that of the specific market:

$$CSE = \sum_i [\sum_j [(\theta_{ij} - \theta_{ij}^*)](g_{ij}^* -]g^*) \tag{A2}$$

where g^*_{ij} is the growth rate of total imports of product i in country j; $\theta_{i,j}$ and θ^*_{ij} represent the shares of product i in country j for the exporting country and world respectively. Further refinements of the analysis (Leamer and Stern, 1970; Richardson, 1971a, 1971b) decompose the structural effect into three terms which account for the geographical (market effect *ME*) and sectoral (commodity effect *CE*) composition of exports as well as for their interaction (*MIX*):

$$CSE = ME + CE + MIX \tag{A3}$$

The latter term is included because the geographical and sectoral distributions are not independent so that the sum of the first two effects does not equal the CSE if either Laspeyres or Paasche weights are used.

The market effect represents the export growth obtained as weighted average of the growth rates of specific markets (net of world growth) with weights given by the initial export distribution by partner:

$$ME = \sum_j (\theta_j - \theta_j^*)(g_j^* - g^*) \tag{A4}$$

Where g_j^* is the growth rate of total imports of country j, θ_j and θ_j^* represent the geographical distribution of exports for the reference country and the world. By the same token, the commodity effect is the effect of total growth of each commodity (net of world growth) weighted by the commodity distribution:

$$CE = \sum_j (\theta_i - \theta_i^*)(g_i^* - g^*) \tag{A5}$$

The interaction effect is given by:

$$\sum_i \sum_j \left[(\theta_{ij} - \theta_{ij}^*) - (\theta_i - \theta_i^*) \frac{\theta_{ij}^*}{\theta_i^*} - \frac{(\theta_j - \theta_j^*)(\theta_{ij}^*)}{\theta_j^*} \right] g_{ij}^* \tag{A6}$$

In simple words this effect represents the impact of the change in both geographical and sectoral weights. Some authors find no economic meaning for the interaction effect (Reymert and Schultz, 1985) while Richardson (1971b) called this effect 'Second Competitiveness Effect'. For each exporting country, the standard competitiveness effect is given by the difference between the growth rate of exports of commodity i in country j and world exports of i in country j, weighted by the initial structure:

$$COMP = \sum_i \sum_j \theta_{ij}(g_{ij} - g_{ij}^*) \tag{A7}$$

This competitiveness effect represents the difference between the growth of exports for a given country and world exports net of differences in relative specialisation.

Appendix 2: Derivatives of the CER Competitiveness Index

By manipulating equation (7), the derivates with respect to the different variables can be expressed as follows:

$$\frac{\partial CCI}{\partial ULC_A} = \frac{k_A P_{EA}}{\left(k_{EA} P_A ULC_{EA} - P_{EA} P_A k_{EA} + P_{EA} P_A k_A \right)^2} > 0 \text{ if}$$

$$\frac{ULC_A}{P_A} > k_{EA} - k_A; \tag{A1}$$

The condition for a positive sign is always satisfied as the term on the left-hand side is always positive and well above realistic differences in capital efficiency. The sign of derivatives with respect to ULC_{EA}, k_A and k_{EA} is determined as shown in equations (A2) to (A4):

$$\frac{\partial CCI}{\partial ULC_{EA}} = -\frac{k_{EA}k_A P_A P_{EA} ULC_{EA}}{\left(k_{EA}P_A ULC_{EA} - P_{EA}P_A k_{EA} + P_{EA}P_A k_A\right)^2} < 0; \tag{A2}$$

$$\frac{\partial CCI}{\partial k_A} = \frac{k_{EA}(ULC_{EA} - P_{EA})}{\left(k_{EA}P_A ULC_{EA} - P_{EA}P_A k_{EA} + P_{EA}P_A k_A\right)^2} < 0; \tag{A3}$$

$$\frac{\partial CCI}{\partial k_{EA}} = -\frac{k_A P_A P_{EA} ULC_A (ULC_{EA} - P_{EA})}{\left(k_{EA}P_A ULC_{EA} - P_{EA}P_A k_{EA} + P_{EA}P_A k_A\right)^2} > 0; \tag{A4}$$

Which states that competitiveness always increases when the own capital efficiency of average ULCs increases, but deteriorates when average ACE increases more than the domestic one. The effect of domestic inflation is show in equation (A5):

$$\frac{\partial CCI}{\partial P_A} = -\frac{k_A P_{EA} ULC_A \left[k_{EA}(ULC_{EA} - P_{EA}) + P_{EA}k_A\right]}{\left(k_{EA}P_A ULC_{EA} - P_{EA}P_A k_{EA} + P_{EA}P_A k_A\right)^2} < 0; \text{ if}$$

$$k_A > k_{EA}(1 - \frac{ULC_{EA}}{P_{EA}}); \tag{A5}$$

Its effect on competitiveness is positive unless a country's ACE is above the average profit rate. As the latter has been basically stable at 0.13 and ACE is always above 0.2 this condition, which underlines the importance of a certain degree of similarity between countries, is always fulfilled. Conversely, the effect of average inflation is always negative:

$$\frac{\partial CCI}{\partial P_{EA}} = \frac{P_A \left[k_{EA}(ULC_{EA} - P_{EA} + 1) + P_{EA}k_A\right]}{\left(k_{EA}P_A ULC_{EA} - P_{EA}P_A k_{EA} + P_{EA}P_A k_A\right)^2} > 0; \tag{A6}$$

The explanation for these effects lies in the nominal nature of the CCE and in the additional effect on ACE. In standard ULCs a domestic price increase raises both nominal labour productivity and nominal wages, with the overall effect uncertain but positive, if wage inflation is higher than overall inflation. In the CCI we have to take into account the positive effect of prices on nominal ACE, which reduces the CCI if is strong enough to counterbalance the effect of higher wage inflation. The overall effect will always be negative if wage inflation is not higher than actual inflation.

Appendix 3: Unit root and cross-sectional dependence tests

Table 2.A1 Results of the Pesaran (2007) unit root test and Pesaran (2004) test for cross-sectional dependency

	Unit root	Cross sectional dependence	Cross correlation
CT	2.8	0.6	0.02
CEU	0.1	−1.8*	−0.06
MKTshT	−1.4	26.8***	0.86
MKTshEU	−1.6*	−2.6**	−0.08
TBT	−1.0	1.3	0.04
TBEU	0.6	−1.0	−0.03
log(CCI)	−0.3	−2.3**	−0.07
log(ULCrel)	1.6	3.0***	0.09
log(RULCrel)	−0.4	−0.4	−0.01
log(REERrel)	−2.2*	18.4***	0.57
log(GDP)	−1.0	32.7***	0.98

Notes
* Significant at 10% level, **significant at 5% level; ***significant at 1% level.

Notes

1 http://ec.europa.eu/economy_finance/economic_governance/macroeconomic_imbalance_procedure/index_en.htm (accessed 29 May 2013).
2 These improvements are not necessarily restricted to investment goods, but consumer imports may indirectly also improve competitiveness by setting quality standards against which local firms have to prove themselves.
3 See the introduction to the book.

References

Aldington Report (1985), *Report from the Select Committee of the House of Lords on Overseas Trade*. London: HMSO.

Bennett, H. Z., J. Escolano, S. Fabrizio, E. Gutierrez, I. V. Ivaschenko, B. Lissovolik, W. Schule, S. Tokarick, Y. Xiao and M. Moreno Badia (2008), 'Competitiveness in the southern Euro Area: France, Greece, Italy, Portugal, and Spain'. *IMF Working Paper* WP/08/112.

Blanchard, O. and F. Giavazzi (2002), 'Current account deficits in the Euro Area: the end of the Feldstein–Horioka puzzle?' *Brookings Papers on Economic Activity,* 2: 147–186.

Boltho, A. (1996), 'The assessment: international competitiveness'. *Oxford Review of Economic Policy,* 12(3): 1–16.

Buckley, P. J., C. L. Pass and K. Prescott (1988), 'Measures of international competitiveness: a critical survey'. *Journal of Marketing Management,* 4(2): 175–200.

Buiter, W. H. (1981), 'Time preference and international lending and borrowing in an overlapping-generations model'. *Journal of Political Economy,* 89: 769–797.

Chen, R., G. M. Milesi-Ferretti and T. Tressel (2013), 'External imbalances in the Euro-zone'. *Economic Policy,* 73: 102–142.

Collignon, S. (2013), 'Macroeconomic imbalances and competitiveness in the Euro Area'. *Transfer: Eurpean Review of Labour and Research*, 19(1): 63–87.

Croci-Angelini, E. and F. Farina (2012), 'Current account imbalances and systemic risk within a monetary union'. *Journal of Economic Behavior and Organization*, 83: 647–656.

De Grauwe, P. (2011), 'The governance of a fragile Eurozone'. *CEPS Working Document*, No. 346, May.

ECB (2005), 'Competitiveness and the export performance of the Euro Area'. *Occasional Paper Series*, 30.

ECFIN (2012), Quarterly report on price and cost competitiveness, 4th quarter 2012. http://ec.europa.eu/economy_finance/publications/pcqr/2012/pdf/pccr312_en.pdf.

European Commission (2011), 'Scoreboard for the surveillance of macroeconomic imbalances: envisaged initial design'. *Commission Staff Working Paper* 8/11/2011.

European Commission (2012) 'Macroeconomic Imbalances Procedure'. http://ec.europa.eu/economy_finance/economic_governance/macroeconomic_imbalance_procedure/index_en.htm.

Fagerberg, J. and G. Sollie (1987), 'The method of constant market shares analysis reconsidered'. *Applied Economics*, 19(12): 1571–83.

Feldstein, M. and C. Horioka (1980) 'Domestic saving and international capital flows'. *Economic Journal*, 90(358): 314–329.

Giavazzi, F. and L. Spaventa (2010), 'Why the current account may matter in a monetary union: lessons from the financial crisis in the Euro Area'. Discussion Paper 8008. Centre for Economic Policy Research, London.

Guerrieri, P. and P. Esposito, P. (2012), 'Intra-European imbalances, adjustment and growth in the Eurozone'. *Oxford Review of Economic Policy*, 28(3), 532–550.

Guerrieri, P., and P. Esposito (2013) 'The determinants of macroeconomic imbalances in the Euro Area: the role of external performance,' in L. Paganetto (ed.), *Public Debt, Global Governance and Economic Dynamism*, Milan: Springer Verlag: 105–125.

Ingram, James, C. (1973), 'The case for European monetary integration'. Essays in International Finance 98, April. International Finance Section, Princeton University.

Kapetanios, G. M. H. Pesaran and T. Yamagata (2011), 'Panels with non-stationary multifactor error structures'. *Journal of Econometrics*, 160(2): 326–348.

Keyder, N., Y. Saglam and K. Ötztürk (2004), 'International competitiveness and the Unit Labour Cost Based Competitiveness Index'. *METU Studies in Development*, 31 (June): 43–70.

Krugman, P. (1994), 'Competitiveness: a dangerous obsession'. *Foreign Affairs*, 73(2): 28–44.

Krugman, P. (1996), 'Making sense of the competitiveness debate'. *Oxford Review of Economic Policy*, 12(3): 1–16.

Leamer, E. F. and R. M. Stern (1970), *Quantitative International Economics*. Chicago: Alpine Press.

Milana, C. (1988), 'Constant-market-shares analysis and index number theory'. *European Journal of Political Economy*, 4(4): 453–478.

Obstfeld, M. and K. Rogoff (1995), 'The intertemporal approach to the current account'. In G. M. Grossman and K. Rogoff (eds), *Handbook of International Economics*, vol. 3. Amsterdam: North-Holland: 1731–1799.

OECD (1992), *Technology and the Economy: The Key Relationships*. Paris: OECD.

Pesaran, M. H. (2004) 'General diagnostic tests for cross-section dependence in panels'. *IZA Discussion Paper* No. 1240.

Pesaran, M. H. (2006) 'Estimation and inference in large heterogeneous panels with a multifactor error structure'. *Econometrica*, 74(4): 967–1012.

Pesaran, M. H. (2007) 'A simple panel unit root test in the presence of cross-section dependence'. *Journal of Applied Econometrics*, 22(2): 265–312.

Pesaran, M. H., Y. Shin and R. P. Smith (1999), 'Pooled mean group estimation of dynamic heterogeneous panels'. *Journal of the American Statistical Association*, 94(446): 621–634.

Reymert, R. and C. E. Schultz (1985), *Export and Market Share*. Report 5/85. Oslo: Central Bureau of Statistics.

Richardson, J. D. (1971a), 'A constant market shares analysis for export growth'. *Journal of International Economics*, 1(1): 227–239.

Richardson, J. D (1971b), 'Some sensitivity tests for a constant market shares analysis of export growth'. *Review of Economics and Statistics*, 53: 300–304.

Sachs, T. D. (1981) 'The current account and macroeconomic adjustment in the 1970s'. *Brookings Papers on Economic Activity* 1: 201–268.

Part II

Competitiveness and external trade

3 Is Germany's model of export-led growth sustainable in a currency union?[1]

Ulrich Fritsche

The European monetary union is in trouble. Economically, the divergence of competitiveness as measured by unit labour cost came to an end by letting some countries in the southern cone of Europe slide into deep depressions which in turn produced political trouble. Germany, however, runs an economic system based on the principles of export-led growth which is still viable due to the fact that the US and some Asian economies recovered fast due to very expansionary monetary and fiscal stimulus. The general aim of this chapter is to give some answers to the question of how to cope with imbalances in the monetary union and the role of a former key currency country therein.

Sustainability dimensions as reference

This chapter is normative in nature. Therefore we need criteria to assess if a model of export-led growth is compatible with long-run aims of the European integration. The monetary union is not an end in itself. It aims to foster prosperity and convergence of income and living conditions and to increase overall economic welfare. However, the problem is more complex as the economic sphere interacts with political and social dimension of the integration process. A natural choice to evaluate the German export-led growth model is therefore found in the sustainability debate.

Traditionally – see Deutscher Bundestag (1998) – the sustainability debate focuses on three pillars: the ecological, economic and social dimensions of sustainability. The classical definition of sustainability dates back to the Brundtland Report of 1987 (United Nations, 1987) and states (p. 2) that 'sustainable development is development that meets the needs of the present without compromising the ability of future generations to meet their own needs'. Usually, sustainable development could be directly linked to the satisfaction of basic needs, active participation and intergenerational and global justice. However several other notions could be added without contradicting and even supporting the general notion of sustainability as defined in 1987. Three of them are important in our context of assessing the viability of the monetary union.

1 Social risk management capabilities: The concept of social risk management was defined by the World Bank (Holzmann and Jorgensen, 2001). Within

the context of this approach, the 'traditional' areas of social protection as labour market institutions, social insurance and social safety-nets are embedded into a broader framework. This broader framework is based on the strategic side on different ways to deal with risk (in the Holzmann–Jorgensen framework the strategies are risk coping, risk mitigating and risk prevention) and on different levels of actors. A functioning social risk management system can be seen as an aspect of sustainable development.

2   Income and wealth distribution: The original notion of sustainability as indicated by the Brundtlandt Report referred to intergenerational balance of interests. Income and wealth distribution aspects are therefore part of sustainability.

3   Political stability: The economic and political spheres are highly interrelated. Social risk management as well as income and wealth distribution aspects feed back into the political sphere. The dramatic loss of confidence in the political class in the countries deeply involved in depression and crisis states endangers the European integration process dramatically. Therefore this dimension should be part of any analysis.

Based on such an extended 'sustainability view' it should be possible to answer the question of whether the export-led growth model of Germany is coherent (i.e. sustainable) with the functioning of the European monetary union as an economic entity.

Export-led growth history

Originally, development economics was based on the idea of scarce physical capital which had to be financed by redirecting savings flows from industrialised countries into developing countries. Insufficient savings were seen as the main source of bottlenecks in the development process (Fritsche, 2004) which was a main result of the interpretation of the Solow growth (Solow, 1956) model. Extended models of this type with several bottlenecks' can be found in the neoclassical-monetarist (Khan *et al.*, 1991) and the post-Keynesian (Taylor, 1991, 1993) literature. To a large extent, developing countries used non-market instruments (e.g. interest rate caps and fund channeling through state-owned institutions to foster development) and financial repression (Fry, 1995) to achieve investment-led growth financed mainly by external savings. This 'debt-cum-development' strategy of the 1960s and 1970s together with global financial deregulation came at a cost – as Diaz-Alejandro put it once 'Good-bye financial repression, hello financial crash' (Diaz-Alejandro, 1985). The direct answer to the failure of the development strategy in the 1960s and 1970s was labeled the Washington Consensus (Williamson, 2000 on the development of the term). This Washington Consensus as a development strategy was the answer of the IMF and the World Bank to import-substitution strategies and was mainly based on supply-side reforms and trade and financial liberalisation measures. The financial crisis of the 1990s – mainly the Asian crisis but also the Russian crisis and the breakdown of the Currency Board in Argentina – led to more subtle views on development strategies (Stiglitz, 1998; Rodrik, 2008). The role of far-reaching financial deregulation was questioned and the focus was oriented towards the development strategy of post-war Germany, Japan and other Asian (Tiger, Flying Goose, whatever) countries. Stiglitz (1998) created the phrase 'post-Washington consensus' for the new view. Main components are the importance of safeguards for the development process, institutions which promote export-led growth strategies, very competitive exchange rates as well as capital controls to avoid appreciation. In a nutshell, such a strategy calls for an active 'beggar-thy-neighbour' strategy based on the undervalued real exchange rates as a driver of accumulation – a strategy which formed the base for the German successful development process after the Second World War (Riese, 1978).

There are three remarkable aspects which make the case of Germany interesting as a role model:

1   The macroeconomic foundation of the development strategy: The undervalued currency – which in turn implies revaluation expectations under the assumption of functioning financial markets – can be to a large extent defended by central bank interventions without necessarily destroying the competitiveness advantage for promoting exports.
2   The microeconomic incentive compatibility: The outward-orientation of the export-led growth model usually leads to dynamic efficiency gains.
3   The social and political aspect: The export-led growth strategy is usually based and enhances/deepens a social consensus which has to be at the root of such a strategy. In a sense export-led growth strategy is a national experiment and can only be successful if the national economic policy institutions play their respective role (i.e. avoid overvaluation of the currency by choosing appropriate wage, monetary and fiscal policies).

However such a strategy creates repercussions in a global context and has limits insofar as there must be at least one big current account deficit country which has a stabilising role for the aggregate demand schedule. Key currency regimes in the past had such 'big spenders' – Great Britain in the gold standard era (Bloomfield, 1959) as well as post-war United States under the Bretton Woods regime performed quite well in that respect. Under the EMS regime, Germany was also seen as a key currency. However there was one important difference with regard to Germany's role in the EMS.

Germany's affinity to tighten the belt

This big difference between traditional key currencies and the role of Germany in the process of EMU creation is the fact that Germany – and the actors relevant for monetary, fiscal and wage policy – always kept the attitude and the behaviour of a developing country using the (once successful) strategy of export-led growth (see Chapter 4). This can be proven by analysing relative unit labour cost developments (Dullien and Fritsche, 2008; Dullien, 2009) and widening current account imbalances over the 2000s as well as the deeply imprinted view among the German public that the level of wages in Germany is way too high compared to 'necessary' levels.

Dullien and Fritsche (2008, 2009) looked carefully at the sources of unit labor cost and divergence before the financial crisis and compared the results to established currency areas as the United States (federal states) or the developments of unit labour costs across the German *Länder* over time. Two results were striking: The deviations were more pronounced and more persistent. This is a well-established result and was also published by the European Commission (2008) in the report 'EMU@10'. Such deviations could be due to several reasons (see Dullien and Fritsche, 2008 for a more extensive discussion) – some of them are summarised in Figure 3.1 below.

The analysis of Dullien and Fritsche (2008, 2009) – published before the climax of the European financial and debt crisis – pointed to unwanted structural divergence as the main driver of the problem. However, a fact that was largely missing in the pre-crisis analysis and is largely missing in the analysis of the recent trouble in Europe (with the possible exception of Flassbeck and Spiecker, 2010) is the fact that such a long period of lasting and widening imbalances became only possible because of Germany's deeply imprinted affinity to 'tighten the belt'. To some extent, this was one of the deep structural reasons for the long-lasting development of imbalances.

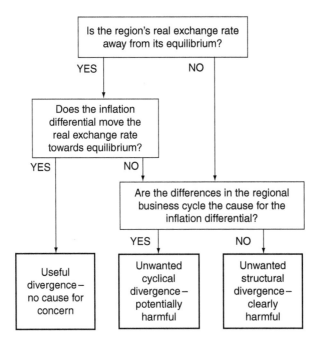

Figure 3.1 Classifying divergences in a monetary union (source: Dullien and Fritsche, 2009).

Governance structures in the EMU

A widely discussed topic in the last years refers to the reorganisation of the governance structure in the EMU (Dullien and Schwarzer, 2011). The proposals are heterogeneous in details but tend to agree on the necessity of avoiding persistent and large competitiveness divergence or current account imbalances. The EU commission tries to monitor signs of divergences more closely and much faster than they did before. However, one point which has not yet been tackled appropriately in the discussion is the deeply imprinted 'tighten the belt' phenomenon in Germany. The reason is clear – any governance structure in EMU focuses on the avoidance of negative development (above average inflation, high budget deficits, increasing current account deficits) but has dramatic weaknesses with regard to the 'tighten the belt' phenomenon. This is quite obvious because, at first glance, this strategy is not rational as the neoclassical standard model implies significant welfare losses. However as long as economic policy governance is based on welfare principles, this weakness remains embedded in policy institutions. A 'beggar-my-neighbor' policy is not punished systematically by rules as it makes no sense at all in the long run. At a second glance, the export-led-growth strategy, based on highly competitive wage negotiations and high productivity increases, of course makes sense from a national (i.e. German) perspective as long as the effective demand schedule from the rest of the world is stable

Export-led growth and sustainability of the currency union

If however, the narrow focus of national interest is given up and we try to evaluate the question if the export-led-growth strategy of Germany is in line with a sensible interpretation of sustainability, we will end up with other conclusions. Let me summarise this in the form of two theses:

> *Thesis 1: Sustainability of the economic development within the currency union calls for an end of the export-led-growth–tightening-the-belt–beggar-thy-neighbour strategy.*

This is due to two reasons. First, any adjustment of persistent imbalances in the currency union without lifting the restriction of a currency union (i.e. giving up the parity) is seriously only possible if the German economy is inflated to some extent (Blanchard *et al.*, 2013). Second, giving up the obsession with export-led growth (i.e. tighten your belt) is a necessary precondition so that imbalances like those of 1998–2008 do not occur again once the imbalances are corrected.

> *Thesis 2: The governance structure of economic policy has to be reoriented towards a concept of sustainable macroeconomic development on a European level.*

So far, the German 'tighten-the-belt' strategy is not punished (not even punishable) within the existing governance structure of the European Union. This is true for two reasons. First, there is no theoretical argument why systematic 'tighten-the-belt' should occur. The governance structure assumes a form of rationality based on the neoclassical synthesis model which has no room for such a behaviour. Second, and more importantly, the analysis of economic governance structures should be focused on a broader understanding of sustainability of development.

Note

1 The author thanks Stefan Collignon, Sebastian Dullien and, most importantly, Ingrid Größl for stimulating discussions. All errors are mine.

References

Blanchard, Olivier, Florence Jaumotte and Prakash Loungani (2013), 'Labor market policies and IMF advice in advanced economies during the great recession'. International Monetary Fund, Staff Discussion Note SDN/13/02.

Bloomfield, Artur, I. (1959), *Monetary Policy under the International Gold Standard, 1880–1914*. New York: Arno Press.

Deutscher Bundestag (1998), 'Abschlußbericht der Enquete-Kommission Schutz des Menschen und der Umwelt – Ziele und Rahmenbedingungen einer nachhaltig zukunftsverträglichen Entwicklung'. Deutscher Bundestag: Drucksache 13/11200, 26 June 1998.

Diaz-Alejandro, Carlos (1985), 'Good-bye financial repression, hello financial crash'. *Journal of Development Economics*, 19: 1–24.

Dullien, Sebastian (2009), 'Divergences in EMU: scope of the problem and policy options'. *Intervention. European Journal of Economics and Economic Policies*, 6(1): 24–32.

Dullien, Sebastian and Daniela Schwarzer (2009), 'Bringing macroeconomics into the EU budget debate: why and how?' *Journal of Common Market Studies*, 47(1): 153–174.

Dullien, Sebastian and Ulrich Fritsche (2008), 'Does the dispersion of unit labor cost dynamics in the EMU imply long-run divergence? Results from a comparison with the United States of America and Germany'. *Journal of International Economics and Economic Policy*, 5(8): 269–295.

Dullien, Sebastian and Ulrich Fritsche (2009), 'How bad is divergence in the euro-zone? Lessons from the United States of America and Germany'. *Journal of Post-Keynesian Economics*, 31(3): 431–450.

Dullien, Sebastian and Daniela Schwarzer (2011), 'Making macroeconomic stabilization work: lessons from the crisis for the EU budget debate'. In Iain Begg, Ansgar Belke, Daniela Schwarzer and Ramūnas Vilpišauskas (eds), *European Economic Governance – Impulses for Crisis Prevention and New Institutions*. Gütersloh: Bertelsmann: 93–118.

European Commission (2008), 'EMU@10: successes and challenges after 10 years of Economic and Monetary Union'. *European Economy*, 2, June 2008. Brussels.

Flassbeck, Heiner and Friederike Spiecker (2010), 'Lohnpolitische Konvergenz und Solidarität oderoffener Bruch. Eine große Krise der EWU ist nahezu unvermeidlich'. *Wirtschaftsdienst*, 3: 178–184.

Fritsche, Ulrich (2004), *Stabilisierungs- und Strukturanpassungsprogramme des Internationalen Währungsfonds in den 90er Jahren: Hintergründe, Konzeption und Kritik.* Berlin: Duncker & Humblot.

Fry, Maxwell, J. (1995), *Money, Interest, and Banking in Economic Development.* Baltimore: Johns Hopkins University Press.

Holzmann, Robert and Steen Jorgensen (2001), 'Social risk management: a new conceptual framework for social protection, and beyond'. *International Tax and Public Finance*, 8(4): 529–556.

Khan, Mohsin, S. Peter, J. Montiel and Nadeem UlHaque (1991), *Macroeconomic Models for Adjustment in Developing Countries.* Washington, DC: International Monetary Fund.

Riese, Hajo (1978), 'Strukturwandel und unterbewertete Währung in der Bundesrepublik Deutschland: Bemerkungen zur theoretischen Position des Instituts für Weltwirtschaft Kiel'. *Konjunkturpolitik*, 24(3): 143–169.

Rodrik, Dani (2008), 'Is there a new Washington Consensus?' *Project Syndicate*, 11 June. Available online at www.project-syndicate.org/commentary/is-there-a-new-washington-consensus.

Solow, Robert Merton (1956), 'A contribution to the theory of economic growth'. *Quarterly Journal of Economics*, 70: 65–94.

Stiglitz, Joseph (1998), *More Instruments and Broader Goals: Moving Toward the Post-Washington Consensus.* Villa Borsig Workshop Series 1998. Helsinki: German Foundation for International Development (DSE).

Taylor, Lance (1991), *Income Distribution, Inflation, and Growth: Lectures on Structuralist Macroeconomics Theory.* Cambridge, MA: MIT Press.

Taylor, Lance (1993), *The Rocky Road to Reform: Adjustment, Income Distribution, and Growth in the Developing World.* Cambridge, MA: MIT Press.

United Nations General Assembly (1987), *Report of the World Commission on Environment and Development: Our Common Future.* New York: United Nations.

Williamson, John (2000), 'What should the World Bank think about the Washington Consensus?' *World Bank Research Observer*, 15(2): 251–264.

4 Intra-European imbalances, competitiveness and external trade

A comparison between Italy and Germany

Piero Esposito and Paolo Guerrieri

Since late 1990s macroeconomic imbalances in the Eurozone increased constantly and became a critical factor in causing the current debt crisis. In these years southern European countries experienced huge losses in competitiveness and persistent accumulation of large current account deficits against northern Europe. In addition, during the global crisis the financing of the stimulus measures caused huge budget deficits, leading public debt to unsustainable levels, especially in Greece after the truth about the real conditions of public finances was found out by the new elected government of Papandreou in 2009.

Before the global financial crisis, little attention was paid to the increase of current account imbalances as they were considered the result of financial integration and liberalisation (Blanchard and Giavazzi, 2002). In addition, they were considered an optimal outcome of private saving and investment decisions (Gourinchas, 2002) justifying the policy of no government intervention (Clarida, 2007; Blanchard, 2006). A remarkable exception is given by Dullien and Fritsche (2009) who already in 2006 warned about the excessive ULC growth in Portugal, and to a lesser extent in Spain and Greece, coupled with the strong fall in Germany.

Following the global financial crisis, with the explosion of current account deficits and public debts in some southern European states, a growing body of research is dealing with the causes of imbalances. While most contributions point to the role of real (Croci-Angelini and Farina, 2012) and financial integration as well as interest rate reductions in southern member states (Schmitz and von Hagen, 2011; Croci-Angelini and Farina, 2012; European Commission, 2012; Chen *et al.*, 2013; Schnabl and Freitag, 2012), some authors suggest that the excessive lending of northern states contributed to such unequal development (Collignon, 2013; Makin and Narayan, 2011) especially when investment is not aimed at increasing the productive capacity (Giavazzi and Spaventa, 2010). Another strand of literature points to the role of wages and unit labour costs developments in European countries (Brancaccio, 2012; Onharan and Stockhammer, 2013; Collignon, 2013), in connection with the performance in external trade (Guerrieri and Esposito, 2012, 2013; Chen *et al.*, 2013). Most of these works conclude for the necessity of symmetric and coordinated policies at European level (Guerrieri and Esposito, 2012), mainly via coordinated wage setting processes (Brancaccio, 2012; Onharan and Stockhammer, 2013; Schnabl and Freitag, 2012).

This chapter investigates the role of the external performance in explaining the increase in imbalances by comparing the two main export-led growth economies in the Eurozone: Germany and Italy. More specifically, we will attempt to assess, on the one hand, the role of global trade integration, not only in terms of outsourcing, but also in terms of penetration of fast-growing markets. Following previous works (Guerrieri and Esposito, 2012, 2013; Chen *et al.*, 2013) we devote particular attention to the role of fragmentation of production with Central and Eastern European countries. In addition, we will focus on the integration with the Asia-Pacific region as it is the most dynamic area of the world in terms of growth and external performance. In a second analysis we will assess whether the introduction of the single currency has had a direct impact on the two countries' net trade and on the widening of imbalances.

The structure of the chapter is as follows: in the second section we will summarise the performance of the two countries and compare it with the evolution of cost competitiveness; in the third and fourth sections we will focus on external performance and stress the role of internationalisation and recomposition of trade flows as result of the increasing importance of emerging economies; in the fifth section we will provide an econometric test of the importance of outsourcing and trade integration in explaining the two countries' net exports; the verification of the impact of the euro introduction is in the sixth section while the seventh section concludes.

Two different performances in the last decade: the role of cost competitiveness

During the period 2000–2010 Germany performed better among advanced economies, with GDP growing by 2.2 per cent every year between 2004 and 2007 and by more than 3 per cent in 2010 and 2011, the highest rate since the unification. In addition, Germany is the only country where per capita GDP is back to the values reached in 2007 and where the employment dynamics are positive. The country managed to reduce its unemployment rate in the decade in question, and in 2011 it was at 6.6 per cent, well below that of United States (9 per cent). By contrast, Italian unemployment has increased continuously since 2008.

This pattern is in striking contrast with the performance from the mid-1990s to the early 2000s, when Germany was still paying the cost of the unification. Between 1999 and 2003 the country experienced a GDP growth among the lowest in the Euro area, with an average rate of 1.2 per cent falling to 1.1 per cent in per capita terms (Table 4.1). During the first part of the decade 2000–2010 Italy shared with Germany a low growth, but for the former the average growth over the period 2004–2007 was 1.6 per cent, more than half a

Table 4.1 GDP, per capita GDP and unemployment rate (annual percentage change)

	Germany			Italy		
	GDP	GDP per capita	Unemployment	GDP	GDP per capita	Unemployment
1993–1998	1.3	1.1	0.5	1.4	1.4	0.4
1999–2003	1.0	0.9	0.1	1.5	1.2	-0.6
2004–2007	2.2	2.3	-0.3	1.6	0.9	-0.6
2008–2009	-2.1	-1.8	-0.5	-3.3	-4.0	0.9
2010	3.6	3.7	-0.7	1.8	1.3	0.6
2011	3.0	3.0	-1.2	0.5	0.0	0.0
2012	0.7	0.5	-0.4	-2.2	-2.5	2.2

Source: AMECO.

percentage point of difference every year. With the global financial crisis the divergence was further exacerbated as Italy experienced a stronger loss in the period 2008–2009 and a lower recovery afterward, while in 2012 the country was again in recession, with a negative growth of 2.2 per cent.

The common feature between the two economies is the positive impact of net export on their growth dynamics over the past decades. This similarity came to an end in the first decade of this millennium as the two countries experienced different trajectories in terms of both export and trade balances. This divergence is clear when looking at their export performance relative to the 35 main industrial countries. As shown in Figure 4.1, in volume terms Germany improved its relative performance by over 30 per cent between 2000 and 2012 while Italian exports moved in the opposite direction, with a relative reduction of 20 percentage points since 1995, when the beneficial effects of the 1993 devaluation started to vanish. Complementary information is given by the evolution of market shares (Figure 4.2). Both countries are on a negative trend because of the increasing importance of emerging economies since the end of the 1980s, but since 1999 the German loss has been relatively small while Italy lost approximately 50 per cent of its share.

The differences between the two countries are even more marked when looking at trade and current account balances and consequently at their contribution to GDP growth. In Germany the current account balance passed from 1 per cent in 1999 to 5 per cent in 2007 thanks to a trade balance above 8 per cent of GDP (Figure 4.5). Even in the years from 2008 German net exports were high, around 6 per cent of GDP, contributing significantly to the overall growth. The Italian trade balance, on the contrary, passed from slightly positive values during the 1990s to increasing deficits in the following years (Figure 4.6). Net exports contributed negatively to the GDP growth over the whole decade and continued especially in 2010 and 2011 while in 2012 the

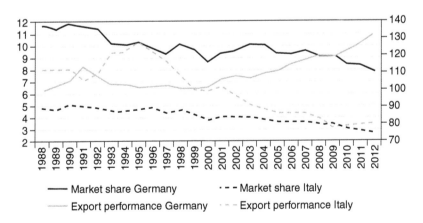

Figure 4.1 Index of real export (2000=100) relative to the main 35 industrialised countries and market shares at current prices (source: AMECO).

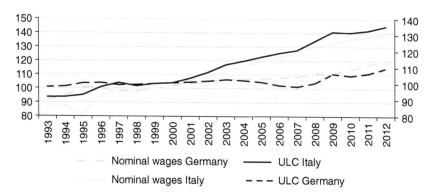

Figure 4.2 Nominal wages index (1999=100) and unit labour costs (source: own elaborations on AMECO).

trade balance turned positive, mainly because of the import reduction induced by the recession.

Traditional cost competitiveness factors are considered the main determinants of the external and overall performance of the two countries. Wage costs increased in Italy by almost 35 per cent between 1999 and 2012, twice as much as in Germany. At the same time the divergence in unit labour costs is even more marked as the gap widened between 1999 and 2012 by 25 per cent. No doubt such divergence in wages was favoured by the implementation of the reforms implemented by Gerard Schröder between 1998 and 2005, especially Agenda 2010, which introduced radical changes to the welfare state and labour market regulations. The Hartz reforms between 2003 and 2005 introduced a higher flexibility in the German labour market, in particular concerning hiring and firing procedures, and eliminated some perverse incentives in the structure of unemployment benefits.[1] The crucial point of the reforms implemented in Germany was the agreement signed with the trade unions by which a slow wage dynamic was accepted in order to keep employment levels stable. This reduction led to a depreciation of the real exchange rate (Marin, 2010b) up to the global financial crisis, boosting the German industry and its exports. The other side of the coin is that domestic demand stagnated over the same period.

The loss of competitiveness of the Italian economy with respect to Germany is due not only to the marked wage dynamics but also to differences in labour productivity. Figure 4.2 shows that the gap between the two countries in terms of unit labour costs (ULC) increased by more than 25 also as result of a 13 per cent gap in productivity over the same period.

Summing up, the divergence of the performances of the two countries over the period 2000–2010 seems to be due to the different contribution of net exports to GDP growth. While cost competitiveness played an important role, it cannot entirely account for the diverging performances. Structural and non-price factors must be investigated in order to explain competitiveness differences between the two countries and the resulting differences in their external performance.

The different degree of internationalisation

Following the vast geo-economic and technological changes affecting the world economy during the first decade of the new millennium, all advanced economies and their firms faced new challenges and opportunities to reorganise internationally their production processes through internationalisation and delocalisation activities. The difference in the ability to adapt to such changes can be analysed by looking at several indicators for Italy and Germany, all together giving a clear picture of the degree of internationalisation of the two countries.

A first indicator of the influence of the international context on the economic performance of a country is given by its degree of openness, measured as the average of export and import to GDP ratios. As clearly shown in Figure 4.3, while in mid-1990s, before monetary unification was completed and before the emergence of China as main world actor, the two countries shared a similar degree of openness. In contrast, in the 15 years from 1997 to 2012 a huge gap was generated as Germany doubled its openness (from 19 per cent to 38 per cent in goods and from 24 to 48 in goods and services) while Italy experienced only a modest increase (from 19 per cent to 23 per cent in goods and from 24 to 29 in goods and services).

Looking at trade flows gives only a partial picture about the process of internationalisation. Forms of deep integration between different economic systems arise from the ability to penetrate foreign markets by mean of both FDI and non-trade agreements. Similarly, the valorisation of the territory is a prerequisite to attract foreign direct investment (FDI; the so-called passive internationalisation).

Figure 4.3 Degree of trade opening (source: own elaboration on Eurostat-COMEXT 2011).

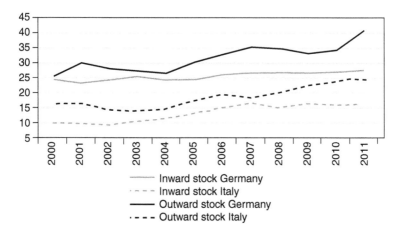

Figure 4.4 Inward and outward FDI stock as % of GDP (source: Eurostat).

The relevance of such phenomena is clear when looking at the world growth of FDI in the last two decades, far exceeding that of world production and trade, as a consequence of the deep historical changes taking place in the world economy in terms of both production and distribution of wealth. FDI data confirm the difference between Italy and Germany. Although, the inward FDI stock between 2000 and 2011 increased in Italy from 10 per cent to 17 per cent, more than the German one (from 25 to 28 per cent) there are still huge differences in levels. If we look at outward FDI the difference is more marked as the Italian stock increased from 16 per cent to 25 per cent of GDP while the German one passed from 25 per cent to 40 per cent.

Sectoral data indicate a higher concentration in the service sector in Germany and in high-tech manufacturing while for Italy FDI is more concentrated in traditional low-tech branches.

Globalisation and demand supply restructuring

The increase in Germany's trade openness is the result not only of growing exports but also of a rise in import penetration. The success of German firms in international markets is the outcome of their deep internationalisation in the form of increasing delocalisation and fragmentation of productions in order not only to penetrate new markets but also to purchase inputs at lower price. Trade relations with the two areas most interested by internationalisation activities, i.e. Central and Eastern Europe (CEEC) and Asia-Pacific, confirm the deeper efforts of the German economy.

As to CEEC,[2] trade integration between Germany and some Eastern European countries – above all Poland, Czech Republic, Hungary and Slovakia (CEEC4) – is mainly the result of a strong exchange of intermediate goods and components, both at the core of the international fragmentation processes started in the second half of the 1990s. Thanks also to the geographical proximity of these countries and their endowment of low-cost skilled workers, German firms moved part of their production processes to CEECs. As we can see from Table 4.2, all CEEC and in particular CEEC4 are among the main suppliers of German firms, replacing in many cases southern European countries, above all Italy. Several studies (Geishecker and Gorg, 2008; Geishecker *et al.*, 2010; Hansen, 2010; Marin, 2010a) suggest that German firms succeeded in cutting their labour costs through the relocalisation abroad of the production of components and processed materials. Some authors argue that such labour cost reduction is as relevant as wage moderation (Marin, 2010b) with the result of stronger productivity gains, up to above 20 per cent, for firms engaged in delocalisation activities (Hansen, 2010; Marin, 2010a).

The intensity of the relocalisation to the east is a crucial factor differentiating the two countries. Italian firms increased their international integration, but on a much smaller scale, keeping both import and export capacities at modest levels. As we can deduce from Figure 4.7 and Table 4.3, the increase in the importance of CEECs as import suppliers and in general the degree of opening toward this area are well below the German levels and the same is true for other dynamic areas like China and Pacific Asia. It is true that Italy did relatively better than other European countries in penetrating emerging markets (see Figure 4.8) but given its higher dependence on manufacturing and exports this result cannot be considered entirely positive.

Table 4.2 Geographical composition of German trade flows (in %)

	Import				Export			
	1999	*2005*	*2010*	*2011*	*1999*	*2005*	*2010*	*2011*
France	10.2	8.6	7.7	7.3	11.3	10.1	9.5	9.5
Italy	7.4	5.8	5.4	5.3	7.4	6.9	6.1	5.8
GIPSI	14.7	12.0	10.7	9.9	14.2	14.3	11.6	10.6
EU15	52.9	48.8	44.2	42.3	56.2	54.7	49.2	46.9
Czech Republic	2.2	2.8	3.7	3.6	1.9	2.4	2.8	2.8
Hungary	2.0	2.3	2.1	2.0	1.6	1.7	1.5	1.5
Poland	2.0	2.7	3.5	3.6	2.4	2.8	4.0	4.1
Slovakia	0.7	1.1	1.2	1.2	0.5	0.8	0.9	1.0
CEEC4	7.0	8.8	10.4	10.4	6.5	7.8	9.2	9.3
EU27	61.2	59.1	56.5	54.7	63.9	64.2	60.2	58.1
China	3.1	6.5	9.5	8.9	1.3	2.7	5.6	6.1
India	0.5	0.5	0.8	0.8	0.4	0.5	1.0	1.0
NIE	2.9	2.6	2.7	2.6	2.2	2.1	2.3	2.2
Dev. Asia	6.4	9.7	12.9	12.3	3.8	5.3	8.8	9.3
Japan	4.9	3.5	2.7	2.8	2.0	1.7	1.4	1.4
USA	8.0	6.7	5.6	5.5	9.9	8.8	6.8	7.0

Source: Own elaboration on COMTRADE.

Note
GIPSI = Greece, Ireland, Portugal, Spain, Italy; NIE = Korea, Malaysia, Singapore, Philippines, Thailand, Indonesia; Dev. Asia = China, India, NIE.

Table 4.3 Geographical composition of Italian trade flows (in %)

	Import				Export			
	1999	*2005*	*2010*	*2011*	*1999*	*2005*	*2010*	*2011*
France	12.6	9.9	8.7	8.3	13.1	12.2	11.6	11.5
Germany	19.2	17.1	16.0	15.6	16.6	13.1	12.9	13.1
GIPSI	6.9	6.5	6.3	6.1	10.5	11.0	8.7	7.6
EU15	61.1	52.7	47.3	45.8	57.8	52.9	47.9	46.3
Czech Republic	0.4	0.8	1.2	1.2	0.6	1.0	1.0	1.1
Hungary	0.7	0.9	1.0	0.9	0.8	1.0	0.9	0.9
Poland	0.8	1.3	2.0	1.9	1.6	1.9	2.5	2.5
Slovakia	0.4	0.5	0.7	0.7	0.3	0.4	0.6	0.6
CEEC4	2.3	3.6	4.9	4.8	3.3	4.2	5.1	5.1
EU27	65.3	58.6	54.6	53.1	63.1	60.3	56.3	54.9
China	2.4	4.6	7.8	7.3	0.8	1.5	2.5	2.7
India	0.6	0.7	1.0	1.2	0.3	0.5	0.9	0.9
NIE	1.4	1.3	1.4	1.5	2.3	2.2	2.2	2.4
Dev. Asia	4.4	6.6	10.3	10.0	3.5	4.3	5.7	6.0
Japan	2.5	1.6	1.2	1.1	1.6	1.5	1.2	1.3
USA	4.8	3.4	3.0	3.3	9.3	8.0	6.0	6.1

Source: own elaboration on COMTRADE.

Note
GIPSI = Greece, Ireland, Portugal, Spain, Italy; NIE = Korea, Malaysia, Singapore, Philippines, Thailand, Indonesia; Dev. Asia = China, India, NIE.

German firms not only restructured their supply side but took full advantage of the new demand for goods and services coming from emerging markets. The composition of demand after the global financial crisis and in particular that of consumption goods is changing at a previously unreached pace thanks to the contribution of the new emerging economies, above all the group of BRICs (Brazil Russia, India and China). The ability to penetrate these markets is fundamental in order to compete in the new multipolar economic order. The country's firms seem to have better exploited emerging markets (Figure 4.7), particularly in China (Tables 4.2 and 4.4). The Asian giant became the main market for equipment goods and for a basket of consumption goods, from cars to other durables, and the German market share in China passed from 2 per cent in 2000 to above 6 per cent in 2010. It is interesting to note that this increase is the mirror image of the market share reduction in the USA, from 10 per cent to 6.5 per cent during the same period. Such developments can be better understood by looking at changes in the revealed comparative advantages (RCA) of the two countries.[3] According to Table 4.4, Germany increased its specialisation towards all groups of emerging economies in consumption and equipment goods as well as parts and components. For consumption goods, in particular, the RCA index became higher than 1 relative to China, while for capital goods and parts and components the index is now strongly above 1 for all groups. Only for intermediate goods the country is despecialising, as a result probably of the feature of

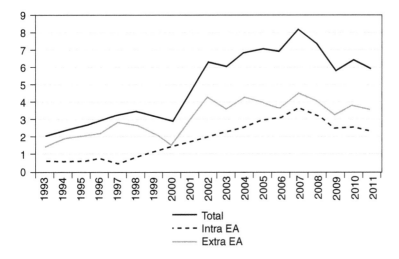

Figure 4.5 Total trade balance and share of the Euro area, Germany (source: own elaboration on COMTRADE).

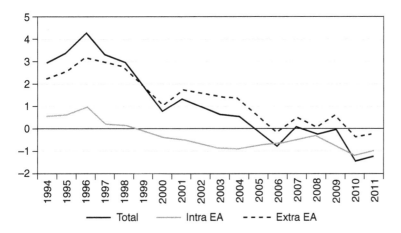

Figure 4.6 Total trade balance and share of the Euro area, Italy (source: own elaboration on COMTRADE).

delocalisation activities of German firms, more specialised in machinery and transport equipments.

Again, the comparison with Italy shows a marked difference. Despite the growth of overall internationalisation, the penetration of new emerging markets is relatively modest although in line with the European average (see Figure 4.8). The geographical specialisation of export (Table 4.3) increased only slowly in China, while from the import side we can observe a strong increase of both

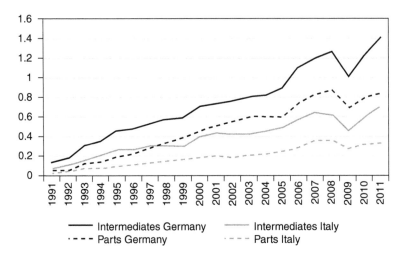

Figure 4.7 Import of intermediates from CEEC4 (% of GDP) (source: own elaboration on COMTRADE).

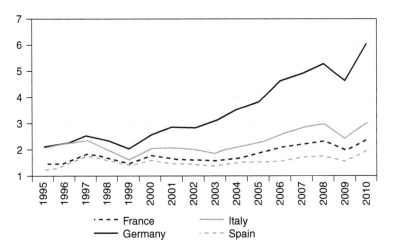

Figure. 4.8 Export toward emerging markets (% of GDP) (source: own elaboration on COMTRADE).

CEEC and Pacific Asia while the contribution of the Euro Area is diminishing. This evidence is an indication of the increasing competitive pressure of emerging market exports on Italian goods (see Guerrieri and Esposito, 2013). Italian RCA are somehow the mirror image of the German ones. Between 1995 and 2011 the index dropped in all cases, except for intermediate goods which, in any case, do not show a clear pattern. It is important to note that in 1995 the index was almost everywhere above 1 while now the opposite is true, meaning that the country is not keeping pace with the other advanced European economies.

As we already mentioned, the introduction of the single currency seems to have played a crucial role in the positive development of the German trade balance. As shown in Figure 4.5, from the end on 1990s net exports within the Euro area were higher than those from the rest of the world, with an increasing gap especially between 2001 and 2007. This result is partly due to the benefits of the fixed exchange rate regime on a country with a strong currency like Germany. In contrast, Italian export competitiveness has historically relied on the possibility of devaluation of the domestic currency, hence, a fixed exchange rate regime, dominated by the German mark, has uncovered the problems of the Italian production structure, causing a continuous loss in competitiveness; the deterioration of the Italian trade balance is due mainly to the result within the Euro Area (Figure 4.6) as the extra-area trade balance kept stable or slightly increasing until 2003; after that, both components dropped to values close to zero. This different behaviour points to the peculiar role of the euro introduction in fostering the German economy at the expense of Italy and the other southern European countries. Empirical evidence of this assumption will be provided in the sixth section.

Summarising, the external performance of the two countries appear to be a reflection of the ability to exploit delocalisation processes and to penetrate fast growing markets, with Germany strongly increasing its integration in the world economy and Italy unable to compete in the world market.

Fragmentation and trade integration: econometric analysis

In the previous sections we showed how Germany seems to have taken better advantage of the new opportunities provided from the world development from the end of the 1990s up to the global financial crisis. On the one hand, the supply side took advantage of an increased fragmentation and international division of labour, especially with Central and Eastern European countries, which boosted the competitiveness of German firms. On the other hand, the country is increasing its degree of internationalisation and exploiting the new opportunities arising from the penetration of emerging markets, above all the Asia-Pacific area, and from the increased importance in the European market.

The aim of this section is to provide empirical evidence on the different micro and macro-economic determinants of net exports of the two countries by using a panel of 14 industries (classification NACE DA-DN) over the period 1993–2010. In a first set of regressions we will estimate the impact of outsourcing, separating the effect of global sourcing from that arising specifically from the integration of production with the group of CEEC4. In a second set of regressions we will test the effect of trade opening, where we will distinguish between global trade integration and the rise of the Asia-Pacific area in total trade of the two countries. In both cases we will estimate two separate coefficients for the group of high- and low-tech industries. This division takes into account first, the different specialisation of the two countries, and second, the possibility that spillovers arising from trade and outsourcing activities are stronger in high tech industries because of a higher concentration of skill biased technical change, as reported in various studies (Haskel and Slaughter, 2002; Esposito and Stehrer, 2009; Cavallaro *et al.*, forthcoming). The two estimated equations are the following:

$$\Delta \log TrBal_{i,t} = \alpha_1 + \beta_1 \Delta(TradeIPCsh_{i,t}) + \beta_2 \Delta(TradeIPCshC4_{i,t}) +$$
$$\beta_3 \Delta(TradeIPCshC4_{i,t}) * Htech + Htech +$$
$$\sum_{k=1}^{K} \lambda_k \Delta x_{i,t} + \gamma_t + \varepsilon_{i,t} \qquad (1)$$

$$\Delta \log TrBal_{i,t} = \alpha_1 + \beta_1 \Delta(Trade_{i,t} / GDP_{i,t}) + \beta_2 \Delta(TradeShEM_{i,t}) +$$
$$\beta_3 \Delta(TradeShEM_{i,t}) * Htech + Htech +$$
$$\sum_{k=1}^{K} \lambda_k \Delta x_{i,t} + \gamma_t + \varepsilon_{i,t} \qquad (2)$$

where *TrBal* is the ratio of export to import of industry i in time t; *TradeIPCsh* is the share of intermediates and parts and components on total trade, which should capture the degree of international fragmentation of production; *TradeIPCshC4* is the share of CEEC4 in total trade in intermediates and parts and components; *Trade/GDP* is the trade to GDP ratio, *TradeShEM* is the share of emerging economies in total trade and, finally, *Htech* is a dummy indicating high-tech industries.[4] Given our focus on the Asia-Pacific area we will test the impact of China and the group of ASEAN countries, both separately and as a single group. As to the control variables included in the vector x, we add in both equation cost competitiveness variables summarised by the growth rate of wages and labour productivity, and technological variables measuring respectively the capital and R&D intensities of each industry in the two countries. Equations (1) and (2) are estimated in differences – representing short-run changes – because of the non-stationarity of most of the variables. Due to missing data for sectoral R&D and investment the sample size is reduced to 224 obesrvations for Germany and 210 for Italy. Trade data are from the UN-COMTRADE database, while data for GDP, wages, productivity, R&D and capital stock are from Eurostat.

Equations (1) and (2) are estimated using the Hausman–Taylor technique (HT; Hausman and Taylor, 1981), which corrects a random effect estimator by assuming that some of the explanatory variables are correlated with the individual-level random effects. This form of endogeneity is addressed by instrumenting the endogenous covariates with their deviation from the group mean. The advantage of the HT compared to the fixed effects (FE) estimator and its IV version is the possibility of estimating the impact of time invariant regressors like the Htech dummy.

Estimation results of equation (1) for both countries are shown in Table 4.5 where, starting from the control variables, we find a positive impact of labour

Table 4.4 Export revealed comparative advantage indexes

Consumption goods	Germany				Italy			
	1995	1999	2007	2011	1995	1999	2007	2011
CEEC	0.52	0.79	0.94	0.92	1.73	1.33	0.86	0.94
CEEC4	0.57	0.69	0.75	0.80	2.25	1.43	1.09	0.91
Balkans and Turkey	0.58	0.91	0.93	1.09	1.98	1.12	1.02	0.85
CIS	0.53	0.85	0.84	0.91	1.94	1.74	1.36	1.25
Dev. Asia	0.51	0.75	0.75	0.77	1.84	1.47	1.52	1.51
China	0.72	0.78	1.20	1.10	0.99	2.44	0.87	0.74
India	0.78	1.07	0.81	0.55	1.47	1.63	0.90	0.77
Latin America	0.46	0.63	0.83	0.89	1.68	0.92	0.72	0.66

Capital goods	Germany				Italy			
	1995	1999	2007	2011	1995	1999	2007	2011
CEEC	0.78	1.15	1.18	1.18	1.23	0.78	0.90	0.84
CEEC4	0.74	0.99	0.99	1.01	1.48	1.02	1.16	1.24
Balkans and Turkey	0.74	1.14	1.23	1.27	1.33	0.83	1.00	0.97
CIS	0.84	1.09	1.18	1.13	1.58	1.28	0.97	1.06
Dev. Asia	0.64	1.16	1.22	1.17	1.21	0.80	0.85	0.85
China	0.70	0.93	1.15	1.15	1.85	1.18	1.05	1.26
India	0.85	1.74	1.46	1.66	1.67	1.72	1.28	1.59
Latin America	0.65	1.02	1.22	1.23	1.68	1.40	1.18	1.27

Intermediate goods	Germany				Italy			
	1995	1999	2007	2011	1995	1999	2007	2011
CEEC	1.13	1.13	0.89	0.92	1.08	1.12	1.23	1.25
CEEC4	1.07	1.04	0.97	0.98	0.82	0.91	1.11	1.13
Balkans and Turkey	1.04	1.07	0.86	0.89	0.99	1.13	1.10	1.04
CIS	1.07	1.14	0.99	0.98	0.87	0.76	0.97	0.93
Dev. Asia	1.02	1.03	0.92	1.00	1.21	1.32	1.32	1.19
China	0.97	0.86	0.83	0.76	0.96	1.26	1.33	1.13
India	1.26	1.53	1.02	0.94	1.44	1.35	1.24	1.05
Latin America	1.13	1.06	0.98	1.00	0.58	0.72	0.89	0.86

Parts and components	Germany				Italy			
	1995	1999	2007	2011	1995	1999	2007	2011
CEEC	0.67	0.95	1.08	1.19	0.89	0.69	0.76	0.67
CEEC4	0.83	1.17	1.21	1.17	1.56	1.06	0.99	1.01
Balkans and Turkey	0.68	0.98	1.26	1.28	1.40	1.11	0.89	0.93
CIS	0.62	1.02	1.08	1.08	1.56	0.69	0.87	0.92
Dev. Asia	0.75	1.10	1.21	1.26	1.13	0.85	0.76	0.77
China	0.63	1.03	1.08	1.18	1.18	0.94	1.02	0.94
India	0.70	1.54	1.31	1.51	1.30	1.74	1.49	1.54
Latin America	0.73	1.09	1.16	1.11	1.39	1.04	1.03	1.17

Source: Own elaboration on COMTRADE.

Table 4.5 Effect of outsourcing with CEEC4 on net exports

	Dependent variable: Δlog(export)−Δlog(import)					
	Germany			Italy		
Δ(TradeIPCSh_C4)	−0.002	−0.023	−0.024	0.089	0.118	0.106
	[0.027]	[0.029]	[0.029]	[0.116]	[0.118]	[0.118]
Δ(TradeIPCSh_C4)*Htech	0.169**	0.216**	0.207**	−0.075	−0.14	−0.145
	[0.059]	[0.067]	[0.067]	[0.193]	[0.196]	[0.196]
Δ(TradeIPC/Trade)	1.229	1.16	1.284	−0.536	−0.74	−0.527
	[0.913]	[1.093]	[1.090]	[1.120]	[1.253]	[1.260]
Htech	0.051**	0.055**	0.055**	0.024	0.052	0.051
	[0.021]	[0.024]	[0.024]	[0.039]	[0.038]	[0.038]
Δlog(LabProd)		0.139**	0.132**		0.488*	0.452
		[0.055]	[0.056]		[0.274]	[0.276]
Δlog(Wage)		0.276	0.301		0.296	0.305
		[0.306]	[0.308]		[0.197]	[0.197]
Δ(GFKF/GDP)			−0.027			−0.023
			[0.040]			[0.025]
Δ(R&D/GDP)			−0.009			0.272
			[0.010]			[0.218]
Constant	−0.009	0.02	−0.154**	−0.009	0.207**	0.064
	[0.058]	[0.060]	[0.053]	[0.063]	[0.075]	[0.066]
N	266	224	224	238	210	210
chi²	58.3	63.5	64.9	32.4	39.6	42.1

Notes
* Significant at 10% level; **significant at 5% level; significant at 1% level. *Trade/GDP* = trade intensity; *TradeIPCsh_C4* = share of CEEC4 in total trade in intermediates, parts and components; *Htech* = dummy for high tech industries; R&D = Research and Development expenditure; *GFKF* = gross fixed capital formation; *LabProd* = labour productivity; estimation technique: Hausman–Taylor Estimator.

productivity but significant at 5 per cent level only for Germany, while wage growth is insignificant in both cases. In addition, none of the technological variables is significant, suggesting a similar impact on import and export flows. Turning to the outsourcing variables, the proxy for total outsourcing is not significant while the share of CEEC4 in total outsourcing is positive and significant only for Germany and only for high-tech industries. In addition, the German trade balance is higher on average in high-tech industries while no significant difference is found for Italy. These results confirm the importance for Germany of productive integration with this group of countries and the sector bias of such effect.

Turning to the impact of trade integration with the Asia-Pacific area, the results are reported in Table 4.6 for Germany and Table 4.7 for Italy. Starting with the former, we find a positive and significant impact of trade opening but not when trade with China alone is considered (columns 1 and 2). The integration with China has a direct negative impact on the trade balance of both

Table 4.6 Effect of trade integration with the Asia-Pacific area for Germany

	Dependent variable: Δlog(export)-Δlog(import)					
	China		Asean		Asean+China	
Δ(TradeSh_EM)	−0.116**	−0.101**	0.194**	0.202**	−0.058	−0.036
	[0.043]	[0.043]	[0.087]	[0.087]	[0.055]	[0.055]
Δ(TradeSh_EM)*Htech	0.144	0.098	−0.149	−0.17	0.073	0.029
	[0.219]	[0.217]	[0.148]	[0.149]	[0.187]	[0.187]
Δ(Trade/GDP)	−0.001	0.007	0.021**	0.024***	0.029**	0.040**
	[0.010]	[0.010]	[0.007]	[0.007]	[0.014]	[0.014]
Htech	0.008	0.006	0.04	0.038	0.067	0.064
	[0.051]	[0.050]	[0.035]	[0.035]	[0.072]	[0.071]
Δlog(LabProd)	0.343**	0.343**	0.311***	0.311***	0.789***	0.786***
	[0.128]	[0.127]	[0.092]	[0.092]	[0.186]	[0.184]
Δlog(Wage)	1.087*	1.289**	0.771*	0.820*	2.442**	2.718**
	[0.640]	[0.639]	[0.441]	[0.444]	[0.911]	[0.911]
Δ(GFKF/GDP)		0.01		−0.044		−0.031
		[0.084]		[0.059]		[0.120]
Δ(R&D/GDP)		−0.055**		−0.017		−0.076**
		[0.023]		[0.016]		[0.033]
Constant	0.046	−0.175	0.453***	0.460***	−0.072	−0.1
	[0.105]	[0.107]	[0.086]	[0.086]	[0.155]	[0.161]
N	224	224	224	224	224	224
chi^2	49.8	56.5	69.2	70.9	49.7	55.8

Notes
* Significant at 10% level; **significant at 5% level; significant at 1% level. Trade/GDP = trade intensity; *TradeSh_EM* = share of trade with emerging economies on total trade; *Htech* = dummy for high tech industries; *R&D* = Research and Development expenditure; *GFKF* = gross fixed capital formation; *LabProd* = labour productivity; estimation technique: Hausman–Taylor Estimator.

low- and high-tech industries, while the share of trade with the group of ASEAN countries accelerates the trade balance's growth in all industries, that when aggregating the two groups their impact turns insignificant. This apparent contradiction can be explained by the fact that ASEAN countries are strongly integrated with China by exporting to the country components and processed goods. These products will be assembled and exported to Western markets, leading to a deterioration of the German trade balance which will be accounted by China and by the increase of export from ASEAN to China. In this way, the ASEAN–Germany flows will include only the demand for capital and consumption goods of the former.

The results for Italy (Table 4.6) return a different picture. The degree of openness (Trade/GDP) is in general negative, indicating that import growth dominates export growth, while there is no generalised effect of trade integration with China or ASEAN when analysed separately. On the contrary, when analysed as single group (columns 5 and 6) the share of trade with the Asia-Pacific region is

Table 4.7 Effect of trade integration with the Asia-Pacific area for Italy

	Dependent variable: Δlog(export)-Δlog(import)					
	China		Asean		China+Asean	
Δ(TradeSh_EM)	0.064	0.063	0.003	−0.005	0.05	0.039
	[0.137]	[0.137]	[0.158]	[0.157]	[0.168]	[0.168]
Δ(TradeSh_EM)*Htech	0.300	0.314	0.146	0.123	−1.020***	−1.063***
	[0.381]	[0.384]	[0.190]	[0.189]	[0.277]	[0.278]
Δ(Trade/GDP)	−0.154***	−0.155***	0.021*	0.019*	−0.158***	−0.163***
	[0.018]	[0.018]	[0.011]	[0.011]	[0.025]	[0.025]
Htech	0.245**	0.247**	0.014	0.017	0.266**	0.271**
	[0.100]	[0.101]	[0.051]	[0.051]	[0.119]	[0.119]
Δlog(LabProd)	0.34	0.392	0.498	0.608	1.243	1.48
	[0.735]	[0.745]	[0.459]	[0.461]	[1.041]	[1.051]
Δlog(Wage)	−0.871	−0.877	−0.444	−0.46	−2.382**	−2.453**
	[0.549]	[0.551]	[0.322]	[0.321]	[0.745]	[0.746]
Δ(GFKF/GDP)		0.023		0.079*		0.147
		[0.064]		[0.042]		[0.095]
Δ(R&D/GDP)		−0.300		−0.053		−0.187
		[0.551]		[0.361]		[0.812]
Constant	0.121	0.158	0.967***	0.063	1.263***	−0.533**
	[0.172]	[0.190]	[0.107]	[0.114]	[0.227]	[0.246]
N	210	210	210	210	210	210
chi²	134	133	120	125	116	119

Notes

* Significant at 10% level; **significant at 5% level; significant at 1% level. *Trade/GDP* = trade intensity; *TradeSh_EM* = share of trade with emerging economies on total trade; *Htech* = dummy for high tech industries; *R&D* = research and development expenditure; *GFKF* = gross fixed capital formation; *LabProd* = labour productivity; estimation technique: Hausman–Taylor Estimator.

strongly negative in high-tech industries, suggesting that Italy is suffering the competition of Asian countries (see Chen *et al.*, 2013, Esposito and Guerrieri, 2013) much more than Germany and especially in industries where the loss of competitiveness over time has been more marked.

Summing up, the econometric analysis provides clear evidence in favour of the importance of trade openness, outsourcing with CEECs and integration with emerging markets in explaining the different external performance of the two countries. Additionally, there is strong evidence that the sectoral dimension of such effects matters, leading to a further divergence between the two countries.

The euro effect and trade balances

The aim of this section is to provide an econometric test of the assumption that the introduction of the single currency favoured German net exports at the expense of most of the other members of the Eurozone. Many studies focused on the determinants of current account balances in the Eurozone (Arghyrou and Chortareas, 2008; Blanchard and Giavazzi, 2002; Giavazzi and Spaventa, 2010). Among them, Arghyrou and Chortareas (2008) analysed individual countries and found a strong and positive effect of external demand for Germany but not for Italy. Other works investigated the export performance of European countries, Danninger and Joutz (2007) in particular found that cost competitiveness and the penetration of fast-growing markets are the keys to the success of German exports. For Italy, a study by the International Monetary Fund (2008) investigated the causes of market share losses and found that technological rigidities, together with the sectoral and geographical specialisation in slow-growing markets, are the main determinants of the disappointing performance of Italian exports.

In our analysis we use bilateral trade flows of the two countries with all partners as it is typically done with gravity models of trade. Such models are particularly suitable for the analysis of the impact of some policy and institutional changes and have been extensively used in order to test the effect of trade agreements on bilateral trade flows.

In the standard version of the gravity equation bilateral trade flows are a function of the economic mass, given by the product of the GDPs of each pair, the bilateral exchange rate and the distance between the two countries. We modify the basic equation in order to adapt it to the estimates of trade balances and to the analysis of a single country against all its trading partners. The final equation is as follows:

$$\Delta \log TrBal_{j,t} = a + b_1 \Delta \log GDP_{j,t} + b_2 \Delta \log EXR + b_3 Euro +$$
$$b_4 \log Dist + contig + \lambda_j + \lambda_t + e_{i,t} \tag{3}$$

where the growth rate of the trade balance (*TrBal*) with partner j in time t is expressed as a function of the partner's GDP growth, the growth rate of the bilateral exchange rate, the geographical distance, a dummy indicating whether the two countries are neighbours and a set of partner- and time-specific fixed effects. The euro effect is captured by the dummy *Euro*, which equals 1 if the partner, in a specific moment in time, is a member of the Eurozone. A positive and significant coefficient for this dummy indicates that the introduction of the euro caused a one-time increase in the average trade balance. We do not include the effect of own GDP as it is partner invariant and collinear with the time dummies λ_t. The sample includes 81 destination countries, accounting for more than 90 per cent of total trade, over the period 1992–2010. All data are from CEPII, trade data as well as GDP and exchange rates are from the CEPII-Chelem database while data for geographical distances and contiguity are from the CEPII-Distances database. Equation (3) is estimated using the fixed effects (FE) and random effect (RE) estimators where the choice of the best estimator is made by mean of the Hausman test. In addition, in order to control for the potential endogeneity of GDP and the exchange rate, we replicate the estimates using the Hausman-Taylor estimator (HT).

Table 4.8 Estimates of the euro effect on the German trade balance

	Dependent variable: $\Delta log(export_{j,t}) - \Delta log(import_{k,t})$					
	FE	FE	RE	RE	HT	HT
$\Delta log(GDP_{j,t})$	0.989**	1.011**	0.813**	0.821**	0.969***	0.990***
	[0.479]	[0.486]	[0.403]	[0.411]	[0.230]	[0.232]
$\Delta log(EXR_{j,t})$	−0.359**	−0.362**	−0.321**	−0.321**	−0.360***	−0.362***
	[0.123]	[0.121]	[0.123]	[0.123]	[0.034]	[0.034]
Log(Distance)			−0.006	−0.006	−0.007	−0.005
			[0.007]	[0.007]	[0.010]	[0.010]
Contiguity			−0.004	−0.005	−0.004	−0.009
			[0.033]	[0.033]	[0.041]	[0.041]
Euro		0.101***		0.010		0.100**
		[0.024]		[0.015]		[0.050]
N	1,450	1,450	1,450	1,450	1,450	1,450
R²w	0.142	0.145	0.142	0.142		
Hausman			7.31	11.99		

Notes
* Significant at 10% level; **significant at 5% level; significant at 1% level. $GDP_{j,t}$ = partner's GDP; $EXR_{i,t}$ = bilateral exchange rate; Distance = geographical distance; Contiguity = dummy for countries having common borders; Euro = dummy for countries adopting the euro.

Table 4.9 Estimates of the euro effect on the Italian trade balance

	Dependent variable: $\Delta log(Export_{j,t}) - \Delta log(Import_{k,t})$					
	FE	FE	RE	RE	HT	HT
$\Delta log(GDP_{j,t})$	1.661**	1.679**	1.368**	1.370**	1.655***	1.670***
	[0.694]	[0.702]	[0.591]	[0.598]	[0.268]	[0.268]
$\Delta log(EXR_{j,t})$	−0.259**	−0.261**	−0.232**	−0.231**	−0.258***	−0.260***
	[0.080]	[0.080]	[0.078]	[0.078]	[0.039]	[0.039]
Log(Distance)			−0.01	−0.01	−0.011	−0.009
			[0.007]	[0.007]	[0.011]	[0.011]
Contiguity			−0.044	−0.045	−0.046	−0.048
			[0.031]	[0.031]	[0.048]	[0.048]
Euro		0.082**		0.003		0.069
		[0.028]		[0.014]		[0.057]
N	1,444	1,444	1,444	1,444	1,444	1,444
R²w	0.166	0.168	0.165	0.166		
Hausman			11.55	14.49		

Notes
* Significant at 10% level; **significant at 5% level; significant at 1% level. $GDP_{j,t}$ = partner's GDP; $EXR_{i,t}$ = bilateral exchange rate; Distance = geographical distance; Contiguity = dummy for countries having common borders; Euro = dummy for countries adopting the euro.

Estimation results are reported in Table 4.8 for Germany and in Table 4.9 for Italy. For both countries, the effect of the partners' GDP and the exchange rate is always significant and of the expected sign. We find a higher demand elasticity for the Italian trade balance, on average around 1.6 against a value slightly below 1 for Germany. On the contrary, the reactivity of the trade balance to accelerations or decelerations of the exchange rate is lower for Italy (0.25 against 0.35 for Germany). Both geographical distance and the contiguity dummy are never significant, probably because they affect imports and exports in a similar way, while important differences arise when looking at the euro effect. For Germany, this effect is positive and significant in the FE and HT cases. Although the Hausman test is in favour of the RE estimator, given the presence of endogeneity we must assume that HT estimates are more reliable, which confirms the significance of the euro effect on the German trade balance. As to Italy, although the FE estimates return a significant coefficient, the above conclusion implies that the effect for Italy is insignificant.

In conclusion, the econometric analysis confirms our assumption of an exogenous benefit of the creation of the single currency area for German net exports. On the contrary such effect is not present for Italy.

Conclusions

Among the many explanations for the increase of macroeconomic imbalances in the Euro Area, in this paper we investigated the role of external trade in explaining difference between the two biggest manufacturing poles of the area: Germany and Italy. More specifically, we were interested in the geographical recomposition of trade flows, which took place in the last 15 years, as a consequence of the emergence of new actors in world trade. While the German economy massively increased its trade opening, the intensity of outward FDI and the share of emerging markets in trade flows, this process took place on a much lower scale for Italian firms. The slow speed of adjustment of Italian trade flows caused a loss in comparative advantages toward emerging markets vis-à-vis the rest of Western Europe, especially in consumption and equipment goods, while an opposite pattern is observed for Germany. In addition, the German economy seems to have benefited from the introduction of the single currency at the expense of the other Euro Area members.

Our econometric results confirm the descriptive evidence. In particular we found that German's high-tech industries strongly benefited from the productive integration with the most advanced group of Central and Eastern Europe (Czech Republic, Hungary, Poland and Slovakia) while for Italy this effect is neutral. As to trade integration with the Asia-Pacific area, we found that Italian high-tech industries are strongly penalised in terms of net exports while for Germany there is no significant effect. As to the traditional cost competitiveness variables, in Germany productivity growth and a slow wage dynamics have fostered net exports while for Italy the wage dynamic has caused a reduction of sectoral trade balances. Finally, we found that the creation of the single currency has benefited German net exports while not affecting Italian ones.

In terms of policy implications we should conclude that the German model should be used as a blueprint for other European countries, but only when considering outsourcing relations and the penetration of emerging markets. The beneficial effect of the euro introduction cannot either be replicated or applied to all countries at the same time as it is a zero-sum game. This means that a rebalancing of the external position of the member countries will necessarily pass through the reduction of the German surplus. In this context, coordinated and symmetrical policy measures must be taken at European level while national policies should focus on improving the external competitiveness.

Notes

1 A study by Farh and Sunde (2009) found that such reforms accelerated job creation significantly and consequently reduced the length of unemployment, especially in manufacturing.
2 On the delocalisation of German and Italian firms see Baldone *et al.* (2007) and Helg and Tajoli (2005), while for German outsourcing to Eastern Europe see Geishecker (2006) and Marin (2006). For studies on other countries see among the others Egger and Egger (2001, 2005); Egger *et al.* (2001); Egger *et al.* (2007); Esposito and Stehrer (2012).
3 RCA are described using the Balassa Index (1965) in comparison with the advanced European economies.
4 High-tech industries are mechanics, electronics, transport equipment, chemicals, coke and petroleum and printing/reproduction of recorded media.

References

Arghyrou, M. G. and G. Chortareas (2008), Current account imbalances and real exchange rates in the Euro Area. *Review of International Economics*, 16(4): 747–764.

Balassa, B. (1965), 'Trade liberalization and revealed comparative advantage'. *Manchester School of Economic and Social Studies*, 33: 99–123.

Baldone, S. F. Sdogati and L. Tajoli (2007), 'On some effects of international fragmentation of production on comparative advantages, trade flows and the income of countries'. *The World Economy*, 30(11): 1726–1779.

Blanchard, O. (2006), 'Current account deficits in rich countries'. Mundell Flaming Lecture, presented at the 7th Jacques Polak Annual Research Conference Hosted by the International Monetary Fund, Washington, DC, 9–10 November 2006.

Blanchard, O. and F. Giavazzi (2002), 'Current account deficits in the Euro Area: the end of the Feldstein–Horioka puzzle?' *Brookings Papers on Economic Activity*, 2: 147–186.

Brancaccio, E. (2012), 'Current account imbalances, the Eurozone crisis, and a proposal for a "European wage standard"'. *International Journal of Political Economy*, 41(1): 47–65.

Cavallaro, E. P. Esposito, A. Matano and M. Mulino (forthcoming), 'Technological catching up, quality of exports and competitiveness: a sectoral perspective'. *Emerging Markets Finance and Trade*.

Chen, R., G. M. Milesi-Ferretti and T. Tressel (2013), 'External imbalances in the Eurozone'. *Economic Policy*, 73: 102–142.

Clarida, R. H. (2007), *Current Account Imbalances: Sustainability and Adjustment*. Chicago: University of Chicago Press.

Collignon, S. (2013), 'Macroeconomic imbalances and competitiveness in the Euro Area'. *Transfer: European Review of Labour and Research*, 19(1): 63–87.

Croci-Angelini, E. and F. Farina (2012), 'Current account imbalances and systemic risk within a monetary union'. *Journal of Economic Behavior and Organization*, 83: 647–656.

Danninger, S. and F. Joutz (2007), 'What explains Germany's rebounding market share?' *IMF Working Paper* 07/24.

Dullien, S. and U. Fritsche (2009), 'How bad is divergence in the Euro Zone? Lessons from the United States and Germany'. *Journal of Post Keynesian Economics*, 31(3): 431–457.

Egger, H. and P. Egger (2001), 'Cross-border sourcing and outward processing in EU manufacturing'. *North American Journal of Economics and Finance*,12(3): 243–256.

Egger, H. and P. Egger (2005), 'The determinants of EU processing trade'. *The World Economy*, 28(2): 147–168.

Egger, P. M. Pfaffermayr and Y. Wolfmayr-Schnitzer (2001), 'The international fragmentation of Austrian manufacturing: the effects of outsourcing on productivity and wages'. *North American Journal of Economics and Finance*, 12(3): 257–272.

Egger, P., M. Pfaffermayr and A. Weber (2007), 'Sectoral adjustment of employment to shifts in outsourcing and trade: evidence from a dynamic fixed effects multinomial logit model'. *Journal of Applied Econometrics*, 22(3): 559–580.

Esposito, P. and R. Stehrer (2009), 'The sector bias of skill biased technical change and the rising skill premium in transition economies.' *Empirica*, 36(2): 351–364.

Esposito, P. and R. Stehrer (2012), 'Effects of high-tech capital, FDI, and outsourcing on demand for skills in west and east', in R. Stehrerand M. Mas (eds), *Industrial Productivity in Europe: Growth and Crisis*. Edward Elgar Publishing: Cheltenham: 386–402.

European Commission (2012) 'Current account surpluses in the EU'. *European Economy*, 9/2012.

Fahr, R. and U. Sunde (2009), 'Did the Hartz reforms speed-up the matching process? A macro-evaluation using empirical matching functions'. *German Economic Review*, 10(3): 284–316.

Geishecker, I. (2006), 'Does outsourcing to Central and Eastern Europe really threaten manual workers' jobs in Germany?' *The World Economy*, 29(5): 559–583.

Geishecker, I. and H. Gorg (2008), 'Winners and losers: a micro-level analysis of international outsourcing and wages'. *Canadian Journal of Economics*, 41(1): 243–270.

Geishecker, I, H. Gorg and J. R. Munch (2010), 'Do labour market institutions matter? Micro-level wage effects of international outsourcing in three European countries'. *Review of World Economics/Welwirtschaftliches Archiv*, 146(1): 179–198.

Giavazzi, F. and L. Spaventa (2010), 'Why the current account may matter in a monetary union: lessons from the financial crisis in the Euro Area. *CEPR Discussion Papers* 8008.

Gourinchas, P. O. (2002), Comment on 'Current account deficits in the Euro Area: The end of the Feldstein–Horioka puzzle?' *Brookings Papers on Economic Activity*, 33(2): 196–206.

Guerrieri, P. and P. Esposito (2013), 'The determinants of macroeconomic imbalances in the Euro Area: the role of external performance', in L. Paganetto (ed.), *Public Debt, Global Governance and Economic Dynamism*. Milan: Springer Verlag, Italy: 105–125.

Guerrieri, P. and P. Esposito (2012), 'Intra-European imbalances, adjustment and growth in the Eurozone'. *Oxford Review of Economic Policy*, 28(3): 532–550.

Hansen, T. (2010), 'Tariff rates, offshoring and productivity: evidence from German and Austrian firm-level data'. *Munich Discussion Paper* 2010–21.

Haskel, J. E., and M. J. Slaughter (2002), 'Does the sector bias of skill-biased technical change explain changing skill premia?' *European Economic Review*, 46(10): 1757–1783.

Hausman, J. A. and W. E. Taylor (1981), 'Panel data and unobservable individual effects'. *Econometrica*, 49(6): 1377–1398.

Helg, R. and L. Tajoli (2005), 'Patterns of international fragmentation of production and the relative demand for labor'. *North American Journal of Economics and Finance*, 16(2): 233–254.

International Monetary Fund. (2008), 'Competitiveness in the southern Euro Area: France, Greece, Italy, Portugal, and Spain'. *IMF Working Paper* 08/112.

Marin, D. (2006), 'A new international division of labor in Europe: outsourcing and offshoring to Eastern Europe'. *Journal of the European Economic Association*, 4(2–3): 612–622.

Marin, D. (2010a), 'The opening up of Eastern Europe at 20 – jobs, skills, and "reverse maquiladoras" in Austria and Germany'. *Discussion Papers in Economics* 11435.

Marin, D. (2010b), 'Germany's super competitiveness'. *Vox-EU*. www.voxeu.org/article/germany-s-super-competitiveness.

Makin, A. J., and P. K. Narayan (2011), 'Have domestic or foreign factors driven European external imbalances?' *Journal of International Money and Finance*, 30: 537–546.

Onharan, O. and E. Stockhammer (2013), 'Rethinking wage policy in the face of the euro crisis. Implications of the wage-led demand regime'. *International Review of Applied Economics*, 26(2): 191–203.

Schnabl, G. and S. Freitag (2012), 'Reverse causality in global and intra-European imbalances'. *Review of International Economics*, 20(4): 674–690.

Schmitz, B. and J. Von Hagen (2011), 'Current account imbalances and financial integration in the Euro Area'. *Journal of International Money and Finance*, 30: 1676–1695.

Part III

The German model of labour market reforms

5 How promising is wage restraint for a large economy?

The example of Germany before and during the current crises

Torsten Niechoj

Introduction

The Euro Area is still suffering from two crises. The first is the 'Great Recession' following the financial market crisis. This financial crisis originated in the USA but became a global phenomenon and spread from the financial markets to the real economy. It hit many economies hard, especially the Euro Area. In 2009, OECD GDP fell by 3.6 per cent and Euro Area GDP declined by 4.4 per cent (data from http://stats.oecd.org). As a follow-up to this crisis, a second crisis has developed, the so-called sovereign debt crisis of the Euro Area. After the financial market crisis, both the financially unstable banking system and the economic downturn required massive state interventions. The governments went considerably into deficit in order to stabilise the banking system and the economy. This together with national failures of the past and the specific institutional constellation of the Euro Area paved the way for rising debt-to-GDP ratios in all countries of the Euro Area (Horn, Joebges, Niechoj *et al.*, 2009; Joebges and Niechoj, 2010).

The political reaction to this second crisis is well known (Niechoj and van Treeck, 2011; Ederer, 2012). Austerity measures are employed in nearly all countries of the Euro Area. The European Central Bank is purchasing government bonds in order to stabilise the market. Moreover, the institutional framework has been modified: a European stability mechanism to provide credits for governments in dire straits has been established, the Stability and Growth Pact has been reviewed and amended by a macroeconomic imbalances procedure and further changes to guarantee sound public finances and a reduction of European current account imbalances, and a fiscal compact to prevent further debt crises has been introduced.

Both the sovereign debt crisis itself and the seeming cure of it, the austerity measures, led to a prolongation of the partly stagnant, partly recessive development in Europe after the financial market crisis.

During the two crises, some export-oriented countries performed relatively well in comparison to the rest of the Euro Area. In this chapter, I will focus on Germany which is one of these countries and, having the largest economy in Europe, strongly influences – only due its mere economic power – the development of the

Euro Area. The main characteristics of its growth model are export orientation and stable industrial relations, which guaranteed low strike intensity and moderate wage developments in the past. It seems that this model is a successful one other countries should follow. In Germany, employment increased after 2009, German government bonds are in great demand and since 2011 public deficits have fallen below the 3 per cent criterion of the European Stability and Growth Pact: a situation other countries like Spain or Portugal, not to mention Greece, can only dream of.

Recommending Germany as best practice for the Euro Area requires at least three qualifications: First, that Germany itself benefited from its growth model; second, that there are no negative side-effects on other European countries; and third, that this model can be generalised and successfully adapted by all European countries. Otherwise, copying the German model in other countries would not increase prosperity in the adopting country, it would deepen the crisis in the Euro Area instead of helping to overcome it and an implementation of the German model would conflict with institutions and conditions in the country in question. As will be shown, the validity of all these three prerequisites is doubtful. To substantiate this, the next section starts with an overview of the economic development of the German economy since the start of the monetary union. Then, the German growth model is explained and put in context, i.e. the institutional setting of the Euro Area. A further section reviews successes and failures of the German model and discusses the effect on other European countries, especially the emergence of intra-European current account imbalances. Against this background, an assessment of the policy approach of the German government is provided in a subsequent section. The last section concludes.

The growth model of Germany in context

A look back on the performance of Germany's economy after 2009, the year of the Great Recession following the turbulences on the financial markets, shows a remarkably good performance up to now (see Table 5.1). Elsewhere, negative growth, rising unemployment, long periods of current account deficits and high public deficits are widespread. In Germany, real GDP growth is in the black again since 2010 and Germany has already reached the pre-crisis level of real GDP in 2010. Unemployment rates are not rising. On the contrary, they are declining and employment has been increasing in Germany despite the crises. Moreover, current accounts have been in surplus since 2002 and since 2011 public deficits are below the 3 per cent level, prescribed by the European Stability and Growth Pact.

In 2009, however, the fall in real GDP was tremendous, absolutely and relatively to other countries. For Germany, with −5.1 per cent the fall in GDP was the largest since the Second World War. It was also more pronounced than in other countries and regions. OECD GDP decreased by 3.6 per cent, the GDP of the USA shrank by 3.1 per cent and the French growth rate, the second-largest economy in Europe next to Germany, also by 3.1 per cent (all data from http://

Table 5.1 German economic situation at the dawn of 2013

	Real GDP growth rate	Harmonised unemployment rate	Current accounts (in % of GDP)	Public deficit
1999	1.9	8.6	−1.3	−1.6
2000	3.1	8.0	−1.8	1.1
2001	1.5	7.9	−0.2	−3.1
2002	0.0	8.7	2.0	−3.8
2003	−0.4	9.8	1.9	−4.2
2004	1.2	10.5	4.7	−3.8
2005	0.7	11.3	5.1	−3.3
2006	3.7	10.3	6.5	−1.6
2007	3.3	8.7	7.5	0.2
2008	1.1	7.5	6.2	−0.1
2009	−5.1	7.8	6.0	−3.1
2010	4.2	7.1	6.1	−4.1
2011	3.0	5.9	5.6	−0.8
2012	0.7	5.5	6.3	0.1

Source: Eurostat (AMECO); European Commission, 2013.

stats.oecd.org). But the impact of this plunge of German GDP on other economic indicators was moderate. The unemployment rate increased only slightly in 2009. Similarly, the effect on current accounts was minimal. Public deficits increased for a period of two years but returned to a low level afterwards.

If we compare the year 2009 with the years before and concentrate on the indicators unemployment, current accounts and public deficits it seems as if the economic crisis of 2009 had no extraordinary impact, a remarkable result. What also strikes the eye is the development of unemployment and current accounts since the start of the monetary union. Up to the mid-2000s unemployment was on the rise but then fell by 5.8 percentage points between the peak in 2005 and 2012.

This performance of the German economy is based on a specific growth model.[1] Since the 1950s, the (West-)German economy has been characterised by export-led growth which was not fostered by a currency depreciation due to exchange rate manipulations but by a depreciation based on a stable price level and higher productivity increases compared to other countries (Herr, 1994). Stable price level and productivity were guaranteed by the German central bank and German industrial relations, a cooperative approach of trade unions and employers resulting in moderate nominal wage increases, a low strike intensity, a tradition of constant technical improvements and high-quality production (Streeck, 1991). As a consequence, German export goods have been very price competitive through the years, which is reflected in trade balance and current account surpluses in most of the years. Such a constellation of current account surpluses is a relatively comfortable one. It implies a positive net investment position and increasing foreign reserves. However, current account surpluses might attract (financial) investors and lead to a conversion of foreign currencies into the own currency by producers in Germany, and thus increase the demand for the home currency. In other words, they lead to a nominal appreciation of the currency in a system of (relative) flexible exchange rates. Then, such a constellation requires a permanent moderation of wages and/or efforts to increase productivity in order to keep the country's position as a forerunner in price competitiveness.

Since the beginning of the 2000s, reforms of the labour market in Germany and the establishment of the monetary union have modified this model (Cesaratto and Stirati, 2010; Niechoj *et al.*, 2011; Lucarelli, 2011; Priewe, 2012: 349–350). In the years 2002 and 2003 the so-called Hartz reforms were designed by a commission led by Peter Hartz, at that time member of the board of the large German car producer Volkswagen, for the social democratic-led government of Chancellor Gerhard Schröder. They became effective in 2003 to 2005 and constituted a paradigm shift in labour market policies towards an activation approach and the establishment of a low-paid sector, impacting on productivity increases and wage developments. The second important modification is a consequence of the establishment of a common currency and monetary policy in 1999. Within the Euro Area, exchanges rates no longer exist. Therefore, nominal depreciations or appreciations are obsolete now. Changes in prices may affect price competitiveness and exports directly, without being dampened by adjusting exchange rates any more. Differences in real interest rates, due to different inflation rates amid a common nominal interest rate policy, have an impact on investment and lead to growth differentials. On the one hand, low real interest rates foster investment, consumption and imports but also inflation when the economy starts to overheat. On the other hand, high real interest rates dampen investment, consumption, imports and inflation. As a result of both factors, the impact of the German growth model is even more pronounced now, within the setting of the monetary union, than before. Real wage increases are dampened and foster increases in price competitiveness which are not filtered through adjustments of the exchange rate anymore. Sluggish growth of wages restricts imports and represses domestic demand and thus investment. German investors are looking for borrowers abroad and exporters of other countries face problems to export to Germany.

Moreover, interdependencies between the German way of stimulating growth and other traditions became clearer against the framework of the Euro Area. Two contrary but mutually dependent models and some middle cases can be identified. A group of countries followed the German example of export-led growth, namely the Netherlands, Austria, Finland and Belgium. In a second group of countries – Spain, Greece and Portugal – growth was based on consumption and investment, partly financed by foreign credits. Therefore, these countries can be classified as a group of domestic demand-led growth. Other countries show characteristics of both models, especially France and Italy. As Table 5.2 shows, this simple typology corresponds to specific import and export patterns. For countries of the first group it holds that exports are in surplus in

Table 5.2 Average of surpluses and deficits of the trade balance in billion euro per year
for two periods and number of years with a surplus (+) and a deficit (−)

	Export surpluses or deficits on average per year		Years with positive and negative trade balance	
	1999–2007	*2008–2012*	*1999–2007*	*2008–2012*
Germany	85.8	136.2	+9	+5
Netherlands	32.7	44.7	+9	+5
Austria	8.5	12.4	+9	+5
Finland	10.3	1.7	+9	+4, −1
Belgium	12.1	5.6	+9	+4, −1
France	5.1	−50.3	+6, −3	−5
Italy	6.8	−23.5	+6, −3	−5
Greece	−20.5	−21.3	−9	−5
Spain	−33.0	−25.3	−9	−5
Portugal	−12.9	−10.0	−9	−5
Ireland	18.4	28.5	+9	+5

Source: Eurostat; own calculations.

nearly all years since the establishment of the Euro Area. In countries with domestic demand-led growth, imports exceed exports continually. The trade balance of Italy and France is roughly balanced over the whole period. A special case is Ireland which is an export-led country with trade balance surpluses but current account deficits caused by profit transfers from Ireland to other countries.

What is important here is the mutual dependency of these two groups. Export surpluses of one country group necessitate the capacity of the second group to import. Sufficient exports to finance imports do not exist in the case of the second group. Thus, a different source of financial means is necessary. Countries with export surpluses have to provide credits to finance the import surplus of the deficit countries.

Successes and failures of the German model

Within this modified setting of the Euro Area, wage developments are a good starting point to explain the tremendous export successes of Germany (see also Niechoj *et al.*, 2011 and Stein *et al.*, 2012 for an in-depth discussion of wage developments within the Euro Area). Wages are both incomes and an important component of prices. As important determinants of private consumption and thus domestic demand as well as price competitiveness they have had a distinct influence on the growth performance of the German economy in the last years.

As Table 5.3 shows, the increase in German wages has been below all other members of the Euro Area since the start of the monetary union, depicted in the table.[2] Moreover, Germany is the only country below the average, in other words, this economy has reduced the average significantly. Greece and Ireland,

Table 5.3 Compensation of employees in the Euro Area, per hour, total economy, 2000q1 = 100

	2000q1	2007q1	2008q1	2009q1	2010q1	2011q1	2012q3
Euro Area (EU17)	100.0	128.0	134.5	135.5	135.9	139.3	142.0
Germany	100.0	106.7	110.3	111.9	113.5	118.7	125.1
Netherlands	100.0	132.0	140.5	143.8	143.2	147.2	148.1
Belgium	100.0	129.8	137.4	140.4	141.5	148.2	155.7
Austria	100.0	122.6	128.0	131.6	133.2	138.2	147.2
Finland	100.0	137.0	148.1	149.9	148.2	155.4	163.9
France	100.0	131.2	136.2	136.9	139.3	143.7	148.6
Italy	100.0	134.0	141.1	141.4	141.8	143.5	143.1
Greece	100.0	172.6	190.2	191.9	192.3	171.6	n/a
Spain	100.0	162.2	177.5	173.7	168.8	167.9	158.3
Portugal	100.0	132.9	138.6	140.5	141.4	140.6	142.0
Ireland	100.0	194.1	204.1	200.8	178.5	173.4	178.3

Source: Eurostat; own calculations.

however, have raised the average significantly. Although the economic downturn of 2009 and the following austerity measures had a dampening effect, both countries still exceed the average drastically.

But what are the consequences of such a diverging development? In countries with high wage increases, rising incomes have contributed positively to private consumption and have fostered a demand-driven extension of investment and imports. In countries with low wage increases, private consumption and investment remained weak. This is one side of the coin. But wages also influence export chances. Wage increases correlate with price increases, if the mark-up is given and rises in wages are not compensated by increases in labour productivity. If wage increases are higher in one country compared to the other member states of the monetary union then this country has to face a loss in price competitiveness vis-à-vis the rest of the Euro Area.

To control for changes in labour productivity, Table 5.4 depicts nominal unit labour costs which take both wage and productivity developments into account. Both for industry, the sector that is the main export-oriented sector in the Euro Area, and for the total economy, nominal unit labour costs show a similar picture compared to the development of the compensation of employees only. Again Germany has remarkably low increases of nominal unit labour costs in case of the total economy; in industry nominal unit labour costs have even decreased. Productivity increases play a role but the main driver for gaining in price competitiveness against the other member states is wage restraint; productivity increases in Germany are roughly in line with the average of the Euro Area, which holds for both industry and the total economy. Within the last decade, the pattern of productivity has changed and wage moderation has become more important when gaining cost advantages against foreign countries. Export-oriented firms can use lower-paid temporary agency workers and

Table 5.4 Nominal unit labour costs in the Euro Area, 2000q1 = 100

(a) per person, total economy

	2000q1	2007q1	2008q1	2009q1	2010q1	2011q1	2012q3
Euro Area (EU 17)	100.0	110.76	113.87	121.13	120.41	120.33	122.94
Germany	100.0	98.00	98.37	106.98	105.80	105.49	109.11
Netherlands	100.0	114.95	117.30	125.01	124.30	125.31	128.98
Belgium	100.0	111.74	115.55	123.17	121.72	123.99	130.65
Austria	100.0	104.70	106.33	114.70	115.29	114.81	120.78
Finland	100.0	109.13	114.69	128.39	126.88	126.65	133.70
France	100.0	114.86	117.34	123.38	124.49	125.44	129.43
Italy	100.0	118.32	123.73	131.78	130.93	131.03	133.06
Greece	100.0	122.55	131.20	134.46	138.78	131.55	n/a
Spain	100.0	124.78	132.49	134.32	132.59	130.82	125.64
Portugal	100.0	120.08	124.37	131.21	129.07	128.04	122.96
Ireland	100.0	125.67	135.13	140.94	128.47	123.99	124.16

(b) per hour, industry*

	2000q1	2007q1	2008q1	2009q1	2010q1	2011q1	2012q3
Euro Area (EU17)	100.0	98.7	101.8	117.4	107.2	104.2	108.1
Germany	100.0	86.7	88.2	110.3	96.5	92.8	97.1
Netherlands	100.0	102.8	103.7	111.9	105.3	105.2	106.2
Belgium	100.0	104.0	105.6	114.3	109.4	108.1	114.9
Austria	100.0	93.2	93.4	109.7	105.0	98.7	100.3
Finland	100.0	82.8	85.1	106.7	96.0	95.5	99.0
France	100.0	99.5	103.2	114.6	109.0	109.5	115.3
Italy	100.0	115.2	119.9	139.2	129.4	127.8	132.0
Greece	100.0	139.7	155.6	161.0	173.9	159.6	n/a
Spain	100.0	119.1	130.3	130.5	122.8	113.8	116.9
Portugal	n/a	n/a	n/a	n/a	n/a	n/a	n/a
Ireland	100.0	88.2	94.1	84.2	68.0	62.4	n/a

Source: Eurostat; own calculations.

Notes
* Belgium, Greece: per person; Portugal: total economy; industry defined as economic activities B (mining and quarrying), C (manufacturing) D (electricity, gas, steam and air-conditioning supply) and E (water supply, sewerage, waste management and remediation) of NACE Rev. 2.

industry-related services, not subject to the collective agreements of the export sectors.

There is, however, a remarkable surge in nominal unit labour costs in 2009. Here, labour productivity played an important role. This jump reflects a temporary fall in labour productivity. In 2009, GDP declined but employment was relatively stable. Labour was hoarded, i.e. surpluses in working time accounts were reduced and short-time work schemes introduced. With the increase in GDP in 2010 labour productivity returned to normal levels.

Besides divergences in private consumption and price competitiveness, different wage developments also contributed to diverging inflation rates and thus to different real interest rates and to GDP growth differentials. Why? Because in the Euro Area the European Central Bank (ECB) sets a single nominal interest rate for all member states. It cannot address country-specific price increases. If wages develop differently and then inflation diverges among the member states, the single nominal interest rate translates into different real interest rates for the economies and thus different environments for financing investments and for consumer credits (see Table 5.5). Although the real interest rate is only one factor among others that influences consumption and investment decisions, *ceteris paribus* it holds that a reduction of the real interest rate results in a higher demand for credits for consumption and investment and thus private consumption and investment.

For Germany, the real interest rate was the highest on average for the period 1999–2012 and in 13 of 14 years above the average. The high costs of credits are reflected in low investment and private consumption. Furthermore, they fostered a run in financial assets, lending to countries with a more promising investment environment, like for example Spain, and a concentration of investment on the export sector. In countries with low real interest rates domestic demand was further amplified besides the direct effect of rising wage incomes. It resulted in high GDP growth rates but massive problems developed also. The housing bubble in Spain is a prime example for this.

Still, the question whether Germany profited from its export-led growth model or not is unresolved. On the one hand, wage restraint impacts positively on price competitiveness and increases the contribution of exports on growth. On the other hand, it impacts negatively on domestic demand.

What the development of GDP, depicted in Figure 5.1, shows is that growth was poor for the whole period since the start of the Euro Area and it was up to 2012 below the average of the Euro Area. Until 2009, Germany, together with Portugal and Italy, were the low performers within the Euro Area. It has changed, however, with the Great Recession. Germany performed relatively well after 2009 in respect to GDP growth.

Employment as a second main indicator of success or failure of a growth model also shows a segmented development for Germany (see Figure 5.2). Until the Great Recession, employment performed worse than the average of the Euro Area. Now, after the recession, it has caught up and is now close to the average. Often, the labour market reforms (Hartz reforms) in the first half of the 2000s are held responsible for this successful increase of employment and reduction of unemployment. The reforms established a low-paid sector and increased the pressure on all unemployed to accept a job, even if qualification and compensation do not match. Concrete measures covered: the merger of unemployment assistance and social assistance to means-tested benefits (Arbeitslosengeld II) and the limitation of unemployment insurance (Arbeitslosengeld I) to one year, which together reduced the reservation wage; the introduction of mini and midi jobs with fixed upper limits for income and no or reduced social contributions; so-called '1-euro jobs' were offered, i.e. employment opportunities outside the normal labour market; criteria of job acceptance were amended in such a way

Table 5.5 Interest rates and inflation

	Nominal interest rate (Euribor, three month fixing)	Inflation rate*	Real interest rate	Deviation of the real interest rate from an EA average	Number of years with a real interest rate above average	Number of years with a real interest rate below average
	Average of the years 1999–2012					
Germany	2.7	1.2	1.5	0.6	13	1
Netherlands	2.7	1.9	0.8	-0.1	5	9
Belgium	2.7	1.8	0.9	0.0	6	8
Austria	2.7	1.7	1.0	0.0	6	8
France	2.7	1.6	1.1	0.2	9	5
Italy	2.7	2.2	0.5	-0.4	0	14
Greece	2.7	2.7	0.0	-1.0	1	13
Spain	2.7	2.5	0.2	-0.8	4	10
Portugal	2.7	2.2	0.5	-0.5	4	10
Ireland	2.7	2.0	0.7	-0.3	6	8

Source: Eurostat; own calculations.

Note

* Harmonised consumer price index without energy prices.

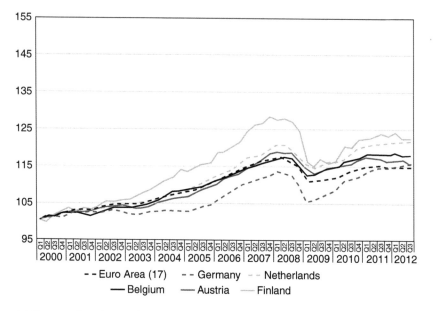

(a) Export-oriented countries.

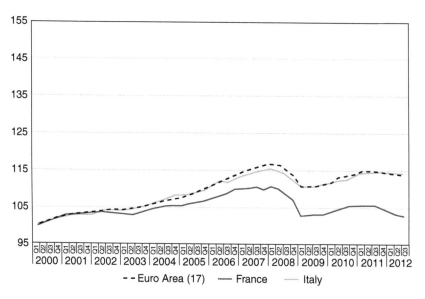

(b) The middle cases: Italy and France.

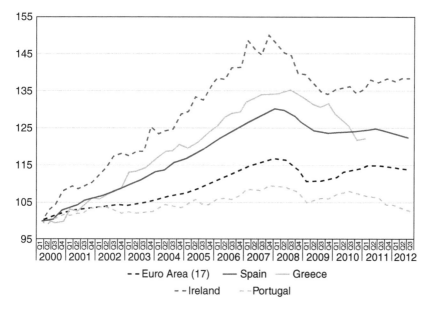

(c) Demand-led and externally debt-financed countries.

Figure 5.1 Development of real GDP before and during the crisis, quarterly values, 2000q1 = 100 (source: Eurostat; own calculations).

that after a while recipients of benefits have to accept jobs below their level of qualification; temporary agency work was facilitated as well as fixed-term employment. It has to be noted that in Germany, contrary to other countries, a minimum wage that could introduce a lower limit to declining wages does not exist.

However, this explanation of declining unemployment based on flexibilised employment and reduced wages has several catches. A coincidence is not necessarily a correlation. Other factors have influenced the employment development after 2005 (Herzog-Stein and Logeay, 2010). This year marked the end of an economic downturn in Germany. Increasing employment afterwards was simply a reflection of the following upswing. Demographic developments and a trend towards shorter working hours and part-time work also influence the unemployment rate: labour supply growth is muted. But the labour market reforms were not ineffective, they aggravated a trend of low-paid employment since the 1990s (Bosch *et al.*, 2008). A lot of the newly created jobs are of low quality and pay. The number of working poor who receive top-up benefits by the state has increased. Temporary agency work is widespread nowadays. Unemployment rates of people aged 55 years and over are still high. So for a lot of employees the Hartz reforms contributed directly to job instability and low wages. Moreover, for others it triggered the fear of income losses. In such a situation,

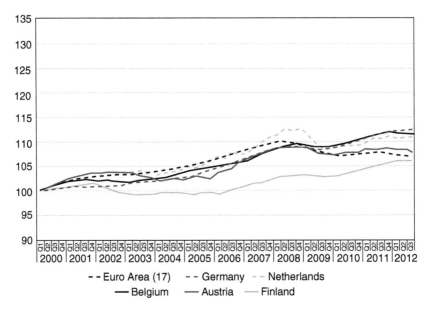

(a) Export-oriented countries.

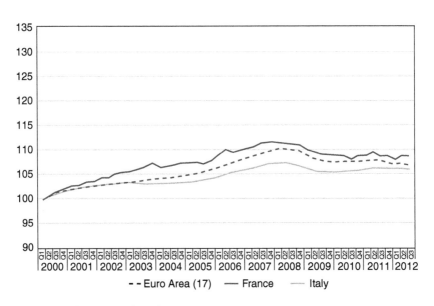

(b) The middle cases: Italy and France.

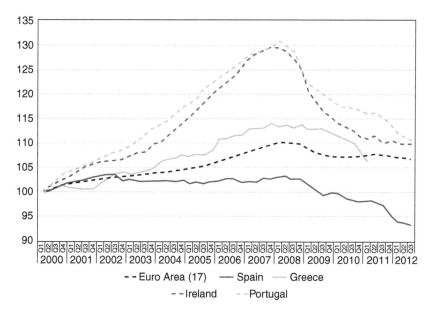

(c) Demand-led and externally debt-financed countries.

Figure 5.2 Development of employment in persons before and during the crisis, quarterly values, 2000q1 = 100 (source: Eurostat; own calculations).

employees and trade unions are willing to accept opening clauses to collective agreements or amendments of collective agreements that worsen working conditions and payments in exchange for employment guarantees. As a result, real wages and voluntary payments by the employers, i.e. locally negotiated payments like holiday pay not covered by the collective agreement, declined in Germany for several years (Schulten, 2008). The consequence was not a rise in employment but sluggish domestic demand that seemingly makes it more necessary to focus on price competitiveness and exports. In other words, the reform of labour markets under Chancellor Schröder fostered the export-led growth model by depressing wage claims. As mentioned above, this politically induced wage restraint is rooted in a long tradition and is supported by state, employers and employees and their organisations, and public and academic opinion as a prerequisite of an export-oriented economy.

Especially the stabilisation of employment after 2009 cannot be ascribed to the structural reforms of the labour market. On the contrary, the conservative-liberal government under Chancellor Merkel prepared the ground for this 'job miracle' with a policy mix that contrasts sharply to the usual pro-market orientation of these two parties. It used instruments to smooth the negative effects of the Great Recession more in the tradition of corporatism and

Keynesianism than those policies which are normally applied by pro-market proponents:

1   The banking sector was stabilised by encompassing state guarantees and financial support for banks. The establishment of Bad Banks was supported and the burden was shifted to the taxpayer. For Germany, a credit crunch and bank runs were successfully avoided (Horn, Joebges, Niechoj *et al.*, 2009).
2   Keynesian deficit spending was introduced. Two fiscal stabilisation programmes dampened the impact of the crisis on growth and employment. Widely known is the car-scrapping premium as one measure among others. The programmes not only dampened the fall in GDP, they also helped to establish the expectation that this sharp decline is only temporary (Eicker-Wolf *et al.*, 2009: 49–58).
3   Employees were not dismissed on a large scale. Labour was hoarded. This safeguarding of jobs was possible due to the specific system of industrial relations in Germany. Working time accounts, managed within the firms and backed by collective agreements, and short-time work, subsidised by the state, have a long tradition. Moreover, in a lot of companies working time accounts of employees were in surplus before the crisis. So for a limited time, it was possible to lower hours worked without reducing employment significantly (Herzog-Stein and Seifert, 2010; Herzog-Stein *et al.*, 2010; Möller, 2010).

This combination of measures stabilised expectations in Germany. Expecting a positive future implied that consumers continued to consume and that firms kept employees for the expected rise of sales after the crisis as well as the level of investment. In this situation running discussions about demographic change and shortage in labour supply supported labour hoarding. The success of these measures and the hope that those expectations would not be disappointed hinged, however, on a quick restart of the economy. It was not planned to issue one fiscal stabilisation programme after another nor was labour hoarding considered as an option for more than a few months. Sometimes working accounts are deeply in minus and without orders dismissals have to follow. Also short-time work is nothing a firm and employees can practise endlessly. What saved the German economy was that a few months after the beginning of the crisis exports to Asia (especially China), the USA and Central and Eastern Europe started to increase again. In anticipation of the forthcoming upswing equipment goods were ordered by these countries – and in equipment Germany has a strong competitive advantage which is based on prices *and* quality. Furthermore, car exports were going surprisingly well. This economic downturn and the upswing afterwards also pronounced a shift in German export patterns from Western Europe to other regions that has been taking place since the mid-1990s (Stephan and Redle, 2010). Since 2010, there has been a strong increase of exports to Asia and also the USA. In 2011 exports to the Euro Area were again roughly at the same level as in 2008 but since 2012 the outlook has been negative due to the austerity measures that at the end of 2012 affected German exports, too.

In this situation, relying on exports has paid off. But since the introduction of the euro German export orientation has also led to a development of GDP growth below average and it implies a significant dependency on growth developments in other countries which is rather unusual for a large economy like Germany and reveals its dangers in the current situation of stagnation or recession in most of the economies of the Euro Area. That employment has not been affected more since the Great Recession and that it has even increased afterwards can be attributed to a policy mix of fiscal expansionism and corporatist institutions in a specific constellation of a fast recovery of demand by important trading partners of the German economy, supported by a weak euro and a specific product portfolio of the German export sector.

This is only one side of the coin and shows to what extent Germany has benefited from its growth model. As the largest economy within the Euro Area, its development has had an impact on the other member states as well, which is the flipside. It has led to the situation that Germany and some other member states of the Euro Area face permanent current account surpluses, others permanent deficits. The sum of the surpluses of Germany and the Netherlands roughly corresponds to all the deficits of the deficit countries (see Figure 5.3). This does not mean that intra-trade within the Euro Area has necessarily to be balanced in the sense that Germany´s surplus has to be the deficit of one or several other member states. Surpluses or deficits are the result of trade relations with economies outside the Euro Area, too. But because of the almost balanced current account of the Euro Area with the rest of the world, deficits and surpluses within the Euro Area roughly correspond to each other.

As Figure 5.3 shows, the composition of the two groups of countries – in deficit and in surplus – does not change much over time. Only Ireland, an export-led country with a collapsed banking system and profit transfers to other countries shows volatile behaviour here. Moreover, even the Great Recession has neither whirled the composition nor the trend towards accumulating and persistent imbalances between the two groups. But if current accounts of a country are permanently in deficit, the difference between the imported value and the exported value plus the income account has to be financed somehow. Thus, external debt is increasing as well as the debt service. The net investment position reflects this rise in current account imbalances and external borrowing. Similar to the current accounts but with a different sign, net investment positions also diverged since the establishment of the monetary union. The export-led countries served as creditors and accumulated more and more assets; the domestic demand-led economies accumulated liabilities, respectively. The net investment position of Germany broadly matches the sum of the net investment positions of Greece, Spain, Portugal and Ireland.

What persistent current account deficits mean for a country can be studied in the cases of Greece, Spain and Portugal. These countries are in dire straits

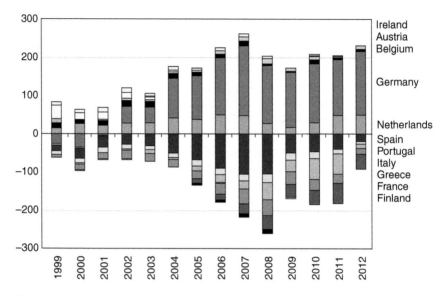

Figure 5.3 Current accounts in the Euro Area (source: Eurostat AMECO).

now. They have to handle an enormous debt service, private and public, and they have accumulated a massive loss in price competitiveness that under-mines exports. Austerity measures were introduced under the auspices of the troika that have deteriorated further production. Unemployment has risen dras-tically. For the export-led economies this situation is, however, dangerous and eroding, too. Credits to the domestic demand-led countries have to be written down and export markets are collapsing. Both country groups are interwoven and not immune to problems of the correspondent group. Even the German economy cannot decouple itself completely from the problems of the Euro Area.

Current account imbalances might not be the sole problem within the Euro Area; there are country specific problems and the burden of the financial market crisis that turned private losses into public debt (Joebges and Niechoj, 2010; Niechoj and van Treeck, 2011). But for a sound and enduring solution of the debt crisis a reduction of these imbalances is essential (Horn *et al.*, 2010; Laski and Podkaminer, 2011). Without it, a further crisis is already looming that will call the existence of the Euro Area again in question.

Blame avoidance

Several initiatives of the German government during the sovereign debt crisis have demonstrated that the negative aspects of the export-led growth model have been ignored and interdependencies within the Euro Area have been underesti-mated (see for a detailed discussion Niechoj, 2012: 409–415):

- Concerning monetary policy, all German members of the ECB council after the financial market crisis – first Axel Weber and Jürgen Stark, now Jens Weidmann and Jörg Asmussen – have repeatedly emphasised their opposition to the purchase of government bonds and financing states through this backdoor by the ECB. Moreover, the idea of Eurobonds was rejected. A common responsibility is out of focus and the interdependency of the growth models in the Euro Area is neglected.
- Fiscally, the German government has pressed for faster and stricter fiscal adjustment paths within the framework of the Stability and Growth Pact. Furthermore and along the lines of the German debt brake, Chancellor Merkel launched an initiative to further strengthen fiscal discipline by enshrining debt caps in all constitutions of the Euro Area member states. In March 2012, this was agreed in a treaty, the so-called fiscal compact. Moreover, it was a German idea to introduce private sector involvement in the case of Greece and future debt restructurings of the European stability mechanism and to introduce an orderly insolvency procedure for states. In other words, the leeway for mutual fiscal support, and especially the fiscal burden Germany is willing to accept, is limited.
- Structural reforms are the key to overcoming the crisis. Therefore, in the beginning of 2011 Angela Merkel and France's President Sarkozy initiated the so-called Euro plus pact, a pact that recommends wage restraint when labour cost growth exceeds productivity growth. Wage indexation is supposed to be abolished and labour markets are supposed to be flexibilised. The public sector was allocated a leading role; in other words, it should act as a forerunner of wage restraint.
- European imbalances are a problem; this is acknowledged. But imbalances are caused by a lack of competitiveness. Political reactions have to be asymmetric, i.e. deficit countries are solely responsible for gaining in competitiveness. This positioning became clear in the negotiations on the supplementation of the excessive deficit procedure of the Stability and Growth Pact by a macroeconomic imbalances procedure. Germany, for a long time, opposed the introduction of such an imbalances procedure. Finally it agreed to a wording that de facto puts most of the responsibility for adaptation on the deficit countries. Based on a scoreboard of indicators, the thresholds for sanctions are asymmetric. For example, a current account deficit of up to 4 per cent but a surplus of up to 6 per cent of GDP is permitted; the net international investment position has only a negative threshold of 35 per cent, not a positive one; the increase in nominal unit labour costs is sanctioned above the level of 9 per cent but negative values are acceptable for all countries, also for surplus countries.

So, from this perspective, fiscal discipline and structural reforms of the labour markets are essential to overcome the sovereign debt crisis and imbalances within the Euro Area. With the adjustment programmes of the troika of International Monetary Fund, ECB and European Commission and the constitutional amendments of the fiscal compact, the German government has achieved a lot in the area of fiscal policies. What is still lacking, from their perspective, is the solution to the competitive disadvantages of several countries, which is important for increasing their ability to repay their debt to Germany and other countries. At the beginning of 2013, at the World Economic Forum in Davos, Chancellor Merkel nicely expressed her vision of competitiveness for the Euro Area:

> What we are still lacking, however – and this is something we must work on in 2013 – is an answer to how, throughout the common monetary union, we can ensure greater coherence over the years ahead in the matter of competitiveness.... What I'm thinking of here – and this is something we're currently discussing in the European Union – is a compact for competitiveness along the lines of the fiscal compact. The way this could work would be that countries would conclude agreements or treaties with the European Commission committing them to become more competitive in areas where they're lagging behind. This could often concern things like non-wage labour costs, unit labour costs, research spending, infrastructure and the efficiency of public administration.
>
> (Merkel, 2013)

In the same speech, she also elaborated on the German view towards European imbalances and clarifies the responsibilities:

> [W]hen we're criticized on account of the imbalances that still exist, it's important to note the reason for these imbalances. Take unit labour costs in Europe: if they were to converge exactly at midpoint on the spectrum, the average of all European countries, Europe as a whole would no longer be competitive and Germany's export industry would be finished. That can't be the goal we're striving for. So up to a point, obviously, current account surpluses show that countries are scoring well on competitiveness. And that's something it would be pure folly to put at risk.
>
> (Merkel, 2013)

In other words, the country with the highest current account surplus, Germany, is suggested as a role model for the Euro Area. Current account surpluses – based on price competitiveness – are key to growth and prosperity. Germany does not share any responsibility for what happened to the other member states; the German model of export-led growth does not imply negative side-effects. Moreover, the country (and its taxpayers) has already taken a lot of burden on its shoulders by granting a huge amount of credits. Now the others have to do their homework to keep up with the German economy.

In doing so, the German government is not only avoiding blame, Merkel puts the case for a generalisation of the German model. There are, however, at least two reasons why this is a cheap recommendation. First, the German model is still based on well-educated employees and an industrial basis. If other countries lacking this would like to copy the German model they would either have to invest massively in the education system and in industry or they would have to get rid of production that is not competitive and they would also have to lower their wages far below the German level to gain in price competitiveness against the German economy. The first option is unlikely; the second is what we see in Greece, Spain and Portugal with all its negative consequences of poverty and unemployment. However, compared to Germany even massive cuts in compensation of employees are not enough to foster exports sufficiently. Indeed, these countries now achieve a reduction of current account deficits but this is mainly due to restricted imports, not successful exports. It takes time to build up a competitive basis. The second reason is that this model cannot be extended to all member states of the Euro Area. For a small economy, wage restraint is possible and might lead to growth and employment via export surpluses, if larger economies tolerate trade balance deficits. In the case of a large economy, however, wage restraint has side-effects on growth and on other countries. It represses domestic demand and fuels current account imbalances, especially in an integrated currency area lacking exchange rate adjustments. If all countries aimed at current account surpluses, following the German growth path, domestic demand would be further devastated by a European-wide wage restraint that might result in deflation and a crisis of investment. The reason for this is that price competitiveness is always a relative concept. If one country starts to decrease wage growth or wages itself and achieves price advantages, this country will expand exports but others will lose market share and might respond with wage restraint in their country. Moreover, book-keeping tells us that all member states could *aim* at surpluses vis-à-vis the other member states but not all can succeed. The sum of all surpluses has to correspond to the same sum of deficits elsewhere. In a simple simulation, Semieniuk *et al.*, 2012 show the futility of aiming at surpluses in all member states of the Euro Area. It is possible, however, that the Euro Area as a whole can aim at and succeed in having a surplus with the rest of the world. But again, this does not necessarily solve the problems of intra-European imbalances and it presumes that the rest of the world tolerates its deficit. It has to be noted that global imbalances are no negligible problem either although exchange rates between the Euro Area and the rest of the world serve as a buffer for accumulating global imbalances (Horn, Joebges and Zwiener, 2009; Priewe, 2011).

Conclusions

At a first glance, the German economy was in a remarkably good position at the time of writing (the turn of 2012 to 2013) – despite the financial market crisis, the economic crisis afterwards and the still looming sovereign debt crisis. Current accounts have been in surplus since 2002, growth has been at the pre-crisis level since 2010, the harmonised unemployment rate was at 5.5 per cent in 2012. Furthermore, public deficits are not only below the 3 per cent level prescribed by the European Stability and Growth pact, but nearly balanced and contrary to other member states of the Euro Area the interest rates of government bonds are not rising but have been decreasing for quite a while, now stabilising at a low level. It seems that, at least in comparison to most of the other member states of the Euro Area, Germany has overcome the heavy burdens of the financial market crisis as well as those of the economic crisis afterwards and is one of the rare solvent anchors within the turbulences of the debt crisis in the Euro Area.

This, however, ignores the role wage restraint has played in Germany under the new rules of the monetary union. In the case of Germany, exports to the Euro Area were fostered by a fixed exchange rate and by low increases in wages and unit labour costs. As a consequence, current account imbalances in the Euro Area have been aggravated and private consumption and thus growth in Germany have been below Euro Area average. This trend was amplified by labour market reforms, the so-called Hartz reforms in the first half of the 2000s, establishing a low-paid sector in Germany.

Wage restraint was not responsible for the stable and later on even positive employment development in and after 2009. What shielded employment from the contraction in growth and exports in the downswing of 2009 was a specific constellation, tripartite corporatist measures and institutions, to be more precise: financial support of the state for short-time work plus public investment programmes and flexible working-time accounts, introduced years before the crises by trade unions and employers. The following upswing in growth and employment originated in a strong demand for German exports from Asia and countries outside the Euro Area. Since the end of 2012, however, it has become clear that Germany also suffers from the desolate situation in the Euro Area.

The policies during the crisis in 2009 might be a role model for other countries; wage restraint, however, cannot be recommended for a large economy in a monetary union against the background of the German experiences.

Notes

1 The term 'model' is used in the sense of 'pattern' and not 'strategy' in order to highlight that there is no central actor – neither government nor business or other candidates – that implements a certain strategy for the whole country. There are indeed several actors with strategies and interests promoting this growth model; some of them I name in the course of this chaper. But in the end the resulting pattern is a common and partly unintended effort of interacting actors, nothing a single actor has planned or is able to introduce.
2 The first quarter of 2000 was used as the base period and as a proxy for the beginning of the monetary union due to missing data for 1999 for some countries.

References

Bosch, G., T. Kalina and C. Weinkopf (2008), 'Niedriglohnbeschäftigte auf der Verliererseite'. *WSI Mitteilungen*, 8: 423–430.

Cesaratto, S. and A. Stirati (2010), 'Germany and the European and Global crisis'. *International Journal of Political Economy*, 39(4): 56–86.

Ederer, S. (2012), 'The euro crisis and the responses to it: Missing the point?' *Intervention. European Journal of Economics and Economic Policies*, 9(1): 13–22.

European Commission (2013), 'European Economic Forecast. Winter 2013'. *European Economy*, 1/2013.

Eicker-Wolf, K., T. Niechoj and A. Truger (2009), 'Vom unerwarteten Aufschwung in den Sog der Weltrezession. Zur makroökonomischen Politik unter der Großen Koalition', in K. Eicker-Wolf, T. Niechoj, S. Körzell and A. Truger (eds), *In gemeinsamer Verantwortung. Die Sozial-und Wirtschaftspolitik der Großen Koalition 2005–2009*. Marburg: Metropolis: 19–73.

Herr, H. (1994), 'Der Merkantilismus der Bundesrepublik in der Weltwirtschaft', in: K. Voy, W. Polster and C. Thomasberger (eds), *Marktwirtschaft und politische Regulierung*, Vol. 1. Marburg: Metropolis: 227–261.

Herzog-Stein, A. and C. Logeay (2010), 'Labour market reforms, hysteresis, and business cycles in Germany: a SVAR approach to explain unemployment developments', *Applied Economics Quarterly* Supplement, 61: 89–120.

Herzog-Stein, A. and H. Seifert (2010), 'Der Arbeitsmarkt in der Großen Rezession – Bewährte Strategien in neuen Formen'. *WSI Mitteilungen*, 11: 551–559.

Herzog-Stein, A., F. Lindner, S. Sturn and T. van Treeck (2010), 'From a source of weakness to a tower of strength? The changing German labour market', *IMK Report*, 56e, available online at www.boeckler.de/pdf/p_imk_report_56e_2011.pdf (accessed on 11 February 2013).

Horn, G. A., H. Joebges, T, Niechoj, C. Proano, S. Sturn, S. Tober, A. Truger and T. van Treeck (2009), 'Von der Finanzkrise zur Weltwirtschaftskrise. Wie die Krise entstand und wie sieüberwunden werden kann'. *IMK Report* 38, available online at www.boeckler.de/pdf/p_imk_report_38_2009.pdf (accessed on 11 February 2013).

Horn, G. A., H. Joebges and R. Zwiener (2009), 'From the financial crisis to the world economic crisis (II). Global imbalances: Cause of the crisis and solution strategies for Germany'. *IMK Policy Brief*, December, available online at www.boeckler.de/pdf/p_imk_pb_12_2009.pdf (accessed on 11 February 2013).

Horn, G. A., T. Niechoj, S. Tober, T. van Treeck and A. Truger (2010), 'Reforming the European Stability and Growth Pact: Public debt is not the only factor, private debt counts as well'. *IMK Report* 51e, available online at www.boeckler.de/pdf/p_imk_report_51e_2010.pdf (accessed on 11 February 2013).

Joebges, H. and T. Niechoj (2010), 'Rettungsmaßnahmen im Euroraum – kurzfristig sinnvoll, aber nicht ausreichend'. *IMK Report* 52, available online at www.boeckler.de/pdf/p_imk_report_52_2010.pdf (accessed on 11 February 2013).

Laski, K. and L. Podkaminer (2011), 'Common mentary policy with uncommon wage policies: centrifugal forces tearing the Euro Area apart'. *Intervention. European Journal of Economics and Economic Policies*, 8(1): 21–29.

Lucarelli, B. (2011), 'German neomercantilism and the European sovereign debt crisis'. *Journal of Post Keynesian Economics*, 34(2): 205–224.

Merkel, A. (2013), Speech by Federal Chancellor Merkel at the World Economic Forum Annual Meeting 2013, available online at www.bundesregierung.de/Content/EN/Reden/2013/2013–01–24-merkel-davos.html?nn=447030 (accessed on 11 February 2013).

Möller, J. (2010), 'The German labor market response in the world recession – demystifying a miracle'. *Zeitschrift für Arbeitsmarktforschung*, 42: 325–336.

Niechoj, T. (2012), 'Germany – best practice for the Euro Area? The Janus-faced character of current account surpluses', in H. Herr, T. Niechoj, C. Thomasberger, A. Truger and T. van Treeck (eds), *From Crisis to Growth? The Challenge of Debt and Imbalances*. Marburg: Metropolis: 389–419.

Niechoj, T. and T. van Treeck (2011), 'Policy responses to the euro debt crisis: can they overcome the imbalances that caused the crisis?' *Intervention. European Journal of Economics and Economic Policies*, 8(2), 245–266.

Niechoj, T., U. Stein, S. Sabine and R. Zwiener, R. (2011), 'German labour costs: a source of instability in the Euro Area. Analysis of Eurostat data for 2010'. *IMK Report* 68e, available online at www.boeckler.de/pdf/p_imk_report_68e_2011.pdf (accessed on 11 February 2013).

Priewe, J. (2011), *Die Weltwirtschaft im Ungleichgewicht. Ursachen, Gefahren, Korrekturen*. WISO Diskurs Series, Bonn: Friedrich Ebert Foundation.

Priewe, J. (2012), 'European imbalances and the crisis of the European monetary union', in H. Herr, T. Niechoj, C. Thomasberger, A. Truger and T. van Treeck (eds), *From Crisis to Growth? The Challenge of Debt and Imbalances*. Marburg: Metropolis: 331–360.

Schulten, T. (2008), 'Europäischer Tarifbericht des WSI 2007/2008'. *WSI Mitteilungen*, 9: 471–478.

Semieniuk, G., T. van Treeck and A. Truger (2012), 'Towards reducing economic imbalances in the Euro Area? Some remarks on the stability programmes 2011–2014', in H. Herr, T. Niechoj, C. Thomasberger, A. Truger and T. van Treeck (eds), *From Crisis to Growth? The Challenge of Debt and Imbalances*. Marburg: Metropolis: 361–387.

Stein, U., S. Stephan and R. Zwiener, R. (2012), 'Zu schwache deutsche Arbeitskostenentwicklung belastet Europäische Währungsunion und soziale Sicherung. Arbeits- und Lohnstückkosten in 2011 und im 1. Halbjahr 2012'. *IMK Report* 77, available online at www.boeckler.de/pdf/p_imk_report_77_2012.pdf (accessed on 11 February 2013).

Stephan, S. and L. Redle (2010), 'Going East. Deutschland setzt auf Handel mit China und den Ländern Mittel- und Osteuropas'. *IMK Report* 54, available online at www.boeckler.de/pdf/p_imk_report_54_2010.pdf (accessed on 11 February 2013).

Streeck, W. (1991), 'On the institutional conditions of diversified quality production', in E. Matzner and W. Streeck (eds), *Beyond Keynesianism. The Socio-Economics of Production and Employment*. London: Edward Elgar: 21–61.

6 Hartz IV and the consequences

Did the labour market reforms destroy the German model?

Joachim Möller

Introduction: characteristics of the German model

In a standard definition, the so-called German model is described as an 'institutionalized high wage economy combining high competitiveness in world markets with strong social cohesion and, in particular, low levels of inequality along a variety of dimensions' (Streek, 1997: 2). In a similar way, Freeman (2000) describes this model as 'Rhenish Capitalism'. There are several characteristics that belong to the German model. These characteristics include at least five dimensions:

1 education and training: the dual training system, long tenure and acquisition of firm-specific human capital;
2 labour relations: high union coverage, co-determination and social partnership, high importance of internal vs. external flexibility;
3 solidarity: moderate degrees of inequality in earnings and financial assets, a comprehensive social security network;
4 industrial structure: export orientation of the economy, relative strength of manufacturing;
5 infrastructure: efficient transport facilities, highly reliable legal system.

These elements should not be considered in isolation because they are interrelated and form a consistent economic system. In more detail, the above dimension could be described as follows.

1 The vast majority of German workers pass through the dual training system, which has a long tradition. The dual system combines the acquisition of theoretical and practical knowledge. Young school-leavers typically choose a specific occupation and sign a contract with a firm (*Ausbildungsvertrag*). These school-leavers receive practical training within a firm and – typically for one day per week – theoretical training at a public school (*Berufsschule*). An important aspect of the dual system is that it offers corresponding training resources; for instance, the working time of experienced workers who are able to transfer firm-specific and general skills to the apprentices.

Although it cannot be excluded that under certain circumstances some firms might consider the apprentices as cheap labour, the firm-specific and general practical training also require a certain investment by the firm in the apprenticeship system. Typically, small firms do not hire all of their apprentices but take some advantage by creaming off the best apprentices. Their interest is to hire the elite of their apprentices whose abilities they have got to know very well and who acquired firm-specific human capital. Those apprentices who are not offered a contract after completing their apprenticeship move to other firms. Furthermore, there is also some poaching between firms. Because the curricula within the professions are codified, standard skills being typical of a specific profession can be expected from a worker with a completed apprenticeship. Hence, a certificate in a certain profession serves as a signal for a bundle of skills and competences.

2   Traditionally, the system of labour relations is of high importance for the German model. In a larger firm, a work council serves as a mediator between the interests of the workforce and those of the management. This conflict-resolving potential is particularly important for firms facing a highly volatile product demand (as is typical of firms with a high exposure to world trade). More particularly, work councils play a key role in organising within-firm flexibility, for instance, through the variation of working hours to stabilise employment.

Moreover, work councils are important in fostering training measures and the implementation of high security standards. In case of necessary employment adjustments, work councils guarantee the consideration of social aspects in managerial decisions.

The system of well-functioning labour relations in Germany is particularly strong in manufacturing industries. This system relies on high unionisation and coverage of collective bargaining.

3   During the period from the German *Wirtschaftswunder* in the 1950s and 1960s to the time of reunification, the degree of earnings inequality in Germany was low. This was also true for skill differentials. With respect to measures of earnings inequality, Germany ranked somewhere in between the Scandinavian and the Anglo-Saxon countries. One of the reasons for historically moderate skill differentials might be seen in the low-skilled bias in technical change being typical of the Fordian production phase that was dominating the industry at the time of the *Wirtschaftswunder*. Thus, low-skilled workers were in relatively high demand during this period. Since the 1980s, the nature of technical progress fundamentally changed towards skill bias. Unions tried to counter these forces by bargaining for a fixed component in wage increases (*Sockelbeträge*) from which the lowest-income groups profit more than proportionally. However, unemployment of low-skilled workers has become an increasingly severe problem since the late 1980s.

From the time of Bismarck in the late nineteenth century, the German model relied on a comparatively generous social network. This network holds true for health insurance, pension schemes and, particularly, for unemployment insurance. For the latter, relatively high replacement ratios and long periods of entitlement for insurance benefits were typical.

4   Among the OECD countries, Germany has one of the highest shares of manufacturing employment. In the past, this industry structure was considered an ambiguous characteristic. On the one hand, Germany was blamed for being a laggard with respect to structural change. For instance, immediately before the Great Recession of 2009, Berry Eichengreen warned that Germany might experience the same fate as Italy or other countries that were losing ground. '[What happened to Italy] as China moved up the technology ladder into the production of more sophisticated consumer goods will happen to Germany as China moves into the production of more sophisticated producer goods' (Eichengreen, 2007: 2). However, manufacturing has always been one of the industries where Germany has had a comparative advantage. Moreover, these industries are known as being highly productive and innovative. Interestingly, many observers today see an advantage in a relatively high share of manufacturing in production and employment. Therefore, it appears that the former drawback is increasingly turning into an advantage, particularly since the financial crisis, which has cast some doubts on the sustainability of a mainly service-driven growth in advanced countries (see Möller, forthcoming). In the aftermath of the financial crisis, Germany, with its seemingly outdated industry structure, performed surprisingly well; whereas countries with a weak industrial basis are still suffering.

5   The division of labour is particularly important in modern manufacturing. Just-in-time or just-in-sequence delivery of parts in the production chain calls for high standards of logistics and an outstanding transportation system. Additionally, a sophisticated system of a highly fragmented production process that comes along with higher economic integration and modern manufacturing production in various branches (Hummels *et al.*, 2001) requires efficient legal structures for creating confidence in a production network.

The rationale behind the Hartz IV reforms

In retrospect, the German model has increasingly moved towards a crisis since the mid-1970s. Since then, mass unemployment became an increasingly menacing phenomenon. In parallel with a striking ratchet effect in the unemployment figures since the first oil price crisis, systemic unemployment was steadily rising. After each recession, the core of unemployed individuals was substantially higher than before. This phenomenon can be described as a result of significant hysteresis effects due to, for instance, depreciation of human capital through periods of long-term unemployment and other mechanisms.

From the early 1990s onwards, an additional challenge related to the high financial burden caused by German reunification became increasingly relevant. Huge transfers to the East put public and private budgets under pressure. As a result, the German economy was plagued with low growth and low job creation rates. Furthermore, the deep structural crisis of the East German economy led to extremely high unemployment rates in almost all regions of the new *Länder*. Labour market institutions were not flexible enough to cope with the huge burden of adjustment after the reunification in the post-socialist economy, which from one day to the next was exposed to the world economy without being able to devalue its currency to regain competitiveness. In the late 1990s, there were some additional negative effects for the German economy immediately after the introduction of the euro. Capital flows were redirected to formerly high interest countries within the Eurozone, which was detrimental to home investment.

Hence, at that time, the German economy was in a critical phase, and it appeared to be not only a laggard in structural change but also the paradigm of Eurosclerosis. Consequently, *The Economist* (1999) blamed Germany as the 'sick man of the euro'. Increasingly, a situation developed that called for a drastic reform. The result was the political program Agenda 2010 that Michael Burda dubbed the 'Teutonic turnaround'. Chancellor Schröder, in his famous speech from March 2003, argued that if Germany refrained from modernising its labour market institutions, it would be modernised through the brute forces of the global markets leaving barely room for a social protection net (see Deutsche Bundestag, 2003). Hence, according to his position, the far-reaching labour market reforms were necessary to keep the German model alive. Here, the fundamental question arises whether the deep structural changes that came along with the reforms sacrificed basic ingredients of the German model. Did the reforms throw the baby out with the bathwater? To assess the situation adequately, we will first describe the reforms and their effects.

The key elements of Agenda 2010 aimed to reform labour market institutions. The so-called Hartz reforms were implemented in different steps between 2003 and 2005. The fundamental concept for improving the functioning of the labour market and reducing the number of the unemployed can be characterised as 'supporting and demanding'. The reform adopted a stick and carrot approach. On the 'carrot' side, there were several instruments for facilitating the integration of the unemployed; for instance, support for training measures, wage subsidies and improved conditions for the placement of workers into new jobs. Concrete elements on the 'stick' side were somewhat lowering job protection standards, reducing the maximum period for the entitlement of unemployment insurance benefits, tightening of job acceptance regulations for the unemployed as well as deregulation for temporary work agencies. Perhaps the most substantial change was the merger of unemployment assistance and welfare (Hartz IV). The implication was that, after 12 months of receiving unemployment benefit, a worker would have to fall back into the basic welfare system. In contrast to the insurance system, basic welfare provides means-tested benefits only. Compared to the pre-reform situation, the new institutional setting meant a substantial deterioration of a worker's position. Three important aspects have to be mentioned in this context. First, workers are status oriented. The new institutional system, however, implies the possibility of a deep fall in social status after only one year of unemployment, creating a credible threat. Second, compared to the pre-reform situation, the position of the long-term unemployed significantly deteriorated because social offices could access the benefit recipients' private assets. Third, the criteria under which workers had to accept a job offer were sharpened.

Taken together, these three reform elements created high pressure on the unemployed to find a new job quickly. This reform undoubtedly led to changes in behaviour. Particularly, effects on the reservation wage of the unemployed, on search intensity and on the willingness of job-seekers to make concessions could be expected. Moreover, it is rather likely that the bargaining power of workers in general was affected by these profound changes in the institutional environment.

A further element of the reform was a redefinition of the criteria for persons being available to the labour market. Welfare recipients were considered to be available in the labour market if they were able to work for at least three hours a day. As a perhaps unintended by-product of this change, there was a 0.5 million increase in registered unemployment. As a consequence, officially counted unemployment peaked at more than five million immediately after the reform was implemented.

Reform effects

General effects

It cannot be doubted that the German labour market reforms were a drastic cure. Although not all parts of the reforms were well designed, strong positive effects on the labour market became rapidly visible. The German economy experienced an extraordinary boom period in the three years following the reform. From 2004:Q4 to 2008:Q2, the growth of real production was 9.4 per cent in the aggregate economy and 18.8 per cent in manufacturing. From 2005 to the eve of the world recession by the end of 2008, unemployment fell from its peak level of more than five million to less than three million. At the same time, the negative ratchet effect disappeared: For the first time since the 1960s, the unemployment rate at the beginning of the economic downturn (2008:Q3) was lower than at the beginning of the previous recession. Moreover, as indicated by Möller (2010) among others, the functioning of the labour market significantly improved as indicated by a marked inward shift of the Beveridge curve, as shown in Figure 6.1. As seen from the figure, the curve was rather stable until the 1980s. Then, three major outward shifts of the curve occurred, with the latest shift being an artificial one due to the aforementioned redefinition of labour market availability in 2005. As a striking demonstration of the reform effect, the curve started to move steadily inwards after the reforms, particularly from the mid-2006 onwards.

The turnaround of systemic unemployment is documented in Figure 6.2. The figure shows the development of unemployment in West Germany since the 1950s. The fat curve connects the peaks and troughs of the unemployment series. As seen, the recession in the 1960s did not lead to an increase in systemic unemployment; i.e. the troughs before and after the recession were at approximately

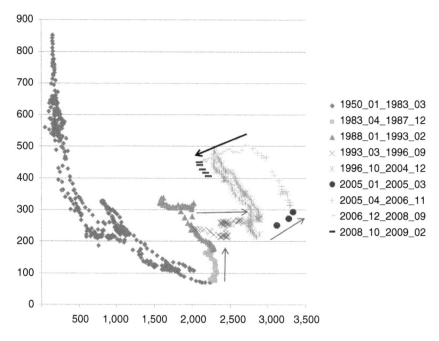

Figure 6.1 The Beveridge curve 1950: M1 to 2009: M3: registered unemployed vs. registered vacancies (source: German National Bank, statistics; data seasonally adjusted).

the same level. With the OPEC I crisis in the mid-1970s, the situation changed markedly. Since that time, the level of the unemployment lows increased from recession to recession, pointing to the existence of hysteresis effects. In the post-reform period after 2005, one can observe that for the first time since the 1960s, the trend was reversed.

Additionally, Figure 6.3 shows that long-term unemployment decreased markedly after the labour market reforms. Note that the steepness of the decline is remarkable given the previous development of the series (in East and West Germany). Because long-term unemployment is an important determinant of systemic unemployment, the decline corroborates the view that the labour market reforms led to a significant improvement of the labour market performance in Germany.

Specific reform effects

As a matter of fact, wage increases in the aftermath of the reform were rather moderate, and workers were more likely to accept unfavourable job conditions. Figure 6.4 provides an impression of the changes in the behaviour of applicants from the view of employers. It turns out that in the post-reform years 2005 and

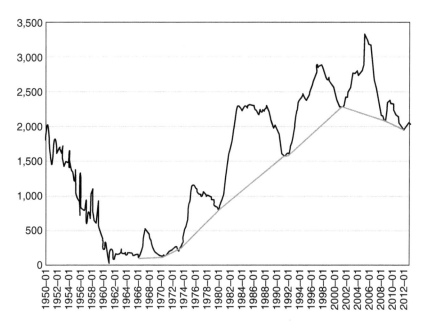

Figure 6.2 Peaks and troughs in unemployment 1950–2009 (unemployed persons, West Germany only. Data source: Deutsche Bundesbank).

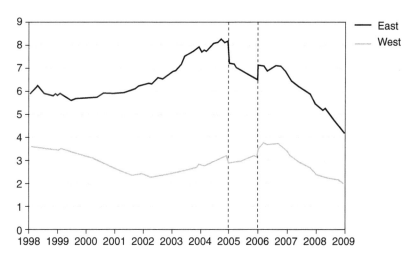

Figure 6.3 Long-run unemployment rate in East and West Germany 1998–2009 (source: Statistics Federal Employment Agency; values for 2005 cannot be interpreted because of a structural break).

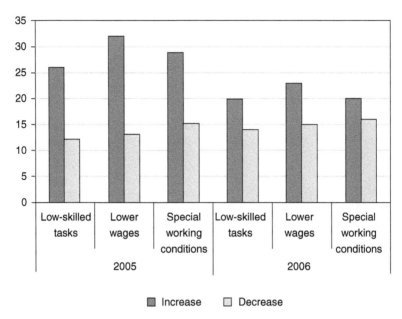

Figure 6.4 Increase or decrease in the willingness of job-seekers to accept unfavourable aspects of job characteristics (source: IAB job vacancy survey, see Kettner and Vogler-Ludwig, 2010).

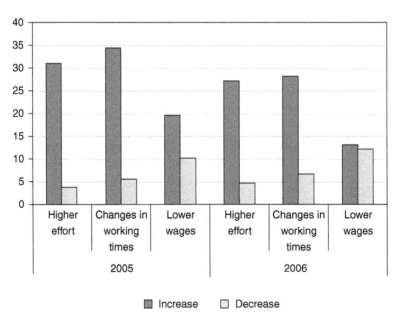

Figure 6.5 Increase or decrease in the willingness of the incumbent workforce to accept unfavourable aspects of job characteristics (source: IAB job vacancy survey, see Kettner and Vogler-Ludwig, 2010).

2006, the overall willingness to accomplish low-skilled tasks and accept lower wages or special working conditions has significantly increased. The changes are particularly strong immediately after the reforms in 2005. As shown in Figure 6.5, the changes in the behaviour of the incumbent workforce are at least as strong as the effects on job-seekers. In the view of employers, this change is remarkable with respect to higher effort and more flexibility such as the willingness to accept changes in working hours and – albeit to a lower extent – even lower wages. Again, the effects are particularly strong in 2005, immediately after the reforms. Note that the net changes in the willingness to accept lower wages are significant in the year 2005 but not in 2006.

Drawbacks of the reform

Although the German labour market performance clearly improved through Agenda 2010, the labour market reforms came at some significant costs. There is some indication that labour market segmentation and wage inequality have increased. These phenomena are well described. For instance, there is a marked decrease in the share of 'normal' contracts in total employment (see Table 6.1).[1] The share of normal working contracts has become particularly low for young workers.

Wage inequality has risen substantially in the top as well as in the bottom tail of the wage distribution. Moreover, some groups of workers suffer from less job stability. Overall, precarious employment has clearly risen.

Critics of the reform have also stressed that the right balance between 'supporting' and 'demanding' has not been found. The strategy is biased towards the stick whereas the carrot plays a minor role. Furthermore, the instruments of active labour market policy – at least in the starting phase of the agenda – do not fit individual needs adequately.

The share of low-wage earners has increased markedly, both for total employment and for subsamples divided by region (East/West) or gender. Figure 6.6 shows that the share of low-pay workers has increased at least since the

Table 6.1 Share of normal employment contracts in total employment by age and skill group (%)

Age	1991	1999	2007
15–24	56.2	35.9	28.1
24–49	75.0	70.4	63.9
50–64	73.9	69.4	65.3
Skill level			
low	54.9	46.9	34.0
intermediate	77.0	71.0	64.8
high	75.7	71.9	67.5

Source: IAB.

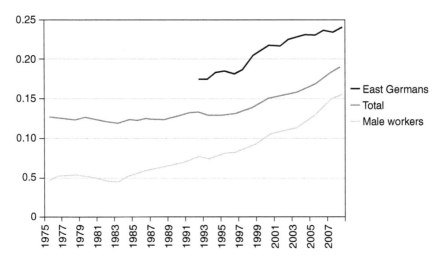

Figure 6.6 Share of low-pay workers in total employment 1975–2008. Low pay is defined as below two-thirds of median earnings; full-time male workers age 25 to 55 only (source: own calculations with SIAB data, see Dorner *et al.*, 2010).

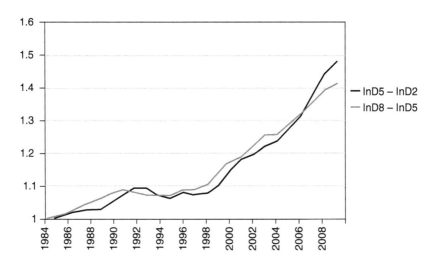

Figure 6.7 Indicators of wage inequality in the lower and upper tail of the distribution (log decile ratio InD5–InD2 and InD8–InD5).Full-time male workers only; age 25 to 55; West Germany (source: own calculations with SIAB data, see Dorner *et al.*, 2010).

mid-1990s. For total employment and male workers, the trend towards a higher share of low-pay employment has accelerated since 2005.

Parallel to the increasing shares of low-pay employment, wage inequality has increased as well. The phenomenon is visible not only in the lower tail but also in the upper tail of the distribution. Figure 6.7 shows that the trend towards higher wage dispersion had already started in the mid-1990s, i.e. long before the labour market reforms. The log decile ratios InD5 – InD2 and InD8 – InD5 essentially moved in parallel for most of the observation period. Interestingly, the increase in wage inequality in the lower tail of the distribution surpassed that of the upper tail in the aftermath of the labour market reforms.

Figure 6.8 depicts the development of an index of real earnings for full-time male workers in West Germany by three skill levels (low-skilled, workers with vocational training and university graduates). Ultimately, until the time of the reunification (1991), the real wages of all skill groups were increasing. In the first half of the 1990s, real wages for all groups were stagnating. Since the mid-1990s, however, the development of real earnings has clearly diverged among the skill groups. Whereas workers with a university degree experienced sharp increases in their real earnings, the earnings of the low-skilled declined, particularly after 2005. For one and a half decades, the real earnings of the intermediate skill group more or less stagnated after 1990 but then decreased as well. Hence, sizeable groups of workers suffered losses in real earnings particularly in the years after the labour market reforms. With stagnating or even declining real earnings for the majority of workers, unit labour costs have fallen considerably. As a result, the competitiveness of the German industry increased markedly

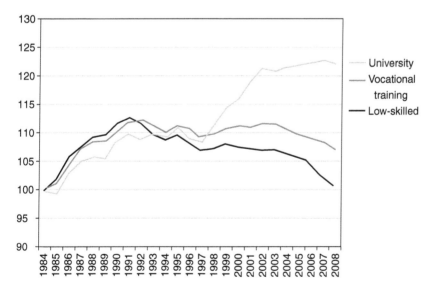

Figure 6.8 Real wage index by qualification type for full-time male workers in West Germany 1984 to 2008 (source: own calculations using SIAB data).

vis-à-vis other countries within and outside the Eurozone. This higher competitiveness led to an unprecedented increase in real exports, partly at the cost of the neighbouring countries in the Eurozone.

Germany during the Great Recession

It is interesting to see how the post-reform German labour market responded to the sharp decline in external demand during the Great Recession 2009. As an export-oriented economy, the country was hit by the collapse of orders for exporters more than other advanced countries. Relative to the trend, the German GDP dropped by approximately 6.5 per cent. Quite remarkably, there was no corresponding decrease in employment. The unemployment rate remained almost stable. Not without reason, this unusual response was called the German labour market miracle. Ultimately, an unprecedented level of within-firm flexibility was the main explanatory factor (see Möller, 2010). In the first place, it was the flexible response of working hours that led firms to keep their workforce stable. Through subsidies of the Federal Employment Agency (the so-called *Kurzarbeitergeld*), the financial burdens to firms and workers were held down. Because the crisis was perceived by firms as a short-lived demand crisis, labour hoarding turned out to be a reasonable strategy. Social partnership was a main prerequisite for managing this high within-firm flexibility. For example, work councils played a major role in communicating the various measures for keeping employment stable between workers and management. From a worker's perspective, keeping their job was in their best interest because of the threat of falling from unemployment insurance payments into means-tested social assistance after only one year of unemployment. Because in earlier recessions, mass layoffs were not unusual and, if anything, employment protection was weakened in the last decade, one can argue that employment protection regulations were not the main reason for firms keeping their workforce stable. It is much more plausible that the labour hoarding behaviour observed under the given circumstances was voluntarily.

Conclusions: did labour market reforms destroy the German model?

Given the evidence presented above, the answer is a 'No, but…'. Some key elements of the German model – such as the dual training system and long tenure – were not affected by the reform. Some elements were strengthened, and some elements were weakened. Labour relations proved to be really strong during the crisis, and social partnership was extremely helpful for organising the high level of within-firm flexibility. This fact was particularly true for the export-oriented manufacturing firms, which through labour market reforms and a long period of wage moderation have reached a high level of international competitiveness. Hence, the export orientation based on a strong manufacturing sector was even strengthened by the direct and indirect effects of the reform. The main element for the German model being substantially weakened through the reforms is solidarity. Traditionally, the German economy was run under a rather low level of earnings inequality. At the same time, at least the important group of trained workers enjoyed quite a comfortable social security network. Social security, however, has deeply changed. Workers are much more in danger of losing their social status in quite a short period of time. Given the regulatory framework after the reforms, workers are much more pressed to accept unfavourable working conditions and low-paid jobs. It comes as no surprise that wage inequality has increased sharply. Moreover, social permeability has also decreased over the years. The heritage of education (*Bildungsvererbung*) is of major concern for critics of the German system. These concerns lead to segmentation tendencies in the society, which are an increasingly important topic in the political debate. In the past, solidarity was a key element of the German model. It is possible that – if no counteraction measures are seized – the menace of an increasingly divided society would be a strong challenge to the survival of the German model. Currently, initiatives for introducing a statutory minimum wage receive growing support. Overall, one can argue that the deep labour market reforms in Germany were necessary as a painful cure to stop the harmful trend in the rise of systemic unemployment. However, the dark side should not be forgotten. A challenge for the future is mitigating the damages that an increasing amount of segmentation has inflicted on the German model.

Note

1 'Normal' working contracts comprise full-time, permanent contracts which are eligible to social contributions and exclude temporary work.

References

Burda, M. (2007), 'German recovery: it's the supply side'. *Vox-EU*, 30 July. www.voxeu. org/article/german-recovery-it's-supply-side.

Deutsche Bundestag (2003), Plenarprotokoll 15/32, Berlin, 14 March: 2481.

Dorner, M., J. Heining and P. Jacobebbinghaus (2010), 'The sample of integrated labour market biographies'. *Schmollers Jahrbuch*, 130: 599–608.

The Economist (1999), 'The sick man of the euro'. 3 June.

Eichengreen, B. (2007), 'The Germany economy: be careful what you ask for'. *Vox-EU*, 30 July. www.eurointelligence.com/news-details/article/the-german-economy-be-careful-what-you-ask-for.html?cHash=050f9ab081c28f7499b4f565d2b00754.

Freeman, R. B. (2000), 'Single peaked vs. diversified capitalism: the relation between economic institutions and outcomes'. *NBER Working Papers*, National Bureau of Economic Research.

Hummels, D., J. Ishii and K.-M. Yi (2001), 'The nature and growth of vertical specialization in world trade'. *Journal of International Economics*, 54: 75–96.

Kettner, A. and K Vogler-Ludwig (2010), 'The German job vacancy survey – an overview', in *First and Second International Workshops on Methodologies for Job Vacancy Statistics. Proceedings.* Eurostat Methodologies and Working Papers. Luxemburg: Eurostat: 7–17

Möller, J. (2010), 'The German labor market response in the world recession – De-mystifying a miracle'. *Journal for Labour Market Research*, 42(4): 325–336.

Möller, Joachim (forthcoming), 'Prosperity, sustainable employment and social justice: challenges for the German labour market in the twenty-first century'. *International Journal for Educational and Vocational Guidance*.

Streek, W. (1997), 'German capitalism: Does it exist? Can it survive?' in C. Crouch and W. Streeck (eds), *Political Economy of Modern Capitalism: Mapping Convergence and Diversity.* London: Sage Publication: 33–54.

7 Hartz IV and the German model

A comment

Enrico Saltari

To the Italian reader, the chapter by Joachim Möller poses a question which is not easy to answer but nevertheless cannot be avoided: Why did the Hartz reform of the labour market succeed in reducing the unemployment rate while the reforms of the Italian labour market (which started at the end of the 1990s but, as it seems, have not yet been completed) have had the only effect of increasing its volatility? What is surprising is not only the drastic reduction in the total German unemployment (in 2005 the rate was 11.3 per cent, in 2012, only seven years later, it more than halved at 5.5 per cent), but the simultaneous fall of long-term unemployment when the Hartz labor market reform was about to be completed (2003–2005). In the same years (2005–2012) the Italian unemployment rate increased from 7 to 11 per cent.

To be sure, as Möller makes it clear, the 'flexibilisation' of the German labour market was not without costs for workers. On the one hand, the Hartz reform acted on long-term unemployment: it entailed a weakening of the welfare status of the long-term unemployed in such a way as to increase their willingness to accept job offers even at lower wages. On the other, it also acted on short-term employment through the liberalisation of temporary contracts and the deregulation of work agencies. For instance, the OECD index for the strictness of employment protection legislation for temporary workers decreased from 2 to 1.25.

Bearing these costs produced at least two positive outcomes. As mentioned above, one of them is the strong reduction of long-term unemployment. This is an important achievement as it meant the reversal of the systemic unemployment which afflicted Germany, and Europe, since the oil shocks of the 1970s. The other positive effect was wage moderation which raised German competitiveness boosting investment and exports. On the other hand, the Hartz reform also produced negative, perhaps undesired, consequences. Labour market flexibility, as often happens, implied an increase in the share of temporary workers, particularly among the young workers. Another side-effect of the reform was a worsening of wage inequality, i.e. a strong rise in wage dispersion.

All in all, this is Möller's conclusion, that the positive effects more than offset the negative ones. And, above all, even if weakened, the German model, one of the pillars of the German society, was not substantially undermined. These very conclusions pose again the question raised at the beginning: Why did the German reforms of the labour market have such an outcome while in Italy they failed? It should be underlined that the labour market reforms carried out in both countries were very similar: liberalisation concerned only the legislation for temporary contracts while leaving untouched the strictness of regulation for regular contracts and collective dismissals.

Even if difficult, this is a question worth trying to answer. I suggest three elements of reflection as ingredients of a possible answer.

The detailed and convincing reconstruction of the recent evolution of the German economy after the Hartz reform offered by Möller can hardly be disputed. Nor can the assessment he gives of the positive effects of the Hartz reform. For instance, in the years following the reform until 2008 the German economy saw an exceptional expansion of production and employment. However, labour market flexibility does not seem to work symmetrically in his historical account. For when it comes to the reaction to the 2009 Great Recession, a different explanation of the German performance is given. Certainly wage moderation induced by the Hartz reform helped the competitiveness of export-oriented firms, thus giving support to employment. Nevertheless, the explanation of employment stability during the recession is an 'unprecedented level of within-firm flexibility'. In a sense, one could say that at the basis of the virtuous performance of the labour market there was the German model, especially in the form of social partnership and internal flexibility, rather than the Hartz reform, which favoured instead external flexibility.

This is the first difference with respect to the Italian labour market reforms based almost exclusively upon external flexibility.

Moreover, in conjunction with the decision of keeping the workforce within firms, the data also shows a marked acceleration in capital accumulation in Germany. Labour hoarding per se, especially when financed through government subsidies (by means of *Kurzarbeitergeld* or *Cassa Integrazione Guadagni*) is subject to ambiguous interpretation since by definition it cannot be a long-term decision. It may be seen as a first step toward a future massive layoff. Or, if the crisis is perceived as temporary, it will be accompanied or followed by a restructuring of the production process. Investment dynamics can be used as litmus paper to distinguish between the two situations. In the years immediately after the 2009 recession, when Germany and Italy were affected by an analogous fall in gross domestic product (more than 5 per cent) and investment (more than 11 per cent), gross fixed capital formation rapidly recovered in Germany in 2010 and 2011 (at some 6 per cent); in Italy it first stagnated and then declined. Although there is still no data to break down aggregate investment into its components in those years, what occurred just after the much more modest 2003 recession leads to the hypothesis that Germany privileged information and communications technology (ICT) investment at the expense of non-ICT investment, while the reverse happened in Italy. The evolution of total factor productivity in the two economies in the same years provides support for this supposition.

Thus, another relevant factor explaining the different response to the labour market reforms of the two economies lies in the indirect effect it produced on the pace (and composition) of the accumulation process. Here, again, the German model may have played a major role.

The last point worth emphasising here concerns the productive structure, especially along the dimension of firm size. As is well known, both economies are export-oriented with a strong manufacturing sector. There is a big difference, however, which is not immediately visible at a first glance. If one looks at the industry composition inside the manufacturing sector, individual industries have a similar distribution with a prevalence for traditional productions in consumption goods in Italy and more innovative ones in investment goods in Germany. Nevertheless, a closer view of the German manufacturing sector reveals that in *all* industries employment is concentrated in large (more than 250 persons engaged) firms; summing the employment figures in medium (50–249 persons engaged) and large firms reinforces this result in the sense that in almost all industries more than 50 per cent of employment is in these firms. The reverse is true in Italy: most of the employment is in micro (1–9 persons engaged) and small (10–19) firms. In fact, more than 75 per cent of employment in the manufacturing sector is in medium to large firms in Germany and less than 45 per cent in Italy. In a nutshell, in Germany most of the employment is found in large firms, in Italy in small firms, independently of the type of production. Now as a matter of fact, firm size is clearly a relevant factor in determining the kind of flexibility to adopt in reducing labour costs. Internal flexibility is a more feasible strategy in large firms; external flexibility appears as the main route for small firms.

To sum up, I think that the extraordinary performance of the labour market in Germany cannot be explained solely by the Hartz reform without considering the political and economic background, whose essential components are the German model and its productive structure.

8 German reforms as a blueprint for Europe?

Sebastian Dullien

Introduction: the new hype about Germany

At the latest since the onset of the euro crisis and Germany's relatively good performance during the global financial and economic crisis of 2008–2009, the federal republic is revered as a new economic role model for other industrialised countries. While economic growth has not been overly impressive, at the time of writing unemployment in Germany is lower than in any other large European country or in the United States and lower than it has been for more than 20 years. The German public budget is almost in balance and the level of public debt measured as a share of GDP is also lower than in any other of the large OECD countries. Moreover, the German economy continues to expand its exports briskly and runs large current account surpluses. These stable macroeconomic conditions have made Berlin the new centre of power when rescue measures during the euro crisis were discussed, as it seems that Germany is the only country left having adequate financial resources to pay for bail-out programmes.

In 2012, *The Economist* thus ran a large piece titled 'Modell Deutschland über alles' (14 April), strongly advocating other ailing economies to follow the German path of labour market reforms which have been implemented under the term Agenda 2010 by the social democratic chancellor Gerhard Schröder from 2003 onward. Volker Kauder, the chairman of the German ruling conservatives' parliamentary group, proudly stated in 2012 that 'all over Europe, German is now spoken', implying that finally everyone was following the German policy approach, especially referring to Germany's austerity stance which it had pre-scribed itself through a constitutional amendment in 2009. This amendment pop-ularly referred to as the *Schuldenbremse* (debt brake) served as a blueprint for Europe's recently passed fiscal compact, which forces euro countries to limit their own structural deficits to 0.5 per cent of GDP.

Even though there is little academic literature to back such a simple narrative, the storyline usually found in the political arena and in the popular press is straightforward: Burdened with an excessive welfare state and sclerotic labour markets, the German economy experienced a protracted economic crisis in the early 2000s, with which the government headed by the social democrat Gerhard Schröder was struggling. After narrowly winning re-election in 2002, Chancellor

Schröder embarked on a comprehensive reform programme (called Agenda 2010) to overhaul the German labour market, the German social security system and an excessively large German public sector. The labour market became thus more flexible in terms of working times, redundancy payments and firing rules. Freed from the burden of the excessive welfare state, the German economy recovered from its year-long stagnation and started to outperform the rest of Europe again in terms of economic growth, employment creation and unemployment.

Reading current comments on the German economy, it is startling how quickly the perception of the German model and the country's economic fate has turned around. Until the middle of the past decade, both the domestic debate as well as the international perception had a completely different tone. In 2003, the Centre for European Reform labelled Germany 'the sick man of Europe' (Barysch, 2003). In the same year, the leading German economist Hans-Werner Sinn published a book titled *Ist Deutschland noch zu retten?* ('Can Germany be saved?'[1]) with the conclusion that unless very radical reforms are implemented, Germany was doomed economically. The book was followed by other works, written by economists or leading journalists, all predicting the German demise. At the time of their implementation even the Schröder reforms were not seen as a game-changer. Hans-Werner Sinn judged them in 2007 as not being 'a real breakthrough' (Sinn, 2007: 109), and the German Council of Economic Advisors repeatedly claimed that they were not far-reaching enough. Interestingly, the same reforms are now often proclaimed at having been crucial for the German economic performance since the middle of the past decade.

This quick change in perception leads one to wonder how far the narrative of strengthening the German economy through decisive reforms of the Schröder years really is accurate. If this narrative was true, why was the recent improvement in economic conditions not seen by leading German economists when the Agenda 2010 package was passed? In addition, if the narrative was accurate, how far can these reforms be copied by the rest of Europe?

In order to answer the above questions this chapter will first describe the elements of the Agenda 2010 labour market reforms and will link them to Germany's macroeconomic performance. Then, some problematic elements of the German performance will be pointed out and in a last step it will be asked what would happen if all countries in Europe followed a similar path.

Elements of Germany's Agenda 2010 reforms

In order to evaluate the German reforms' impact one first has to distinguish what really has been part of the Agenda 2010 package. Some of the elements regularly attributed to the social democrats' economic reforms in Germany have just not been present in the legislative reform packages of the Schröder government.[2] The weight of other elements of the reform package has been exaggerated, possibly due to a lack of understanding of the specificities of the German labour market. German labour market institutions have been changing endogenously over the past two decades, without government intervention, but through marginal changes in collectively bargained wage contracts (Carlin and Soskice, 2009). This process has been much more gradual and must not be confused with the changes brought about by the Schröder reforms.

The Schröder reform package of the years 2003 to 2005 contained the following elements:

- *It merged the old unemployment assistance with the general social welfare system.* Prior to the crisis, the unemployment assistance had been paid to unemployed people who had exhausted the duration of their unemployment insurance benefits, while social welfare had been paid to those which had no prior claim on unemployment insurance benefits. While the unemployment assistance was set as a proportion of past wages, the social welfare was paid to whoever did not have sufficient income or wealth to cover his or her subsistence. While the social welfare was means-tested, unemployment assistance was not. The social welfare was a complicated system of lump-sum payments for food and other items of daily use plus payments for rent and occasional payment for special needs, such as new furniture or winter clothes, depending on individual need. One special feature of the social welfare was that any earnings of the individuals were directly subtracted from the transfer payments, making especially part-time work for those in the system very unattractive.

    The reforms did four things to this system: They first abolished any reference between past income and payments received after individual unemployment insurance payments had run out (usually after 12 months) and replaced them with a lump-sum payment called *Arbeitslosengeld* II plus a rent subsidy. Second, they merged all payments for special needs into one single monthly lump-sum payment. Third, they made the payments in the system means-tested, forcing individuals with substantive savings to tap into them before claiming public benefits. Fourth, they allowed persons receiving *Arbeitslosengeld* II to work and to keep a certain share of their wages, turning the system effectively into a low-wage subsidy.
- *It reformed the German labour office and active labour market policies.* Within the package, the organisational structure of the German labour offices was completely overhauled and the office was renamed *Arbeitsagentur* (labour agency). While prior to the reforms municipalities were in charge of looking after those receiving social welfare and the old labour office was responsible for placement and payments to those receiving unemployment assistance, after the reforms all recipients of *Arbeitslosengeld* II were placed under the responsibility of the labour agency.
- *It liberalised market access to certain professions.* Prior to the reforms, market entry in a large number of professions in Germany was strictly regulated, so that only those who had worked for a certain time in established companies and were able to provide documentation of training were allowed for example to open a business laying parquet or tiled floors. For

53 professions this requirement was scrapped, yet not for the heavily regulated white-collar professions, such as legal services, pharmacies or tax consultants.

- *It liberalised the market for temporary work agencies.* The Schröder reforms relaxed the rules for temporary work agencies. This sector was heavily regulated prior to the reform. Rules for limiting the time of employment in a temporary work agency were scrapped, and a number of other restrictions were relaxed.

- *It marginally reformed the provisions for firing.* The reforms basically restored the company size threshold level for which dismissal provisions are effective. It was raised from five to 10 employees, that is to a level which had already been in place before 1998. Also, some recent court rulings were put into the letters of the law, especially introducing the dismissed employee's legal right for a defined severance payment, which previously had to be fought for in the courts. In general, it is agreed by experts in labour law that these changes did not have large material effects.[3]

- *It lowered social security contributions for marginal jobs.* A reduced but progressive rate of social security contributions was introduced for employees earning between €400.01 and €800 per month.

In addition, although not officially part of the Agenda 2010 reforms, austerity budgets were passed by the Schröder government with the aim of bringing the German public deficits back in line with the Stability and Growth Pact's provision of limiting the government deficit to 3 per cent of GDP.

Note, however, what the Schröder reforms did *not* do: They did not touch the German system of collective wage bargaining. They did not change the rules on working times. They did not make hiring and firing fundamentally easier. They also did not introduce the famous working time accounts and the compensation for short working hours which helped Germany through the crisis of 2008–2009. These rules all remained virtually untouched by the Schröder government's legislation.[4]

This conclusion might be surprising, given the predominant narrative of the German reforms, but it is backed by economic research. The OECD for example compiles a widely regarded index for employment protection.[5] According to this index, employment protection for regular work contracts actually became *more strict* in 2004 (exactly the opposite of what one would expect in case of labour market deregulation) and has not changed since. The index for the protection of temporary jobs dropped somewhat, but compared to prior changes and changes in other countries in other reform periods, this drop seems marginal (see Figure 8.1). Going into the subcomponents of the synthetic employment protection indicator, one can see that the fall in the index is entirely due to the changes in regulations on temporary work agencies, while dismissal rules for regular contracts were actually tightened.

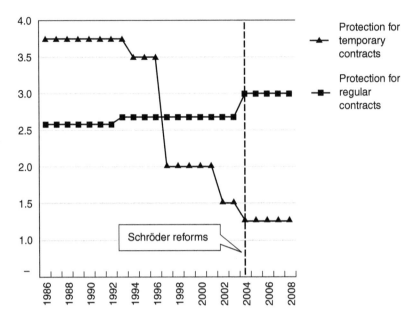

Figure 8.1 Employment protection in Germany, OECD indicators (1=least strict; 6=most strict) (source: OECD).

Macroeconomic elements of the German success

The lauded German success has manifested itself in the past years in good export performance of German companies: While many other European countries lost market shares in world export markets, Germany was able to defend market shares or even increase them. In addition, Germany has been able to turn around its current account from a deficit of 1.7 per cent of GDP in 2000 to a whopping surplus of 7.4 per cent of GDP in 2007 and was able to maintain its surplus at above 5 per cent of GDP in 2012 (IMF, 2012).[6]

In Germany, there has been an ongoing debate on the underlying reasons for this development. Two elements are usually noted: First, the German manufacturing sector with its specific specialisation has been especially well positioned to benefit from the ascent of large emerging markets such as China, Brazil or Russia. As Germany is exporting mainly capital equipment, industrial chemicals and (up-market) cars, the investment surge in the emerging markets and the emergence of a large middle class craving for luxury goods has pushed up demand for German products abroad. Especially since the onset of the euro crisis, this has also been credited in the public debate to the high quality of German products, German talent and the high standards of German stock of knowledge.

Second, an element often quoted and strongly debated among academics has been the increased price competitiveness of German companies, especially compared to other Euro Area countries. Measured in nominal unit labour costs, Germany has improved its price competitiveness relative to the rest of the Euro Area by more than 10 per cent (see Figure 8.2). Relative to some countries in the euro periphery such as Spain or Italy, the improvement has been a whopping 25 per cent. As can be seen when looking at the two elements of unit labour costs, which are nominal wages and productivity growth, this increase in competitiveness did not stem from overly large increases in productivity (in fact, growth in labour productivity in Germany was significantly lower in the 2000s than it had been earlier – see Figure 8.3), but from nominal wage restraint.

In Germany, there has been a controversial debate about how far this wage restraint has been at the heart of the country's large and persistent current account surpluses. While some authors claim that the significant improvement of the German companies' price had a decisive impact on the current account position (Dullien *et al.*, 2009 or Priewe, 2013), others point to weak aggregate demand, especially in investment (European Commission, 2012) or to capital flows as determinants of overall current account balances (Erber, 2012).

In fact, there are some very plausible reasons that in addition to the improvement in price competitiveness, other factors also had an important influence in explaining strong export growth and the large improvement in the current account position. First, export growth has almost certainly also been influenced by Germany's unique geographical position between a high-income, highly integrated European market (the old EU member states) and poorer new EU member states, which have joined the single market only in 2004 and subsequently experienced an especially strong increase in their import demand, from which Germany could benefit.

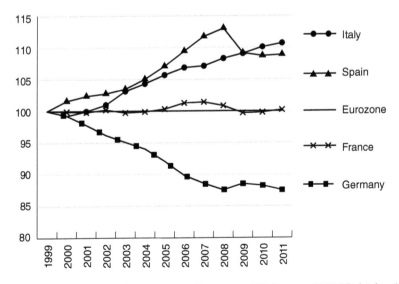

Figure 8.2 Nominal unit labour costs. Eurozone = 100 (source: AMECO database).

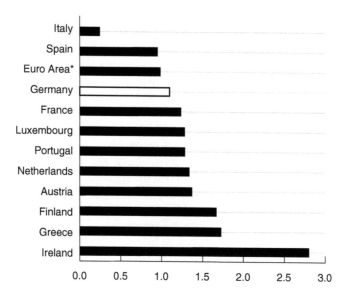

Figure 8.3 Average annual productivity growth 1999–2010, in % (source: AMECO database).

Note
* Without Cyprus, Estonia, Malta, Slovenia.

Moreover, there are crucial indications that the high current account surpluses stem at least as much from weak domestic demand as from superior price competitiveness. Just by accounting logic, weak domestic absorption leads to higher net savings of the German economy and hence larger current account surpluses. While the weakness of German consumption has often been mentioned (and can be traced as a side-effect of the wage restraint), the persistent weakness in domestic investment has been less well publicised. In fact, as can be seen in Figure 8.4, Germany's fixed asset formation as a share of GDP has underperformed the rest of the Euro Area from the year 2000 onwards. While it has sometimes been argued that this weak performance is related to lacking profitability of the German corporate sector and hence shows the need for more wage restraint (Sachverständigenrat, 2002: 329; Sachverständigenrat, 2010: 103), this view is actually not very plausible given other data, especially on the profitability of German companies or the wage share, which all point to very good profit situations.

If one looks in contrast into the details of the statistics on gross fixed capital formation, two elements stick out. First, public investment in Germany has been extremely weak. Net investment of the general government fell further from an already weak 0.4 per cent of GDP in 1995 and actually turned negative in 2003, the year when the Schröder reforms were passed. Only with the onset of the economic and financial crisis of 2008–2009 (and the passage of large stimulus

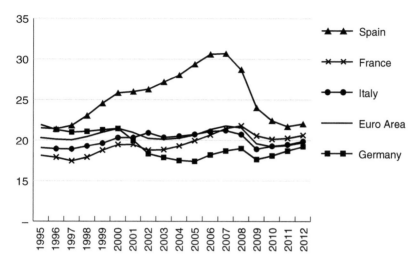

Figure 8.4 Gross fixed investment, total economy, in % of GDP (source: AMECO
database).

packages which included significant public investment) did this component turn
positive again. Yet until the onset of the euro crisis (which depressed public
investment in the crisis countries as they were forced to cut public expenditure),
German public investment lagged significantly behind that of other European
countries. Second, investment in housing has been extremely weak until the
beginning of the Great Recession of 2008–2009. As has been discussed in
Dullien and Schieritz (2011), this development can also be traced back to economic policy as subsidies for individual home construction have been repeatedly reduced over the past years and finally scrapped in 2006. Hence, one can
conclude that the current account surplus has been caused to a significant extent
by tight fiscal policies.

However, the combination of austerity and wage restraint has not only
helped to improve export performance and the current account position. It has
also had some important negative economic and social side-effects. The most
striking one is the rather low productivity growth. German labour productivity
not only grew more slowly in the years 1999–2010 than in the past, but it also
underperformed most other Euro Area countries (see Figure 8.3), as well as the
USA. Modern growth theory would predict that countries can improve their
productivity either by catching up to the technological frontier and hence
adapting technology, organisation and management methods from further
advanced economies or – especially if they are already close to the technological frontier – by investing in human capital and research and development.
Given that Germany is already rather close to the technological frontier, the
latter is especially relevant for this country. However, in European comparison, spending on education and research and development combined is only

mediocre (see Figure 8.5). Especially spending on education in Germany is rather meagre, with Germany in a similar league as countries such as Italy and Spain and only slightly in front of Slovakia and Greece, all countries with a long-reported underinvestment in education.

Finally, over the past decade, Germany has developed one of the largest low-wage sectors in Europe. In 2008, almost seven million Germans or almost 20 per cent of all employees worked for low wages, defined as wages below €9 per hour (Kalina and Weinkopf, 2010). The lower two quintiles saw their real wages fall between 2000 to 2006 (Dullien *et al.*, 2009).

Even though the German wage bargaining system has not been touched by the reforms, it can be argued that this growth in the low-wage sector is at least partly a result of the Schröder labour market reforms. German unions and employers have always taken the labour market situation in different segments into account when negotiating wages; moreover, important parts of low-wage industries have not been covered under the collective-bargaining contracts since the early 1990s. Hence, it can be argued that in this segment of the market a simple neoclassical supply-and-demand analysis can be applied to wage setting (albeit with a delayed adjustment towards equilibrium as existing nominal wages are usually sticky). The impact of the reforms on this labour market segment was two-fold: First, they have increased supply of low-wage workers as pressure has been put on workers to take up an employment even if the job did not adequately match their qualifications. Second, the reforms have lowered the reservation wage as the new rules allowed welfare to top up low wage earning, effectively introducing a de facto low-wage subsidy. This has further increased supply in the labour market which has led to a fall of real wages in the low-wage sector.

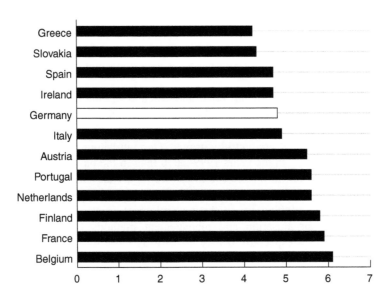

Figure 8.5 Spending on education 2006, in % of GDP (source: OECD).

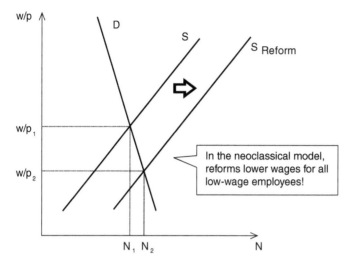

Figure 8.6 Supply and demand diagram for low-wage sector (source: own elaboration).

Figure 8.6 shows this process in a simple supply and demand diagram of the low-wage sector: The supply curve is shifted to the right, lowering the real wage for all low-qualified workers, while at the same time the number of hours worked in this sector is increased.

What if everyone followed the German approach?

As mentioned before, especially in the euro crisis from 2010 onwards, other European countries have often been told to follow the German model and pass similar reforms to Germany's. However, that Germany has been doing well is not a sufficient condition for making it a blueprint for everyone. To remain in the German tradition of thought, we can put this argument into the language of the famous philosopher Immanuel Kant (1785/1993: 30) whose categorical imperative states: 'Act only according to the maxim whereby you can, at the same time, will that it should become a universal law.'

So, how well do Germany's reforms fare by these standards? What would happen if all countries in Europe followed the German approach?

For the rather low investment both in research and development as well as education, the answer is pretty straightforward. According to a large share of the broad body of literature of the new growth theory, technological progress is closely linked to spending on research and development as well as education.[7] Moreover, technological progress usually has positive spillover effects to the countries with which an innovating country is trading (Keller, 2004). Translated to Europe, this means that following the German pattern of low spending on research and development and education would mean a much lower rate of technological progress and hence lower long term growth rates than would be otherwise possible. Against the background of the admittedly now largely defunct Lisbon Agenda, this means moving further away from the idea of making Europe the technologically most advanced region in the world.

The second important element of the German model has been nominal (and consequently real) wage moderation. Here again, the important question is what would happen if every country in Europe would follow this approach. The answer to this question depends crucially on the economic paradigm one adheres to. In approaches based on the standard neoclassical textbook models, such as the neoclassical synthesis or AS–AD model, a fall in nominal wages usually leads to higher output, as it brings the actual real wage closer in line with the equilibrium real wage compatible with full employment. The fall in nominal wages would hence shift the AS-curve to the right as shown in Figure 8.7.

According to what contributions such as Coricelli *et al.* (2006) or Soskice and Iversen (2000) claim, a fall in nominal wages might also increase aggregate demand. The implicit logic here is that lower nominal wages lead to lower prices. With a fixed nominal money stock, these lower prices translate to higher real money holdings (M/P) and through the Keynes effect or the Pigou effect to higher investment demand or higher consumption demand and hence to overall higher aggregate demand and higher output.[8] If one follows this interpretation, falling nominal and real wages and consequently a falling price level in the European monetary union as a whole would be beneficial, leading to higher output.

The problem with this approach, however, is that a broad body of literature questions whether the nominal money stock can be seen as exogenously fixed

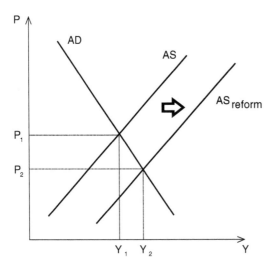

Figure 8.7 Impact of wage restraint on output and prices in the AS–AD model (source: own elaboration).

and as net wealth of the private sector. As Dullien (2004) shows, if money is mostly endogenous inside money, falling prices in a closed economy do not increase aggregate demand. Instead, in situations of fragile banking systems (which one can well argue is the case in Europe at the moment), falling prices lead to debt deflation which creates problems in the financial system, leading to less credit supply and hence *less* aggregate demand.

If only one country in a monetary union follows such a deflationary policy, this counter-argument against wage deflation is less important. Here, a deflationary wage policy might well increase aggregate demand for the country's products as the country gains market shares from its trading partners (a typical beggar-thy-neighbour policy of real devaluation), compensating for weak domestic demand. This is exactly what Germany has done according to its critics since the middle of the past decade.However, if such a deflationary wage policy were followed by all European countries, the negative effect on aggregate demand might dominate. Hence, employment effects from nominal wage restraints can be expected to be much less beneficial for the Euro Area as a whole than for Germany alone.

Conclusions

To summarise, the evidence presented here hints that the German success in terms of its large current account surplus, low unemployment rate and acceptable economic growth stems from a combination of nominal wage restraint, supported by labour market reforms which have brought down the reservation wage and have put downward pressure on wages, and severe spending restraints both on public investment as well as on research and development and education. On the whole, this cannot serve as a blueprint for Europe. Some of the elements of the German model have negative externalities on its partners in Europe, some others depress economic growth at home. The nominal wage restraint bears elements of a beggar-thy-neighbour policy which could even turn into a negative-sum game if followed by all European countries. The reluctance to spend on research and development and education lowers potential growth rates not only in Germany, but through the existence of spill-over effects also in the rest of Europe as the overall technological progress slows. This effect would be amplified if everyone acted similarly. Finally, the weak spending on public infrastructure lowers the potential for productivity increases at home.

Rather than trying to copy the German approach as a whole, European leaders should carefully examine which of the elements of German reforms might actually increase productivity, output and employment without detrimental effects on the partners or on long-term growth.

Notes

1 An updated translation was published under exactly this title as late as 2007, not long before the subprime crisis hit and completely turned around the perception of the German economy. See Sinn (2007).
2 For example, the short-work compensation, which has been deemed as being central to

Germany's labour market performance in the Great Recession of 2008–2009 had already been introduced in the 1950s and has been expanded as part of the stimulus package of 2009.

3 See Nägele (2003).

4 One should mention here that during the first Schröder years (1998–2002) a number of tax reforms had been pushed through. For example, the top marginal tax rate had been cut, sales of cross-holdings of corporations and banks had been made easier (and cheaper) and corporate tax rates had been lowered. However, these reforms were not part of the Agenda 2010 package and did not have large effects on the labour market.

5 The OECD has a separate website with data and explanations for this indicator which can be found at www.oecd.org/employment/emp/oecdindicatorsofemploymentprotection.htm.

6 Of course, large current account surpluses are highly problematic as they endanger the stability of the global and European economy. However, as these surpluses are generally perceived in the public debate as 'successes', they will be treated as such in this paper.

7 Standard references include Romer (1990), Grossmann and Helpman (1991) and Aghion and Howitt (1992).

8 For a more detailed description of these underlying assumptions and a criticism from an endogenous-money perspective, see Dullien (2004).

References

Aghion, P. and P. Howitt (1992), 'A model of growth through creative destruction'. *Econometrica*, 60(2): 323–351.

Barysch, K. (2003), *Germany – The Sick Man of Europe?* London: Centre for European Reform Policy Brief.

Carlin, W. J. and D. Soskice (2009), *German Economic Performance: Disentangling the Role of Supply-Side Reforms, Macroeconomic Policy and Coordinated Economy Institutions.* Open access publications from University College London.

Coricelli, F., A. Cukiermanand and A. Dalmazzo (2006), 'Monetary institutions, monopolistic competition, unionized labor markets and economic performance'. *Scandinavian Journal of Economics*, 108(1): 39–63.

Dullien, S. (2004), *The Interaction of Monetary Policy and Wage Bargaining in European Monetary Union*, Basingstoke: Palgrave Macmillan.

Dullien, S. and M. Schieritz (2011), 'Die deutsche Investitionsschwäche: Die Mär von den Standortproblemen'. *Wirtschaftsdienst*, 91(7): 458–464.

Dullien, S., H. Herr and C. Kellermann (2009), *Der Gute Kapitalismus*, Bielefeld: Transcript.

Erber, G. (2012), 'Irrungen und Wirrungen mit der Leistungsbilanzstatistik'. *Wirtschaftsdienst*, 92(7): 465–470.

European Commission (2012), 'Current account surpluses in the EU'. *European Economy* 9/2012, Brussels.

Grossmann, G. M. and E. Helpman (1991), *Innovation and Growth in the Global Economy*, Cambridge, MA: MIT Press.

IMF (2012), *World Economic Outlook Database*, Washington, DC: IMF. www.imf.org/external/pubs/ft/weo/2013/01/weodata/index.aspx (accessed on 22 March 2013).

Kalina, T. and C. Weinkopf (2010), 'Niedriglohnbeschäftigung 2008: Stagnation auf hohem Niveau – Lohnspektrum franst nach unten aus'. *IAQ Report* 1010–06, Essen.

Kant, I. (1785/1993), *Grounding for the Metaphysics of Morals*, 3rd edn, translated by James, W. Ellington. Indianapolis: Hackett.

Keller, W. (2004), 'International technology diffusion'. *Journal of Economic Literature*, 42(3): 752–782.

Nägele, S. (2003), 'Neuerung durch die Agenda 2010 – Kündigung mit Abfindungsanspruch'. *Der Arbeitsrechtberater*, 9: 274–276.

Priewe, J. (2013), 'Anmerkungen zu "Irrungen und Wirrungen mit der Leistungsbilanzstatistik" von Georg Erber'. *Wirtschaftsdienst*, 93(1): 52–59.

Romer, P. (1990), 'Endogenous Technological Change'. *Journal of Political Economy*, 98(5): 71–102.

Sachverständigenrat (2002), *20 Punkte für mehr Wachstum und Beschäftigung*, Jahresgutachten 2002/2003, Wiesbaden.

Sachverständigenrat (2010), *Chancen für einen stabilen Aufschwung*, Jahresgutachten 2010/2011, Wiesbaden.

Sinn, H.-W. (2003), *Ist Deutschland noch zu retten?* Munich: Econ.

Sinn, H.-W. (2007), *Can Germany Be Saved? The Malaise of the World's First Welfare State*. Cambridge, MA: MIT Press.

Soskice, D. and T. Iversen (2000), 'The Non-Neutrality of Monetary Policy with Large Price Setters'. *Quarterly Journal of Economics*, 115: 265–284.

Part IV

Regional development

The Italian Mezzogiorno and former East Germany

9 Fiscal federalism

What lessons can Italy learn from Germany?

Kristina van Deuverden

Introduction

Government structures vary broadly among countries. While some countries show a more unitary structure others are widely decentralised. In Germany, for historical reasons, the federal character of political and administrative relations is pronounced. Consequently a highly independent and powerful position of the federal states, the Länder, is intended by the Basic Law (*Grundgesetz*). However, the constitution also always aimed for establishing nationwide uniform living conditions. In the proper sense both objectives generate an inherent target conflict. On the one hand the diversity of regions is pronounced. On the other hand uniform standards are desired. The conflict manifests itself within a type of competitive federalism. While Basic Law assigns formal autonomy to the Länder, their scope to act is limited. An increasing number of federal laws predominate the expenditure side while the tax setting power of the Länder – which had always been limited – has been reduced during the last six decades.

Unsurprisingly, the German federal arrangements have ever been a complex system. But the high number of realignments resulted in an even more complicated and sophisticated set of rules. This paper reviews the assignment of powers to governmental levels by Basic Law and lines out the major regulations of the fiscal equalisation schemes. In fact, the system exhibits a notable number of shortcomings. Besides, new challenges will become more and more pressing within the next years. The Solidarpakt, which constitutes special grants to the new Länder, will end in 2019 and the German debt brake will be completed in 2020. Finally, the Federal financial equalisation system itself has to be realigned until 2020 because the standard act is limited in time. Focusing on the German experience, at least, the question will be whether there are any lessons that can be drawn.

Fiscal federalism in Germany

Fiscal federalism covers a variety of aspects. Constitutional law considerations and political decisions whether to centralise or decentralise structures as well as the assignment of fiscal relations between governmental levels play an important role. When the theory of fiscal federalism was developed the major interest focused on the efficient assignment of functions, expenditure and revenue to governmental levels (e.g. Musgrave, 1959; Oates, 1972). Basically this theoretical approach assumed a benevolent (federal) government and, thus, concentrated on the discussion as to which level functions should be executed at for a most efficient, fair and equal result of public activity. From this point of view a more or less centralised system (of functions, expenditure and revenue) where the federal level exhibits the competences in the main part and bears the interest of the sublevels in mind which in turn cooperate with the federal level would be an efficient federal system. Probably, this approach would result in more or less equalised levels of public spending.

In the next years several trends in fiscal theory started to emphasise aspects of self-interests. From this point of view politicians first and foremost want to be re-elected. Thus, their decisions would always try to mirror the preferences of their (median) voters. If these preferences vary over regions, various levels of public goods or heterogeneous life-conditions will be an optimal result of fiscal policy (Tiebout, 1956). From this point of view an efficient outcome requires that each level of government is responsible for its own functions and, thus, its own expenditure. Consequently, each level should be free to dispose of its own revenue sources. Allowing for the self-interests of politicians and, thus, governmental levels and regions, means that governance is no longer assumed to be benevolent. Single levels now compete against each other. In a world where selfish behaviour of governmental institutions cannot be excluded, a prerequisite for an efficient outcome is the principle of fiscal equivalence. The region which decides on expenditure should be congruent with the region that finances it (Olson, 1969).

There have been recent and sophisticated developments in fiscal federalism theory since then but finally these two basic approaches still mark the range for evaluating existing systems. Unsurprisingly, existing systems will in general not purely follow the one or the other principle. Also the German type of federalism never mirrored a pure type of fiscal federalism. Moreover, it has been practised over six decades and faded even more. Today, the system runs a variety of shortcomings and there is evidence for the need of reforms.

Distribution of power and functions between the Federation and the Länder

The German federal financial equalisation system (FFES) had been implemented in 1950 but heavily modified by the reform of 1969. The fundamental regulations are constituted in the Basic Law. The German state is organised as a federal republic with the federation (Bund) on one hand and 16 federal states (Länder) on the other. Due to historical reasons the Länder constitute an independent and powerful level.[1] This is reflected in Article 30 of the German Constitution:

> The exercise of governmental powers and the discharge of governmental functions is incumbent on the Länder insofar as this Basic Law does not otherwise prescribe or permit.
>
> (German Constitution)

With other words: if the Basic Law does not explicitly designate the federation as the level in charge, the responsibility falls on the Länder which therefore are endowed with all basic power. This regulation should insure that the federation only acts on matters that are in the interest of the country as a whole as e.g. a uniform legal framework or countrywide decisions on public expenditure that is supposed to have spillover effects. Thus, German constitutional law basically assigns an essential role to the Länder. Consequently, a decentralised state structure and a competitive type of federalism should be implemented. This, in fact, is only partly the case.

Articles 71, 72, 73 and 105 of the German Constitution specify in which areas the federation is assigned exclusive power and in which the federation is endowed with some concurrent legislative power. In the first case the Länder may not act unless a federal law explicitly gives them permission; in the second case the Länder may operate unless the Bund has taken action – when this happens federal rules are decisive. In fact, the German Constitution establishes a cooperative federalism that should prevent and allow for the heterogeneity of regions. Basic Law intended to endow the Länder with the highest possible degree of power but to ensure the functioning of the system, some freedom to act had to be given to the federation. In this way, the capability to act despite of possible – and, as time goes by, probable – fundamental changes in the political, social and economic environment should be ensured.

However, despite the pronounced role of the states, German Basic Law always aimed to attain a close convergence of living conditions (Lenk, 2008). This objective proved to be a general clause: whenever questions of inequalities in living conditions have been referred to, federal action has been justified.[2] Within more than 60 years – the Constitution was enacted in 1949 – the federation widely exercised its concurrent legislative power. As a consequence, today the scope of action left to the states is more than ever limited and over the years an increasing number of federal laws have tightened more and more the financial funds of the Länder.[3]

Expenditure

The allotment of functions widely predetermines the structure of expenditure. On the level of the Länder three types of expenditure items can be distinguished (Federal Ministry of Finance, 2011). The first is mainly connected to regional decisions. For example, education was assumed to depend basically on regional priorities. Spending on education has, therefore, to be financed by the Länder (universities) or the municipalities (schools).[4] The second type of spending item is connected to a major task of Länder duties. The states have to execute federal legislation and to bear the costs of administration. A large part of spending on the Länder level is tied by this kind of expenditure. Third, there are so-called joint tasks that are estimated to be in a countrywide interest. These joint tasks are commonly financed by the federation and the particular Land. Federal expenditure on these items is shown in Table 9.1.[5]

Table 9.1 Overview of federation/Länder joint financing arrangements

	Federal budget in € billion[a]	
	2008	*2009*
	Actual figure	Target
Joint tasks (Article 91a of the Basic Law)	1.4	1.4
Breakdown:		
Regional economic structure	0.7	0.7
Agrarian structure and coastal preservation	0.7	0.7
Cooperation on education programmes (Article 91b of the Basic Law)	0.06	0.04
Cooperation on research promotion (Article 91b of the Basic Law)	4.7	5.3
Breakdown:		
Major research facilities	1.6	1.9
Other research facilities	0.4	0.5
Other research promotion	2.7	2.9
Laws providing for money grants (Article 104a paragraph (3) of the Basic Law)	12.5	12.5
Breakdown:		
Federal student aid	1.2	1.4
Housing benefit	0.8	0.6
Parental benefit (including wind-down financing of the previous childraising allowance)	4.8	4.4
Advance on child maintenance to single parents	0.3	0.3
Federation's contribution to housing and heating benefits	3.9	3.7
Other	1.6	2.1
Financial assistance (Article 104a paragraph (4) of the old version of the Basic Law[b] and Article 104b paragraph (4) of the new version of the Basic Law)	1.4	0.8
Breakdown:		
Urban development	0.5	0.4
Investment programme for all-day schools	0.6	0.0
Other financial assistance	0.3	0.4
Sum	20.1	20.0

Source: German Federal Ministry of Finance, 2011: 15.

Notes
a Differences through rounding.
b Wind-down financing. Note: Joint financing does not include the tied payments that the federation makes to the Länder under Article 13 of the Concomitant Act on the Federalism Reform to compensate for federal funding that was discontinued with effect from 2007. The funding had been for municipal transport infrastructure financing, the promotion of housing construction, university construction and education planning. Also not included in joint financing is the financial assistance that is to be paid from a special federal fund to expand childcare for infants from 2008 to 2013. The fund was created by the federation in the 2007 fiscal year with a total volume of €2.15 billion.

The second and the third type of expenditure are barely in the responsibility of the Länder. The largest part of expenditure is determined by federal regulations. From this point of view there should be evidence that per capita expenditure of the Länder converges over time. De facto spending diverges widely (Figure 9.1). First of all, there is a fundamental difference between the city states and the territorial states;[6] the level of expenditure in the city states is notably higher. This is partly generated by the geographical situation. As a result of the limited suburban hinterland these Länder not only provide public goods to their own citizens but also to the citizens of their neighbouring territorial states. Second, there is still a difference between the old and the new Länder. Although this distinction has been much more remarkable in the 1990s of the last century the new Länder still spend a notably higher share per capita.[7]

Power to legislate on taxation and the distribution of tax revenue

The distribution of responsibilities and powers among the levels is closely followed by expenditure. It is obvious that revenue is in the main interest of governments. The distribution of tax revenue and, thus, the distribution of power on tax legislation belong to the most pressing subjects. There are two pure systems for distributing tax revenue (Oates, 1972). On the one hand each level of government can have available and decide on its own tax resources. This would be an adequate way to allocate responsibilities if the financial equalisation system

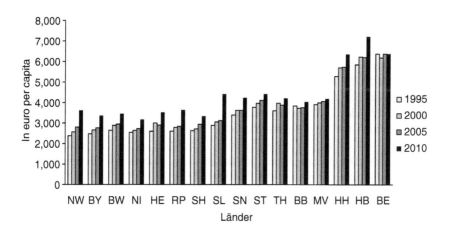

Figure 9.1 Per capita expenditure of Länder (Länder budgets only) (source: German Ministry of Finance and own calculations; applicable law of 2010: preliminary).

Note
BB = Brandenburg; BE = Berlin; BW = Baden-Württemberg; BY = Bavaria; HE = Hesse; HH = Hamburg; MV = Mecklenburg-Western Pomerania; NI = Lower Saxony; NW = North Rhine-Westphalia; RP = Rhineland-Palatinate; SH = Schleswig-Holstein; SL = Saarland; SN = Saxony; ST = Saxony-Anhalt; TH = Thuringia.

implemented was of the decentralised type. On the other hand a joint system where tax revenue accrues to the central level would be the appropriate finance system if there was a centralised state structure with a benevolent federal level that bankrolls the states with grants.

The system implemented in Germany is – again – a mixed one. For some taxes revenue is assigned to a specific level while there are joint taxes which accrue to multiple levels. Tax competences are concentrated at the central level. Since the fundamental reform of Basic Law in 1969 the Länder have nearly no scope to decide autonomously on tax affairs.[8] Tax bases as well as tariffs are uniform. Even though changes in taxes which affect the Länder budgets need to pass the chamber of the states (Bundesrat) the initiative for amendments has to be taken by the federation. Furthermore, decisions of the Bundesrat depend on the majority situation in the federation as well as in parliament itself and often represent the result of complex bargaining processes. At least since 2007 the Länder have the right to ascertain the tax rate of the real property transfer tax but this tax generates only a small fraction of tax revenue.[9] Table 9.2 shows which taxes accrue to which level.

Obviously the minor share of revenue arises by taxes that accrue to a single level of government. The major share of tax revenue is collected in the form of joint taxes – in 2010 63 per cent of total tax revenue originated from this source. The participation rates on these taxes are defined by law and have been relatively constant over time, even though there have been few changes due to structural considerations.[10] However, the German Constitution declares that each level of government is equally entitled to be adequately supplied with revenue in order to execute its functions. Thus, there has to be an instrument to adjust financial needs and cash receipts. These adjustments are performed by alterations of the participation rate in value added tax (VAT) revenue which has been changed several times. The participation rates in 2010 are shown in Table 9.3.

In general the regional distribution of cash revenue of joint taxes will for some reasons, i.e. the administration of taxes, diverge from the regional distribution of tax incidence. While wages tax is collected at the place of employment, it should burden the wage-earner and, thus, cash should accrue at the place of residence. While cash receipts of the final withholding tax on income and capital gains are allotted in accordance with the banking system, the incidence should be borne by the shareholder and, thus, should arise at the place of residence. While corporate tax is paid at the location of the headquarters, it should be collected at the place where the business operates. Consequently, revenue of joint taxes is apportioned with respect to the regional distribution of incidence. Also VAT revenue does not occur in accordance with final private consumption. This is because the tax is collected during the manufacturing process and, thus, it is the regional distribution of value added on certain production stages that determines its regional revenue. Hence, VAT has also to be allotted which is done with respect to population.[11]

After the apportionment of tax revenue, the financial power (measured by revenue per capita) is very heterogeneously distributed among the Länder

Table 9.2 Tax revenue in the years 1995, 2000 and 2010 (in billion euro)

	1995	2000	2010
Taxes accruing to the federation			
Mineral oil duty	33.18	37.83	39.84
Electricity duty	–	3.36	6.17
Tobacco duty	10.53	11.44	13.49
Insurance duty	7.21	7.24	10.28
Motor vehicle tax	–	–	8.49
Surtax/solidarity charge	13.43	11.84	11.71
Other taxes accruing to the federation[a]	28.54	29.42	42.75
Sum	92.89	101.13	132.74
as per cent of total tax revenue	*22.2*	*22.1*	*25.4*
Taxes accruing to the Länder			
Capital tax	4.02	0.43	0.00
Inheritance tax	1.81	2.98	4.40
Real property transfer tax	3.10	5.08	5.29
Motor vehicle tax[b]	7.06	7.01	–
Betting and lottery tax	1.42	1.80	1.41
Fire protection tax	0.39	0.29	0.33
Beer duty	0.91	0.84	0.71
Sum	18.71	18.44	12.15
as per cent of total tax revenue	*4.5*	*4.0*	*2.3*
Taxes accruing to the municipalities			
Trade tax	21.55	27.03	35.80
Class A and B real property tax	7.03	8.85	11.31
Real property transfer tax	0.15	0.16	–
Other municipal taxes	0.58	0.62	0.75
Sum	29.31	36.66	47.87
as per cent of total tax revenue	*7.0*	*8.0*	*9.2*
Joint taxes			
Wages tax	144.54	135.73	127.90
Assessed income tax	7.16	12.70	31.18
Non-assessed income tax	8.65	13.51	12.98
Interest income deduction/final withholding tax	6.55	7.33	8.71
Corporation tax	9.27	24.84	12.04
Value added tax	101.49	107.14	136.46
Sum	277.66	301.26	329.27
as per cent of total tax revenue	*66.3*	*65.8*	*63.1*
Total tax revenue	418,6	457,49	522,0

Source: German Federal Ministry of Finance, own calculations.

Notes
a Spirits duty, sparkling wine duty, intermediate products duty, coffee duty, standard-rate import duties, other taxes accruing to the federation.
b Since July 2009 the motor vehicle tax accrues to the federation.

Table 9.3 Participation rates in revenue of joint taxes in 2010

	Federation	Länder	Municipalities
Wages tax	42.5	42.5	15.0
Assessed income tax	42.5	42.5	15.0
Final withholding tax	44.0	44.0	12.0
Non-assessed taxes on earnings	50.0	50.0	
Corporate tax	50.0	50.0	–
Value added tax[a]	53.9	44.1	approx. 2.0

Source: German Federal Ministry of Finance.

Notes

a First of all 4.45 per cent of VAT accrues to the federation which transfers this amount to unemployment insurance, second 5.05 per cent is transmitted in the same way to the pension system and approximately 2 per cent is transferred to the municipalities. The remaining VAT revenue is shared between the federation and the Länder.

(Figure 9.2). Obviously there are again three categories of Länder. The old Länder Hessen, Bavaria and Baden-Württemberg and in some years North Rhine-Westphalia collect taxes that were above average. The new Länder are still today far below this average but Brandenburg performs better. Within the city states the tax capability of Hamburg is outstanding. Starting at this initial situation substantial revenue shifts follow.

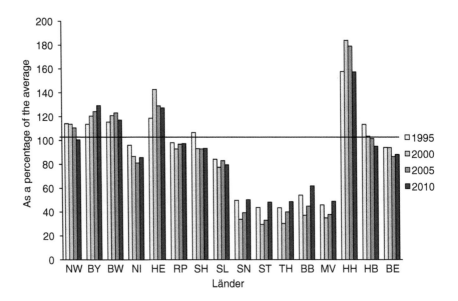

Figure 9.2 Cash tax revenue in the years 1995, 2000, 2005 and 2010 per capita before allotment of VAT as percentage of the average of the Länder (source: German Ministry of Finance and own calculations; applicable law of 2010: preliminary).

The German federal financial equalisation system

The FFES has been implemented in 1950. Since then there have been several reforms, because those Länder that are contributing started numerous initiatives to change regulations.[12] This chapter will mainly focus on current arrangements agreed in 2005 which will be in force until 2019.

Pre-sharing of VAT

After tax revenue (inclusive of 75 per cent of VAT) has been allotted to the federation and the Länder as well as among the Länder by roughly reproducing the distribution of local tax incidence the pre-step of the FFES follows. On this step the remaining 25 per cent of VAT that accrues to the Länder as a whole is realigned between them. Länder that are faced with tax receipts per capita below average receive supplementary revenue fractions. By this redistribution 'exceedingly high differences' between tax revenue should be lessened (§7 Standard Act). The additional VAT shares are calculated by a linear-progressive schedule. Afterwards the gap between the single Land's tax revenue per capita and the average of the Länder is closed by 60 to 95 per cent. At this pre-stage a tax volume of more than €10 billion or a narrow 6 per cent of overall tax revenue of the Länder has been reallocated in 2010.

Figure 9.3 gives an impression of the extent of redistribution on the pre-stage. While VAT should be (strictly) allotted on a per capita basis the Länder participate in revenue by different magnitude. Länder with low per capita tax revenue – as the new Länder – received more than 180 per cent at the top.

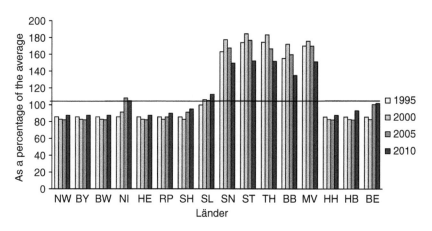

Figure 9.3 Per capita VAT revenue distribution in the Länder in the years 1995, 2000, 2005 and 2010 (as a percentage of the average) (source: German Ministry of Finance and own calculations; applicable law of 2010: preliminary)).

Financial equalisation among the Länder

Horizontal equalisation among the Länder is based on two fiscal indicators: the financial capacity index and the equalisation index. The financial capacity index should represent the 'real' financial power of a Land. It is generated by adding up the tax revenue of the Land (after the distribution of VAT) and 64 per cent of the tax revenue of their municipalities' joint tax share while 64 per cent of the municipal trade tax apportionment is deducted.[13] The equalisation index is the sum of two indicators. The first is the average tax revenue per capita of the Länder as a whole.[14] The second considers the municipal tax revenue weighted by the inhabitants of the Land.[15] The composed indicator of average tax revenue is taken as an indicator for the 'real' financial needs of a Land.

The financial capacity indexes of the Länder calculated in this way are shown in Figure 9.4. Despite of the volume of €10 billion that had already been redistributed at the pre-step of the FFES, financial capacity still diverges between the Länder by more than 20 percentage points at the top.

By now, the FFES in a proper sense follows. If the financial capacity indicator exceeds the equalisation index the Land will have to contribute to the equalisation system otherwise it will receive a grant. A linear-progressive tax schedule is used. Shortages below 75 per cent of the average are completely equalised. From 75 per cent to 80 per cent there is a compensation of 75 per cent. Between 80 per cent and 93 per cent shortfalls are adjusted by decreasing grants between 75 per cent and 70 per cent. Missing amounts from 93 per cent to 100 per cent of the average are topped up between 70 per cent and 44 per cent. Contributions are calculated by a mirror-inverted scheme. By this complex proceeding seven billion euros have been redistributed in 2010.

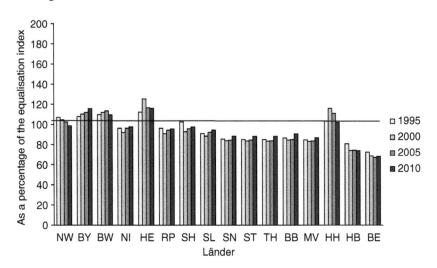

Figure 9.4 Financial capacity after sharing VAT between the Länder in the years 1995, 2000, 2005, 2010 (source: German Ministry of Finance and own calculations; applicable law of 2010: preliminary).

After this step a high degree of inter-state equalisation is realised. This is shown by Figure 9.5. The capacity indexes differ by less than 10 percentage points. Since 1950 the number of contributing states reduced while the volume of transfers between the Länder increased significantly. During the decades regional disparities proved to be relatively persistent and the weak states were not really successful in catching up. With the integration of the new Länder in the FFES the circle of beneficent Länder expanded while the number of contributing states shrank to four (Figure 9.6).[16]

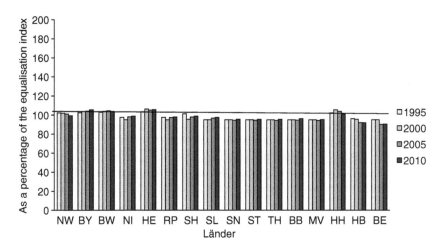

Figure 9.5 Financial capacity before the application of financial equalisation between the Länder in the years 1995, 2000, 2005, 2010 (source: German Ministry of Finance and own calculations; applicable law of 2010: preliminary).

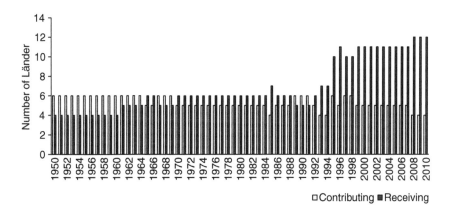

Figure 9.6 Number of receiving and contributing Länder in the FFES (source: German Ministry of Finance and own calculations; applicable law of 2010: preliminary).

Supplementary federal grants

At a third step, an appreciable volume of funds is transferred from the federation to several Länder. These supplementary federal grants (SFG, *Bundesergänzungszuweisungen*) are connected to special attributes. Currently there are four types of grant.[17] First of all, there are SFG for shortfalls. These are directed to the financially weak Länder which do still not attain 99.5 per cent of the equalisation index. These shortages are closed to a degree of 77.5 per cent. This kind of SFG approximately has a volume of €3 billion. Second, there are special need SFGs for the Länder that are faced with high administrative costs due to their small size (10 of the 16 Länder are acknowledged to be small). Third, there are special grants for the new Länder which bear the cost of the German partition period. This burden has been acknowledged to be in the countrywide interest and a new kind of SFG was established in 1995 (SFG on German unification).[18] Finally, there are special need supplementary grants for structural unemployment. These grants have been implemented in 2005 and are directed to the new Länder (except Berlin). Their amount is limited to one billion euros per year.

After this third stage the FFES is completed and the financial capacity of the Länder has significantly converged. As is shown in Figure 9.7 each single state finally achieves a financial capability in a range between 97.5 per cent (Berlin) and 105.5 per cent (Bavaria, Hesse). The last step of the FFES especially benefits the new Länder and, finally, they achieve 98.5 per cent of the financial capability index. However, with the realignment rules in force until 2005 the degree of equalisation has even been higher. A financially weak state attained at least 99.5 per cent of average while the capability of the financially

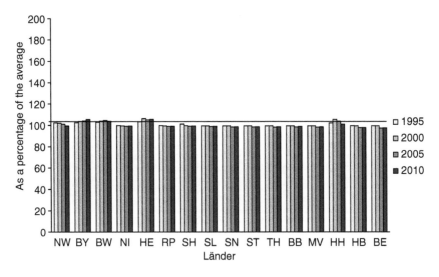

Figure 9.7 Financial capacity after the application of supplementary federal grants in the years 1995, 2000, 2005, 2010 (source: German Ministry of Finance and own calculations; applicable law of 2010: preliminary).

stronger states fluctuated over the cycle. Hence, in a cyclical downturns the difference between the weakest and the strongest Land declines to less than 5 percentage points.

Excursus: the integration of the new Länder

After unification it soon became obvious that integration of the new Länder into the existing transfer scheme would be likely to overstrain the old ones. The tax power of the new Länder was on such a low level that the old Länder, even the financially weak ones, would have had to afford high transfers. Thus, the federation and the states agreed on a transition period in which the FFES between the old Länder remained unchanged. Instead a fund had been raised, the German Unity Fund (Fonds Deutsche Einheit) which has been partly financed by the old Länder, partly by the Bund and partly by borrowing (Table 9.4). At the end of 1994 financial transfers of €82.2 billion had been financed by the fund, 40 per cent of these transfers where paid to the municipalities. At this time the fund had accumulated debt amounting to €49.1 billion. Until 2005 the Bund and the old Länder amortised this debt in annual rates. Then the Bund took over the liabilities and the amortisation rates until 2019, while the states (inclusive the new ones) relinquished on a fix sum of VAT revenue. At the end of 2019 the residual debt will be divided between the Bund and the old Länder.

The German Unity Fund was limited until the end of 1994. Since 1995 the new Länder have beem integrated in the FFES. However, as revenue in the new Länder still was a fraction of the receipts in the old states, the Länder felt unable to cope with the needed transfer volume. Bearing the burden of 40 years of German separation was considered to be a matter of national interest and the so-called Solidarpakt was established. The federation waived seven points of VAT revenue in favour of the Länder. They, on their part, agreed on additional amortisation payments of €1.1 billion to the German Unity Fund. Beyond this, SFGs justified by the German unification were established (see above).

However, the old Länder again felt overstrained by the integration of the new ones in the existing redistribution system. Thus, in 2005 the FFES was reformed again. While the degree of equalisation was slightly lowered, the Solidarpakt II

Table: 9.4 Transfer payments within the German Unity Fund (in million euro)

	Payment to		Source of finance			
	New Länder	Berlin	Federation	Old Länder	Berlin	Borrowing
1990	10,431	817	1,023	0	0	10,226
1991	16,595	1,300	1,533	494	18	15,850
1992	16,074	1,259	3,758	1,259	45	12,271
1993	16,671	1,329	8,090	2,141	100	7,669
1994	16,371	1,320	9,938	4,867	329	2,556

Source: Blum *et al.*, 2009.

was enacted to support the new states. From 2005 to 2019 €105 billion are paid to the new Länder in terms of SFG. These transfer payments decrease on a diminishing scale, from €10.6 billion in 2005 to €2.1 billion in 2019.

Performance of public finance on the Länder level

Budget balances and debt levels

There is a high degree of revenue equalisation in Germany and there is also a high share of expenditure that is determined by federal-wide laws or by joint tasks. Assuming that the enforcement of political projects usually depends on public funding, the dilemma becomes obvious. The capability of the Länder to act is limited – although Basic Law explicitly assigns them to represent a powerful level. States which want to shape political, social or economical parameters on their own will regularly rely on the only escape: borrowing.

Moreover, there is evidence that it can be rational for a state to increase its debt. In general, territorial authorities like other debtors have to keep in mind that their credit costs will increase if their debt increases. Furthermore, there is always the danger of bankruptcy. However, the German Länder experienced other circumstances. In 1992 the federal court decided that the federation as well as the Länder were responsible for each other. As a result of this judgement the federation had to afford SFGs for budget consolidation to the suing states – Bremen and the Saarland.[19] On the whole, the German states face soft credit conditions.[20] The situation constitutes a classical free-rider problem and the setting notably bears the danger of escalating debt.

To prevent increasing debt levels some kind of a golden rule was in force on the federal level until 2010. The Länder experienced similar fiscal rules – whether in their constitutions or in their budget codes. Strictly speaking these rules required net borrowing not to exceed gross fixed investment unless the economic equilibrium was endangered. Obviously, these rules have two weak points (Sachverständigenrat zur Begutachtung der geamtwirtschaftlichen Entwicklung, 2007). On the one hand, net fixed investment would be a adequate reference point for a golden rule. On the other hand, the exemption was too vague and had been exercised many times.

In fact, there has been notable deficit spending. This is illustrated by Figure 9.8. First of all, budgets are clearly determined by cyclical developments mainly because a large part of tax revenue accrues to income taxes and VAT that fluctuate over the cycle. Beyond this, there are obviously strong differences between the states. The new Länder show a slightly homogenous group of weak states that were permanently depending on credit financed expenditure. Until the new Länder were included in the federal financial equalisation system net lending even played a larger role than for the old Länder. However, after 20 years of unification some tendencies appear. While after 2005 Saxony and Mecklenburg Pomerania were able to realise a surplus in most years, the other states still experience deficits.

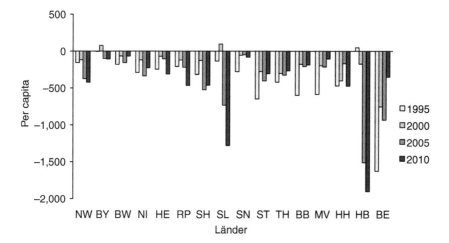

Figure 9.8 Budget balances per capita in the years 1995, 2000, 2005, 2010 (only Länder budgets) (source: German Ministry of Finance and own calculations; applicable law of 2010: preliminary).

The city states as well as the old Länder constitute a more mixed group. Since the beginning of the 1990s the city of Bremen and the Saarland received additional SFGs with respect to budget consolidation. These grants proved not to be adequate to enhance the financial situation basically. Even today both states show the largest deficits. Bayern, the only Land that had managed to change its position from a receiving to a contributing state, marks the opposite and shows a surplus in most years. In contrast, the state with the highest financial capacity, Hesse, realised a deficit in each fiscal year since 1995.

A reflection of these budget deficits is the development of debt. While in 1991 the new Länder started without debt they soon caught up. At present their debt level per capita is above average (Figure 9.9). The only exemption is Saxony where policy has clearly been oriented on sound public finances. The city states realise debt levels that are notably higher than in the territorial states. Bremen particularly, the Land which received additional SFGs until 2004, experienced the highest increase of debt. The old territorial states are again a mixed group. The Saarland, as the counterpart to Bremen concerning additional SFG, is the Land in which debt per capita accumulated most. Remarkably, financially strong states like Hesse or Baden-Württemberg show nearly the same level of debt per capita as Mecklenburg-Western Pomerania.

Altogether, debt per capita on the Länder level amounted to €2,957 in 1994. Until 2010 debt per capita rose to €7,341. In relation to gross national product the debt of the states increased from 14 to 24 per cent. Bearing in mind that the German Länder have almost no scope of action concerning their tax revenue and that there is only a limited degree of freedom for expenditure this performance is

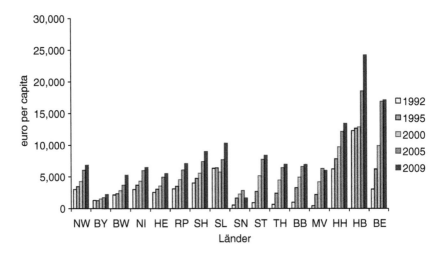

Figure 9.9 Debt per capita in the years 1992, 1995, 2000, 2005, 2009 (only Länder
budgets) (source: German Federal Statistics Office (destatis), own
calculations).

more severe than it seems. The Länder will have to readjust their budgets markedly – also because new challenges are at the front door.

New challenges: end of the Solidarpakt, revision of the FFES and the German debt brake

Obviously, fiscal federalism in Germany is a highly complex and technical
system of relations and exhibits some shortcomings. The apportionment of functions and legislative powers – especially when the legislation and execution of
taxes are considered – had not been as well constituted as would have been
desirable from a scientific point of view. As a result of competitive federalism,
competences centralised more and more at the federal level. This, in turn implies
that an increasing number of federal laws require a majority in the federal parliament as well as in the Bundesrat which becomes a problem when the federal
government in Berlin and the majority of the Länder belong to different coalition
parties.[21] The federal government depends more and more on consent among the
Länder while the capacity of the Länder for independent action is limited. A possible inability to act alone is a reason to enhance the attempts to disentangle
federal relations.

In 2003 a commission on federalism was established with the mandate to
realign those relations. The commission worked for nearly two years but did not
manage to arrive at a common agreement. Nevertheless, after the federal election
in 2005 some of the agenda items were picked up in the coalition treaty.
However, especially with respect to fiscal relations there were only very limited
consequences. In 2007 the second commission on federalism was implemented.

In 2009 this commission drew its conclusions, leaving a broad and far-reaching concept to politicians.[22] As a result the federation adopted the German debt brake. Until 2016 the structural deficit of the federal budget has to be reduced to at least 0.35 per cent of GDP. During a transition period that started in 2011 the structural deficit has to be limited in equal steps. The Länder are required to abolish structural deficits until 2020 completely.[23] With regard to operating the debt brake on the level of the Länder there are various outstanding questions (van Deuverden and Freye, 2010). In any case, the interdiction of borrowing will reduce the remaining autonomy of the Länder evidently. On the one hand, the influence of the federation can be assumed to increase as Länder become more dependent. On the other hand, it may also become more difficult for the federation to find the affirmation of both houses if Länder identify denial followed by a bargaining process as a suitable strategy. Anyway, the German debt brake will limit policy options. However, the commission has not been successful in disentangling fiscal relations among different levels. Thus, the distribution of competences and the distribution of functions will further coincide to a lesser degree than would be suitable. Strengthening the principle of fiscal equivalence could be a useful parameter in the FFES.[24]

However, the FFES itself will have to be realigned because the Standards Act, by which the details of the proceeding are administered, is limited in time until the same year. Negotiations will be determined by two factors. First, the contributing Länder have become more and more unwilling to share tax revenue. Second, the demographic development will issue a challenge to public budgets. While the new Länder have already suffered a high loss of population since unification which – in turn – has reinforced a severe consolidation process in these states, the western part will increasingly be faced with demographic challenges in the near future. In the next years the old Länder have to undertake similar efforts to adjust public activity and probably their willingness to pay will diminish more and more.

Finally, the new Länder will lose the SFG on German unification. These grants were established when the new Länder were integrated in the FFES and aimed at cushioning the consequences of 40 years of planned economy. Since 2005 the funds have begun to run out on a diminishing scale until 2019. This kind of grant still plays an important role for the new Länder; in 2010 they raised the financial capacity of the new Länder by 4.5 percentage points. Any follow-up facilities are not likely. Moreover, tax revenue per capita will probably remain a fraction of that collected in the old states. Thus, for the new Länder the inter-state tax realignment will become even more essential than today. Considering these challenges it is absolutely predictable that political debates will aggravate the second half of this decade.

Are there any lessons Italy can learn from Germany?

The German FFES is often held up as an example for the equalisation of differences within a federal state. However, despite undeniable good attempts there are severe shortcomings of the system. First of all, the apportionment of functions and legislative powers – especially the legislation and execution of taxes – is not as thorough as it should have been. The system as it is shaped does not prevent single states taking free-rider positions, it does not keep the Länder from accumulating debt while their financial scope to realign budgets is limited, and it does not help to preserve or sustain sustainable public finance. Thus, a first lesson could be: Define the system carefully.

The German FFES is a very complex system. Before the redistribution of revenue starts a considerable volume of tax revenue has to be allotted to the states and cash tax receipts are heightened or curtailed by several amendments. The FFES itself consists of several steps. Moreover, the proper distribution among the states follows a complex procedure. From a political point of view a transparent proceeding would be preferable. Thus, a second lesson could be: Like fiscal rules, a financial equalisation system should be clearly defined and easy to understand. Otherwise,the public will not be able to control political agreements.

Besides, German recent history gives rise to the assertion that the lower the disparities of regions should be, the higher the intended degree of equalisation is, which the revenue sharing scheme can attain without rejection. Even before unification disparities in Germany had been high. After unification there was a transitional period but when the new Länder were integrated in the FFES, disparities were still marked. Convergence became a long process and even today productivity in the new Länder is 80 per cent compared to productivity in the old Länder. However, tax revenue converged to a much lesser degree. In 2008 tax revenue in the new Länder was only 52.5 per cent compared to tax receipts in the old Länder while productivity had increased to nearly 79 per cent (van Deuverden, 2010). In Germany tax revenue is highly determined by progressive income taxes. Such a tariff not only burdens individuals with respect to their ability to pay; the same holds true for regions.[25] Thus, the tax system that has been tailored for a high industrial country can only provide a lower level of revenue in a transitional economy and still does today.

In the old Länder, especially in those that have to contribute to the transfer scheme, there was serious resistance to the integration of the new Länder in 1995 and controversial discussions arose. Thus, the federation decided to intervene particularly also because there was the political understanding that the level of expenditure should be considerable higher in the new Länder. Forty years of socialism left a rotten infrastructure behind that had to be rebuilt. Thus, the role of the SFG was enlarged drastically. But again this did not prevent further debates. Hence, the possible level of equalisation heavily depends on the economic disparities between states. If these are large, the system – or rather the contributing states – will soon feel overburdened. Thus, either the degree of equalisation will have to be reduced or the federation will have to engage itself. The smaller the number of donating states relative to receiving regions, the quicker the willingness to pay will fade. Thus, the third lesson is simple: Do not overburden the willingness of single states. Disparities of regions should be the lower the higher the intended degree of equalisation is.

Notes

1 While other European countries experienced an age of national states in the nineteenth century, the German-speaking states constituted the German Confederation which had been a more or less loose association of independent states. When the German Empire was constituted in the late nineteenth century the states retained a powerful position and when the Federal Republic of Germany was built in 1948 the constitution again emphasised the independent position of the Länder.

2 Before the integration of the new Länder the constitution not only required the equalisation but requested the ensuring of the homogeneity of living conditions in all regions (Article 125 Basic Law).

3 Even though legal changes that impinge the Länder budgets need to pass the states chamber (Bundesrat), a single state may face difficulties preserving its interests. Decisions of the Bundesrat depend on majority situations in parliament itself as well as in the federation and often represent the result of complex bargaining processes.

4 This allotment became a problem when the federation wanted to expand childcare services. While this item is the responsibility of the municipalities, direct grants from the federation to the municipalities are not allowed by Basic Law.

5 The co-financing share of the Länder varies with the joint task and over time.

6 This chapter focuses on the relations between the federation and the Länder. Financial relations between the Länder and its municipalities vary widely and, thus expenditure does. Hence, comparing expenditure of both would show a higher degree of equalisation notably between the states and the city states. This has to be taken into account when only the Länder are compared. Nevertheless, the general discussion in this chapter would not be changed substantially.

7 This is financed by supplementary federal grants to lessen the consequences of German separation.

8 The power of tax legislation at the municipal level is also limited but the scope to act is slightly larger. The municipalities can determine the collection rate of trade tax as well as the real property taxes by fixing a multiplier that is applied on the countrywide uniform tax law and they can raise small local taxes.

9 This has been an implication of the Federal Commission (Föderalismuskommission) which was established in 2003. The commission had the mandate to realign fiscal relations in Germany. Its findings were incorporated into the coalition treaty in 2005 (Koalitionsvertrag, 2005).

10 For example, in 1980 the share of the municipalities' participation in income tax revenue was enlarged by 1 percentage point because the municipal payroll tax had been abolished. In 1998, when the municipal trade tax on capital was abolished, the municipalities were instead entitled to a share of VAT revenue. On the other hand they had to transfer a share of the trade tax to the federation and the Länder.

11 This holds true for at least 75 per cent of the VAT share of the Länder. The remaining 25 per cent of the Länder's VAT revenue is used on the pre-stage of the federal financial equalisation system to give a top-up to those Länder that have the lowest per capita tax receipts (excluding the VAT share).

12 Even the federal constitutional court (Bundesverfassungsgericht) had been called in some cases by one or more of the Länder.

13 In addition, the extraction levy under mining law and the compensation for the motor vehicle tax are added. If an increase in the tax revenue of a Land (exclusive of VAT) exceeds 12 per cent above average the excess is deducted.

14 Next to the additions and deductions mentioned for the calculation of the financial capacity index, the tax revenue is again corrected by generalising real property transfer tax to a countrywide average. In addition, the inhabitants of the city states Berlin, Bremen and Hamburg are weighted at 135 per cent.

15 For the average municipal tax revenue, the population of Mecklenburg-Western

Pomerania is weighted at 105 per cent, the Land of Brandenburg at 103 per cent and the Land of Saxony-Anhalt at 102 per cent.

16 In early 2011 it even appeared for some time as if the number of contributing Länder has finally been reduced to three.

17 There have also been SFGs for the administration cost of harbours as well as supplementary special federal grants for budget consolidation in the Saarland and in Bremen. Those two Länder had been successful in complaining that the FFES was not constitutional and in 1992 the federal court decided that, due to the federal principle, the federation as well as the Länder are responsible for each other. However, in 2006 a similar legal action undertaken by Berlin failed. There have also been transitional supplementary federal grants for the old Länder after the integration of the new Länder into the FFES.

18 When the new Länder were integrated in the FFES the old Länder feared they would be overburdened. Hence, there had been several realignments (see below).

19 In 2006 the court partly abandoned this perception when it refused a similar suit by the state of Berlin. However, the judgement had been justified by denying the existence of a budget crisis.

20 Moreover, there have never been large spreads compared to the interest rates the federation had to pay. However, this has changed since mid-2011. While federal bonds issued in November 2011 offered a return of 0.8 per cent, credit costs were notably higher for the states.

21 E.g. in the 1990s when former chancellor Kohl was confronted with a majority of governing coalitions lead by the oppposstion party, essential decisions were hardly possible for nearly a decade.

22 For details: Deutscher Bundestag, Bundesrat (2010).

23 Five Länder (Berlin, Bremen, Saarland, Saxony-Anhalt and Schleswig-Holstein) receive additional grants during the transition period from the federation. In turn, they agreed on a transition period in which they reduce their structural deficits at equal ratios until 2020.

24 If a single Land is burdened with the cost while the federation or the Länder as a whole benefit, the result is suboptimal. For example, in Germany the burden of the administration of taxes is taken by the states. As additional tax revenue has to be shared in the FFES it may be rational to forego some tax receipts because the additional administration costs are higher than the part of the revenue that remains within the state. The federation has tried to establish a federal agency for tax administration since years but has not been successful yet.

25 Moreover, some taxes as interest income deduction or the inheritance tax depend on assets and for their accumulation time is an essential factor. In the western part, 40 years of freedom and economic miracle cannot be caught up easily.

References

Basic Law of Germany, available at www.gesetze-im-internet.de/englisch_gg/index.html.

Blum, U., J. Ragnitz, S. Freye and L. Schneider (2009), 'Regionalisierung öffentlicher Ausgaben und Einnahmen – Eine Untersuchung am Beispiel der Neuen Länder'. *IWH-Sonderheft*, 4: 79.

Deutscher Bundestag, Bundesrat (2010), *Die gemeinsame Kommission von Bundestag und Bundesrat zur Modernisierung der Bund-Länder-Finanzbeziehungen*. Berlin: Die Beratungen und ihre Ergebnisse.

Federal Ministry of Finance (2011), The Federal Financial Equalisation System in Germany', available at www.bundesfinanzministerium.de/nn_4480/DE/BMF__Startseite/Service/Downloads/Abt__V/The_20Federal_20Financial_20Equalisation_20System_20in_20Germany,templateId=raw,property=publicationFile.pdf, 2011.

Koalitionsvertrag zwischen CDU, CSU und SPD vom 11.11.2005, available at www.bundesrat.de/cln_179/nn_8344/DE/foederalismus/bundesstaatskommission/Mitglieder/Koalitionsvertrag,templateId=raw,property=publicationFile.pdf/Koalitionsvertrag.pdf.

Lenk, T. (2008), 'Reform des deutschen Länderfinanzausgleichs – eine unendliche Geschichte'. Position paper of the Liberalen Instituts der Friedrich-Naumann-Stiftung für die Freiheit, available at www.freiheit.org/files/152/56-Lenk_Laender_innen-print.pdf.

Musgrave, R. (1959), *The Theory of Public Finance*, International Student Edition. New York: McGraw-Hill.

Oates, W. E. (1972), *Fiscal Federalism*. New York: Harcourt, Brace, Jovanovich.

Olson, M. (1969), 'The principle of "fiscal equivalence": the division of responsibilities among different levels of government'. *American Economic Review*, 59: 479–487.

Sachverständigenrat zur Begutachtung der gesamtwirtschaftlichen Entwicklung (Council o Economic Experts) (2007), *Staatsverschuldung wirksam begrenzen, Expertise im Auftrag des Bundesministeriums für Wirtschaft und Technologie*. www.sachverstaendigenrat-wirtschaft.de/fileadmin/dateiablage/Expertisen/Staatsverschuldung_wirksam_begrenzen.pdf

Tiebout, C. M. (1956), 'A pure theory of local expenditure'. *Journal of Political Economy*, 5: 416–424.

van Deuverden, K. (2010), 'Auch nach 20 Jahren: Steuereinnahmen in den Neuen Ländern schwach'. *Wirtschaft im Wandel*, 2: 91–104.

van Deuverden, K. and S. Freye (2010), 'Schuldenbremse: Bisherige Beschlüsse stellen Gelingen auf Länderebene infrage'. *Wirtschaft im Wandel*, 9: 438–447.

10 Economic development in East Germany since German unification

Results, shortcomings and implications for economic policy

Gerhard Heimpold and Mirko Titze

Introduction

When the Berlin Wall came down, the lack of competitiveness of East Germany's economy became obvious overnight. This lack found its expression in the form of a considerable gap in terms of productivity when compared to the western part of Germany. In the first half of the 1990s, productivity increased rapidly. But the speed of convergence has decreased considerably since 1995. Economists have tried to explain East Germany's slowdown in terms of productivity by highlighting macroeconomic reasons, in particular the extra-ordinary wage increases of the 1990s, the disincentives stemming from large fiscal transfers from West to East, and the lack of infrastructure (e.g. Sinn and Westermann, 2000: especially 12–22). In Sinn and Westermann's view, these fiscal transfers led to a kind of 'Dutch disease' in East Germany which prevented the export-oriented industries from becoming competitive (Sinn and Westermann, 2000: 21–24). However, in the meantime, the shortcomings mentioned above disappeared, or lost some of their former importance. The unit labour cost of the East German manufacturing sector fell, and is now lower than those in West Germany (Blum *et al.*, 2010: 13, 77). Infrastructure has been modernised through public investment (IWH *et al.*, 2011: 6ff., 89). Transfers still occur, but large-scale job creation schemes (German abbreviation: ABM) and schemes for sending employees into early retirement and for retraining workers have been considerably reduced or stopped altogether. Because the earlier limitations have become less important, it is to be assumed that there must be other shortcomings of a primarily structural nature which have exacerbated the stagnation in productivity. Against this background, this chapter will focus on the structural shortcomings of East Germany's economy, since an understanding of these may contribute to a better idea of what is behind East Germany's decelerated catch-up in productivity. The chapter presents research findings elaborated on at the Halle Institute for Economic Research (IWH), which has analysed economic development in East Germany empirically since the early 1990s. Before identifying these structural shortcomings a brief look at recent theoretical concepts of new growth theory and new economic geography is necessary because these go some way towards explaining why regions do not necessarily converge.

Regional convergence and divergence from the perspective of regional economics

The public might regard the limited progress made by East Germany in catching up as unsatisfactory. However, regional economic theories show that regions do not necessarily converge. Instead, they may show a divergent development, or former disparities may persist. From a theoretical viewpoint, growth can be enhanced by a quantitative increase of resources (especially capital, labour, natural resources), by qualitative improvements in the respective production factors as well as by combining them more efficiently, based on technological progress (e.g. Cezanne, 2005: 499ff.). Depending on the factors considered, regional development theories predict either convergence or divergence (for an overview see, e.g. Maier and Tödtling, 1996: 37–168). Neoclassical growth and trade theories predict convergence, based on diminishing returns of capital use or on exchange of goods or mobility of production factors (Maier and Tödtling, 1996: 61–83). Endogenous growth theories explain why regions do not necessarily converge. They indicate that externalities, if they are of a spatially limited dimension and if initial conditions regarding human capital, research and development (R&D) or infrastructure differ between regions, may lead to increasing disparities. A self-driven positive or negative development may take place (for an overview on the implications of new growth theories for spatial development: see Bröcker, 1994: 29–50). Nonetheless, the theories mentioned do not exclude catching up; it may also be possible through technological 'leapfrogging' (Brezis *et al.*, 1993).

Another strand of regional economics, the new economic geography (NEG), explains that under certain circumstances the distribution of economic activity across space predicts a path-dependent growth of existing spatial agglomerations. Centres may gain by attracting production factors at the expense of the periphery. Hence, in this case centripetal forces work. Nonetheless, these theories do not exclude centrifugal tendencies at the expense of existing agglomerations. Whether centrifugal or centripetal forces prevail depends on the relationship between agglomeration forces on the one hand and transportation costs on the other (Krugman, 1991/1993, 2009).

In the following section an overview of economic results and the factors behind them is provided; with respect to these underlying factors the focus is placed, apart from capital endowment, on structural characteristics which reveal the potential to reap benefits from internal and external economies of scale, research and development and innovation.

East Germany's economic performance 20 years after German unification

Economic results

After German unification, the productivity gap between the eastern and the western parts of the country became the indicator which reflected, in a very condensed manner, the weak performance of East Germany's economy. East Germany's *productivity* was only 45 per cent (Berlin excluded: 35 per cent) compared to West Germany in 1991. Gross domestic product (GDP) per capita has shown a considerable increase since 1991. East German productivity reached 79 per cent (Berlin excluded 75 per cent) of the West German level in 2010 (Figure 10.1).

However, the rapid catch-up in terms of productivity took place mainly in the first half of the 1990s. Catching up slowed down in the second half of the decade and it stagnated – more or less – in the 2000s.

This lower productivity corresponds with backwardness in terms of *export intensity*. When the centrally planned economy collapsed, the former state-owned companies lost their traditional market areas in the COMECON countries. They were forced to seek new sales opportunities which required increasing their competitiveness. The latter was undermined by an extreme increase in

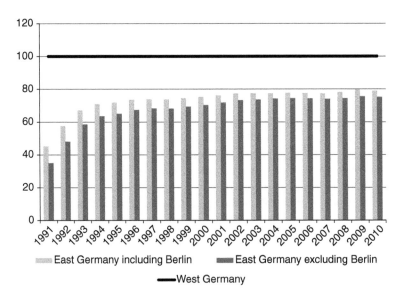

Figure 10.1 Relative productivity in East Germany (West Germany = 100 per cent). Productivity = gross domestic product (unadjusted prices) per employee (source: Regional Accounts VGRdL, 2013, authors' calculations).

Note
Classification of economic activities: WZ, 2008.

production costs, induced by a de facto revaluation when the Deutschmark was introduced, and a rapid wage increase in the early 1990s which far exceeded productivity growth. As a consequence, competitiveness decreased. The export intensity, i.e. the proportion of export turnover in total turnover of the East German manufacturing sector (mining and quarrying industries included) was less than half (12.8 per cent) of the West German export intensity (27.4 per cent) in 1991 (authors' calculations based on Statistisches Bundesamt, 1992: 28f.). It grew to 31.8 per cent, representing 69.2 per cent of the West German value, in 2010. Although some progress in terms of export activity has been achieved since 1991, the West German manufacturing sector has not slowed down over this period. Its export share was 46 per cent in 2010 (authors' calculations based on Statistisches Bundesamt, 2011: table Länder-2).[1]

Empirical studies have attempted to establish why regions and enterprises are different in terms of export activity. A study by Zeddies reveals that structural shortcomings can explain the lower export intensity of East Germany. This study pointed to the small firm size and the relatively low proportion of the manufacturing sector in total gross value added as reasons for a lower export intensity (Zeddies, 2009: 241). Schultz, who used the IAB Establishment Panel (IAB-Betriebspanel), identified the following factors which have an impact on export intensity: economies of scale, specialisation, wages and embeddedness in MNE structures (Schultz, 2010: 163).

Shortcomings underlying economic results

When the centrally planned economy collapsed in East Germany, the obsolete capital stock formed the most obvious weakness underlying the productivity gap. Under the centrally planned economy, modernisation of fixed assets in enterprises and in infrastructure had been widely neglected. In 1989, 54 per cent of the machinery in the East German manufacturing sector was worn out (Deutscher Bundestag, 1998: 67). The obsolete capital stock had required huge efforts of repair and maintenance, including a corresponding proportion of the workforce. Moreover, this obsolete machinery and equipment had led to considerable environmental damage, causing massive pollution of air, soil and water. When the Wall came down, the inadequate capital stock was a significant legacy of the communist past, and there was a pressing need for replacing the old-fashioned with modern fixed assets. Against this background, economic policy supported the modernisation of fixed assets in the enterprise sector in East Germany by investment grants, special depreciation allowances and loan and guarantee programmes. In addition, considerable efforts were made to modernise the infrastructure. As a result, provision of fixed assets has been considerably improved (Figure 10.2).

This stock of fixed assets is currently above the national average in the production sectors. However, taking all sectors together, there has been little progress in the 2000s, and a gap of 15 percentage points has persisted since 2006. The previous dynamism in terms of investment has tapered off.

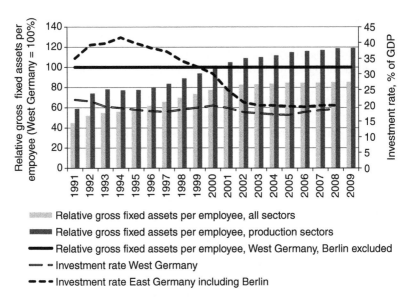

░░░░░ Relative gross fixed assets per employee, all sectors

▓▓▓▓▓ Relative gross fixed assets per employee, production sectors

━━━━ Relative gross fixed assets per employee, West Germany, Berlin excluded

━ ━ Investment rate West Germany

━ ━ ━ Investment rate East Germany including Berlin

Figure 10.2 Relative gross fixed assets per employee in East Germany (replacement prices) and investment rate in East and West Germany (sources: Regional Accounts VGRdL, 2010, 2011a, 2011c, authors' calculations).

Note

East Germany including Berlin; Investment rate = share of gross fixed asset investments in GDP (unadjusted prices); classification of economic activities: WZ, 2003. Production sectors include: mining, quarrying, manufacturing, electricity, gas and water supply, construction.

As mentioned above, regional economic theories reveal that internal and external economies of scale play an important role when it comes to the question of why regions surge ahead or lag behind. With respect to internal economies of scale, enterprises in East Germany have disadvantages. The East German economy consisted of large industrial trusts (*Kombinate*) at the end of the 1980s, but these were uncompetitive. Under the centrally planned economy, the establishment of these large units was a consequence of a scarcity of resources and the lack of hard currency. Thus, the question of 'Make or buy?' was usually answered in favour of 'Make'. This kind of division of labour, following the autarky principle, became obsolete after German unification. The privatisation of the large industrial trusts as entire units was not possible and they were split up in the course of this process. In addition, numerous new firms were founded in East Germany after German unification. The booming start-up activities were faced with a backlog in demand because the small business sector had been marginalised in the communist past. It is in the very nature of start-ups that they are rather small and fragile in the early years of existence, and firm growth takes time. As a result of privatisation and start-up activities, a very fragmented, *small-scale firm landscape* has emerged in the eastern part of Germany. Taking the

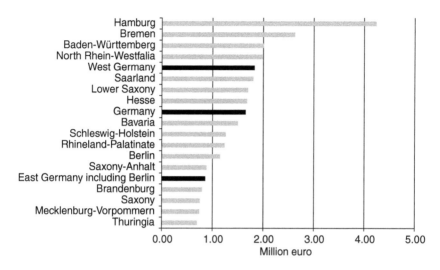

Figure 10.3 Average firm size in terms of turnover, 2010. Turnover per unit liable to turnover tax (prepayment notice) (source: Statistisches Bundesamt, 2013b, authors' calculations).

average turnover per company in East Germany as a proxy for firm size, it is currently (2010) only half of the West Germany value (Figure 10.3).

The small firm size in East Germany can, at least partly, explain the productivity gap. This is due to a capacity unequal to achieving economies of scale. Moreover, small firms can be expected to possess less market power compared to larger ones, a phenomenon which finds its expression in different scopes for price setting.

Conversely, there is a lack of large enterprises, especially large enterprises with their own research and development (R&D) activities. This shortage of large firms concerns not only the sheer number of firms. In addition, East Germany's proportion in total employment is lower than in the western part of the country (Bechmann *et al.*, 2010: 11). This lack of large enterprises coincides with the small number of headquarters in East Germany. The list of the top 500 companies in Germany in 2011 reveals that only 30 have their domicile in East Germany, and 17 of these are in Berlin (authors' calculations based on *Die Welt*, n.d.). The absence of headquarters is partly a consequence of the development after World War II when the headquarters of numerous German companies moved to the western part of the country. In part, the shortage of headquarters is also a result of privatisation in the early 1990s. Companies from West Germany or from abroad were often interested only in buying the pure production unit. This lack of headquarters has an impact on the per capita income (Blum, 2007: 187–194) and the prevalence of small firms also affects the capacity for R&D.

There is a gap in terms of R&D input measured by R&D expenditure in East Germany (Figure 10.4). The figure indicates that, other than Berlin and Saxony, East German states show a lag in terms of R&D expenditure. In Saxony in particular, R&D expenditure has experienced a considerable increase since 1999 which was greater than the average development in Germany (Sächsisches Staatsministerium für Wissenschaft und Kunst [ed.], 2013: 110). As a result, Saxony's proportion in 2010 was above the national average (2.9 per cent vs. 2.8) (Figure 10.4).

Another particular feature of R&D is the large proportion of universities and of the state (non-university) sector in total expenditure. This proportion is greater than the proportion of the enterprise sector, whereas the opposite is the case in the leading West German states (Figure 10.4). Strengths in public R&D and weaknesses in R&D in the enterprise sector require intensive intra- and inter-regional knowledge transfer and cooperation. The case of Saxony reflects some progress: the science-industry cooperation among partners located in Saxony has increased significantly since 2005 (Sächsisches Staatsministerium für Wissenschaft und Kunst [ed.] 2013: 181). The gap in terms of R&D input results not only from the prevalence of small firms, as shown above. Another reason concerns the lower proportion of research-intensive manufacturing industries in East Germany in comparison to West Germany (Günther *et al.*, 2010: 6f.). On the other hand, East Germany's specialisation in labour-intensive industries is above average (Heimpold, 2009: 431).

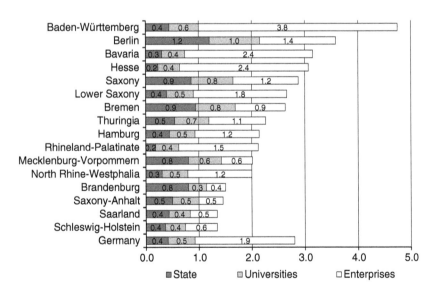

Figure 10.4 Share of R&D expenditure in GDP by sector in 2010 (%) (source: Statistisches Bundesamt 2013a based on: Federal Statistical Office, Stifterverband, Wissenschaftsstatistik, Essen, Regional Accounts VGRdL).

Note
The original data comprise two decimal places; to keep the figures readable they were reduced to one decimal place. GDP data as of August 2012.

Surprisingly, when considering innovation output, the East–West gap disappears. With respect to the proportion of East and West German enterprises introducing new products and services to the market (survey results by IAB Establisment Panel) there are no shortcomings in East Germany. The proportion of firms introducing new products or services is even greater in East Germany than in West Germany (Crimmann *et al.*, 2010: 395). At first glance, this sounds paradoxical, taking into account the low R&D input. However, having numerous East German subsidiaries in mind which have their parent companies in West Germany or western Europe, this pattern seems plausible. Obviously, East German subsidiaries can introduce innovations based on technology transfer provided by their parent companies (Günther *et al.*, 2010: 19 and the source cited there). In this respect, intra-company technology transfer may compensate, at least partly, for the disadvantages of a branch plant economy which shows a lack of own R&D activities, as is the case in East Germany.

External economies of scale in the form of urbanisation and localisation effects are also important when it comes to an explanation of spatial disparities. One might have the expectation that urban agglomerations would play a pioneering role in catching up economically as a result of the benefits of the diversified industries located in urban regions (Jacobs, 1969). Surprisingly, this is not the case in East Germany as far as their contribution to closing the productivity gap is concerned. Making a comparison between the productivity level of East German core cities compared to that of West German core cities, the relative difference is much greater than in rural spaces (Figure 10.5). In other words, East German cities do not fulfill the role of pioneers when it comes to catch-up to West Germany in productivity. The opposite is true; they lag further behind than rural regions.

Positive spatial agglomeration effects may also emerge in the form of localisation effects, i.e. spatially concentrated industries (Marshall, 1920/1962). Benefits can arise from a specialised pool of labour, industry-specific suppliers and by intensive knowledge flows between economic players located there (Marshall, 1920/1962: especially 222–227). Regional science and policy often uses the notion of 'clusters', made popular by M. Porter's contributions (e.g. Porter, 1990; 2008), when it comes to the phenomena of spatially concentrated industries. The IWH developed a quantitative method to identify the potential of clustering at regional level and applied it to German regions (Titze *et al.* 2011). This method uses qualitative input–output analysis in combination with spatial concentration measures. The findings show that potential for clustering is a relatively rare feature in East Germany when compared to West Germany. The proportion of districts which do not possess a concentration of industries is much greater in the eastern part of Germany (72 per cent vs 57 per cent) (IWH *et al.*, 2011: 70, 116). There are only a few districts which have the potential for clustering in the form of value added chains (two in East Germany – Berlin excluded – vs. 27 in West Germany) (IWH *et al.*, 2011: 70, 116).

Moreover, East Germany's regions are poor in clusters which have an inter-regional dimension (Brachert *et al.*, 2011: especially 432–434). The widespread

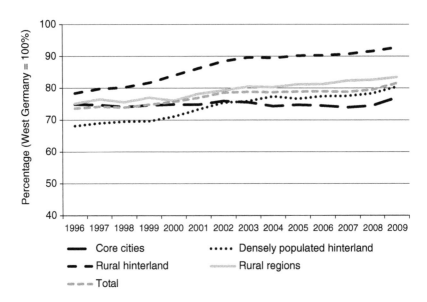

Figure 10.5 Relative productivity by types of district (source: Regional Accounts VGRdL 2011b, Federal Institute for Research on Building, Urban Affairs and Spatial Development (n.d.); authors' calculations).

Notes
Productivity = gross domestic product (unadjusted prices) per employee; classification of economic activities: WZ, 2003. Aggregated district classification 2008 by the Federal Institute for Research on Building, Urban Affairs and Spatial Development.

absence of clustering may be regarded as an additional reason for the persistence of the East–West productivity gap.

Implications for economic policy[2]

The question is whether and how economic policy can contribute to mitigating the shortcomings highlighted above – the prevalence of small firms, the limitations in R&D and export intensity, the absence of headquarters and the problems city regions experience in catching up economically.

In the first years after German unification, the toolbox of economic policy comprised a wide range of enterprise-oriented subsidy schemes and infrastructure programmes. These met the needs of modernising the obsolete physical capital stock which represented the most obvious shortcoming in those early years. As indicated in the section above, thanks to generous investment subsidies and public investment in transport and other infrastructure, considerable progress has been made in improving the capital stock.

To date, the obstacles remaining, especially in terms of small firm size and the lack of headquarters which have led to weak private R&D and low export intensity, cannot be rectified directly or in the short term by economic policy. Further progress in R&D and export intensity will largely depend on firm growth. But there is no simple cause–effect relationship between economic support schemes and further firm growth. Instead, 'natural', market-driven firm growth is required and this takes time. If firm growth is hampered by market failures, such as information asymmetries, state programmes could perhaps help to mitigate them. However, abolishing market failures poses a challenge which is a Germany-wide challenge. Firm growth which can only be achieved in the medium or long term will also contribute to mitigating the shortcomings in terms of private R&D and low export intensity.

According to a study on East Germany prepared on behalf of the Federal Ministry of the Interior, the sources of further firm growth are twofold: internal and external (IWH *et al.*, 2011: 94). This means that firms may also grow as a result of mergers and thus gain increasing economies of scale. Securing companies' succession sets another challenge in the context of firm growth. This challenge is of particular importance given the demographic challenges, especially in the eastern part of Germany. Making skilled labour available is a rapidly emerging challenge both for companies and for public policy.

Finally, this study points to the relevance of tax law, especially to taxation of companies. Tax law should be neutral in terms of firm size and legal form (IWH *et al.*, 2011: 94). This issue goes well beyond subsidy schemes. There is an urgent need for an economic environment that is generally growth-friendly. The benefits of this, however, will be long term and not short term.

In order to bridge the gap, particularly between current shortcomings in R&D and long-term changes, public research entities could transfer knowledge to small firms to enhance innovations here. However, the challenges of tackling shortages in terms of innovation in small firms exist not only in East Germany; they occur in structurally weak West German regions, too. Therefore, if policy regards size-specific innovation barriers as worth tackling by supporting public–private knowledge transfer, it should cover all the structurally weak regions in Germany.

The gap in terms of headquarters mentioned above can hardly be closed in a direct way. Once located in a certain place, headquarters are likely to remain there for some time. Hence, policy efforts to attract headquarters do not appear to be a realistic option. Instead, establishing favourable conditions for further growth in firms, either internally by mobilising endogenous resources or externally through mergers is the more promising option for encouraging the 'emergence' of headquarters. Apart from this, direct R&D support schemes can devise incentives for respective activities in small and medium-sized firms.

The development of firm growth which was highlighted above as a precondition for achieving progress in terms of productivity is embedded in a regional environment. Thus, local development policy has an impact on the development of the enterprise sector. Local development policy could affect the enterprise sector, especially through certain regulatory measures. Therefore, economic aspects should be integrated in an appropriate manner in the overall urban development strategies (IWH *et al.*, 2011: 90).

Notes

1 Due to different classifications of economic activities, the data on export intensity in 1991 and in 2010 are not fully comparable. The data in 1991 are based on the SYPRO classification, the data in 2010 on the classification of economic activities WZ, 2008.
2 The thoughts presented in this sub-section are based mainly on IWH *et al.*, 2011, especially 86–99.

References

Bechmann, S., V. Dahms, A. Fischer, M. Frei and U. Leber (2010), *20 Jahre Deutsche Einheit – Ein Vergleich der west- und ostdeutschen Betriebslandschaft im Krisenjahr 2009*. IAB-Forschungsbericht 6/2010. Nürnberg: Institut für Arbeitsmarkt- und Berufsforschung. Online. Available http://doku.iab.de/forschungsbericht/2010/fb0610.pdf (accessed 6 March 2013).

Blum, U. (2007), 'Der Einfluss von Führungsfunktionen auf das Regionaleinkommen: eine ökonometrische Analyse deutscher Regionen'. *Wirtschaft im Wandel*, 13: 187–194.

Blum, U., H. S. Buscher, H. Gabrisch, J. Günther, G. Heimpold, C. Lang, U. Ludwig, M. T. W. Rosenfeld and L. Schneider (2010), *Ostdeutschlands Transformation seit 1990 im Spiegel wirtschaftlicher und sozialer Indikatoren*. 2nd edn. Halle (Saale): Institut für Wirtschaftsforschung Halle. Online. Available www.iwh-halle.de/d/publik/sh/dkompendium.pdf (accessed 29 June 2011).

Brachert, M., M. Titze and A. Kubis (2011), 'Identifying industrial clusters from a multidimensional perspective: Methodical aspects with an application to Germany'. *Papers in Regional Science*, 90: 419–440.

Brezis, E. S., P. R. Krugman and D. Tsiddon (1993), 'Leapfrogging in international competition: a theory of cycles in national technological leadership'. *American Economic Review*, 83: 1211–1219.

Bröcker, J. (1994), 'Die Lehren der neuen Wachstumstheorie für die Raumentwicklung und die Regionalpolitik', in U. Blien, H. Herrmann and M. Koller (eds), (1994), *Regionalentwicklung und regionale Arbeitsmarktpolitik. Konzepte zur Lösung regionaler Arbeitsmarktprobleme?* Beiträge zur Arbeitsmarkt- und Berufsforschung, BeitrAB 184. Nürnberg: Institut für Arbeitsmarkt- und Berufsforschung der Bundesanstalt für Arbeit: 29–50.

Cezanne, W. (2005), *Allgemeine Volkswirtschaftslehre*, 6th revised edn. Wolls Lehr- und Handbücher der Wirtschafts- und Sozialwissenschaften. Munich and Vienna: R. Oldenbourg Verlag.

Crimmann, A., K. Evers, J. Günther, K. Guhr and M. Sunder, M. (2010), 'Aktuelle Trends. Ostdeutschland ähnlich innovativ wie Westdeutschland'. *Wirtschaft im Wandel*, 16: 395.

Deutscher Bundestag (1998), 13. Wahrperiode. *Schlussbericht der Enquete-Kommission 'Überwindung der Folgen der SED-Diktatur im Prozess der deutschen Einheit'*. Drucksache 13/11000.

Die Welt (n.d.), *Die größten 500 deutschen Unternehmen 2011* (electronic source).

Federal Institute for Research on Building, Urban Affairs and Spatial Development (n.d.), *Downloads. Raumabgrenzungen: Referenzdateien und Karten. Siedlungsstrukturelle Gebietstypen (frühere Gliederungen). Zusammengefasste Kreistypen*. Online. Available www.bbsr.bund.de/cln_032/nn_1086478/BBSR/DE/Raumbeobachtung/Raumabgrenzungen/SiedlungsstrukturelleGebietstypen/Kreistypen__zus/Download__ref__krs09__kty08__xls,templateId=raw,property=publicationFile.xls/Download_ref_krs09_kty08_xls.xls (accessed 6 March 2013).

Günther, J., K. Wilde, M. Sunder and M. Titze (2010), *20 Jahre nach dem Mauerfall: Stärken, Schwächen und Herausforderungen des ostdeutschen Innovationssystems heute*. Studien zum deutschen Innovationssystem Nr. 17–2010. Berlin: Expertenkommission Forschung und Innovation (EFI). Online. Available www.e-fi.de/fileadmin/ Studien/Studien_2010/17_2010_SWOT_Ostdeutschland.pdf (accessed 29 June 2011).

Heimpold, G. (2009) 'Von der De-Industrialisierung zur Re-Industrialisierung: Sind Ostdeutschlands industrielle Strukturen nachhaltig?' *Wirtschaft im Wandel*, 15: 425–434.

IWH, DIW, ifo Dresden, IAB, HoF and RWI (2011), *Wirtschaftlicher Stand und Perspektiven für Ostdeutschland. Studie im Auftrag des Bundesministeriums des Innern*, IWH-Sonderheft 2/2011. Halle (Saale): Institut für Wirtschaftsforschung Halle. Online. Available www.iwh-halle.de/d/publik/sh/PDF/SH_11–2.pdf (accessed 14 March 2013).

Jacobs, J. (1969), *The Economy of Cities*. New York: Random House.

Krugman, P. (1991/1993), *Geography and Trade*, Gaston Eyskens Lecture Series, fourth printing, 1993. Cambridge, MA: MIT Press.

Krugman, P. R. (2009), 'The increasing returns revolution in trade and geography'. *American Economic Review*, 99: 561–571.

Maier, G. and F. Tödtling (1996), *Regional- und Stadtökonomik 2. Regionalentwicklung und Regionalpolitik*. Springers Kurzlehrbücher der Wirtschaftswissenschaften. Vienna and New York: Springer-Verlag.

Marshall, A. (1920/1962), *Principles of Economics. An introductory volume.* 8th edn. London: Macmillan & Co.

Porter, M. E. (1990), *The Competitive Advantage of Nations*. Basingstoke: Macmillan Press.

Porter, M. E. (2008), 'Clusters and competition. new agendas for companies, governments, and institutions', in M. E. Porter, *On Competition*, updated and expanded edn. Harvard Business Review Book Series. Boston, MA: Havard Business School Publishing: 213–303.

Regional Accounts VGRdL (2010), *Arbeitskreis, Volkswirtschaftliche Gesamtrechnungen der Länder' 'Bruttoanlageinvestitionen in den Ländern und Ost-West-Großraumregionen Deutschlands 1991 bis 2008'. Reihe 1, Band 3. Erscheinungsfolge: jährlich. Erschienen im November 2010. Berechnungsstand des Statistischen Bundesamtes: August 2010.* Stuttgart: Statistisches Landesamt Baden-Württemberg. Online. Available www.vgrdl.de/Arbeitskreis_VGR/tbls/WZ2003R1B3.zip (accessed 8 March 2013).

Regional Accounts VGRdL (2011a), *Arbeitskreis 'Volkswirtschaftliche Gesamtrechnungen der Länder' 'Anlagevermögen in den Ländern und Ost-West-Großraumregionen Deutschlands 1991 bis 2009'. Reihe 1, Band 4. Erscheinungsfolge: jährlich. Erschienen im Mai 2011.* Stuttgart: Statistisches Landesamt Baden-Württemberg. Online. Available www.vgrdl.de/Arbeitskreis_VGR/tbls/WZ2003R1B4.zip (accessed 6 March 2013).

Regional Accounts VGRdL (2011b), *Arbeitskreis 'Volkswirtschaftliche Gesamtrechnungen der Länder' 'Bruttoinlandsprodukt, Bruttowertschöpfung in den kreisfreien Städten und Landkreisen Deutschlands 1992 und 1994 bis 2009'. Reihe 2, Band 1. Erscheinungsfolge: jährlich. Erschienen im Juli 2011; Tabellen 'BIP je ArbStd. ET' und 'ArbStd. ET' ergänzt im Oktober 2011. Berechnungsstand des Statistischen Bundesamtes: August 2010.* Stuttgart: Statistisches Landesamt Baden-Württemberg. Online. Available www.vgrdl.de/Arbeitskreis_VGR/tbls/WZ2003R2B1.zip (accessed 6 March 2013).

Regional Accounts VGRdL (2011c), *Arbeitskreis 'Volkswirtschaftliche Gesamtrechnungen der Länder' 'Bruttoinlandsprodukt, Bruttowertschöpfung in den Ländern und Ost-West-Großraumregionen Deutschlands 1991 bis 2010'. Reihe 1, Band 1. Erscheinungsfolge: jährlich. Erschienen im März 2011. Berechnungsstand des Statistischen Bundesamtes: August 2010/Februar 2011.* Stuttgart: Statistisches Landesamt Baden-Württemberg. Online. Available www.vgrdl.de/Arbeitskreis_VGR/tbls/WZ2003R1B1.zip (accessed 6 March 2013).

Regional Accounts VGRdL (2013), *Arbeitskreis 'Volkswirtschaftliche Gesamtrechnungen der Länder' 'Bruttoinlandsprodukt, Bruttowertschöpfung in den Ländern der Bundesrepublik Deutschland 1991 bis 2010.' Vorabversion zu Reihe 1, Band 1, Erscheinungsfolge: jährlich, Erschienen im Februar 2013, Berechnungsstand des Statistischen Bundesamtes: August 2012.* Stuttgart: Statistisches Landesamt Baden-Württemberg. Online. Available www.vgrdl.de/Arbeitskreis_VGR/tbls/R1B1.zip (accessed 28 February 2013).

Sächsisches Staatsministerium für Wissenschaft und Kunst (ed.) (2013), *Sächsischer Technologiebericht 2012.* Autoren: aus IWH, EuroNorm, Fraunhofer ISI. Online. Available https://publikationen.sachsen.de/bdb/artikel/17991/documents/24055 (accessed 7 March 2013).

Schultz, B. (2010), 'Wandel der betrieblichen Einflussfaktoren auf den ostdeutschen Export'. *Wirtschaft im Wandel*, 16: 158–163.

Sinn, H.-W. and F. Westermann (2000), *Two Mezzogiornos*, CESifo Working Paper Series, Working Paper No. 378, December. Online. Available www.cesifo-group.de/portal/pls/portal/docs/1/1190816.PDF (accessed 10 June 2011).

Statistisches Bundesamt (ed.) (1992), *Statistisches Jahrbuch 1992 für die Bundesrepublik Deutschland*, Wiesbaden: Statistisches Bundesamt. Erschienen im September.

Statistisches Bundesamt (2011), *Jahresbericht für Betriebe – Arbeitsunterlage. Betriebe von Unternehmen des Verarbeitenden Gewerbes sowie des Bergbaus und der Gewinnung von Steinen und Erden mit 20 und mehr tätigen Personen. 2010.' Erscheinungsfolge jährlich. Erschienen am 15.04.2011.* Wiesbaden: Statistisches Bundesamt. Online. Available www.destatis.de/DE/Publikationen/Thematisch/IndustrieVerarbeitendesGewerbe/Strukturdaten/Jahresbericht5422701107005.xls?__blob=publicationFile (accessed 13 March 2013).

Statistisches Bundesamt (2013a), *Forschung und Entwicklung: Anteil der Ausgaben für Forschung und Entwicklung 2010 am Bruttoinlandsprodukt (BIP) nach Bundesländern und Sektoren in %.* Online. Available www.destatis.de/DE/ZahlenFakten/GesellschaftStaat/BildungForschungKultur/ForschungEntwicklung/Tabellen/BIPBundeslaenderSektoren.html (accessed on 12 March 2013).

Statistisches Bundesamt (2013b), *Umsatzsteuerstatistik (Voranmeldungen). Umsatzsteuerpflichtige Unternehmen. Steuerpflichtige und deren Lieferungen und Leistungen 2010 nach Bundesländern.* Online. Available www.destatis.de/DE/ZahlenFakten/GesellschaftStaat/OeffentlicheFinanzenSteuern/Steuern/Umsatzsteuer/Tabellen/Voranmeldungen_Laender.html (accessed 15 March 2013).

Titze, M., M. Brachert and A. Kubis (2011), 'The identification of regional industrial clusters using qualitative input–output analysis (QIOA)'. *Regional Studies*, 45: 89–102.

WZ (2003) *Klassifikation der Wirtschaftszweige mit Erläuterungen.* Wiesbaden: Statisches Bundesamt.

WZ (2008), *Klassifikation der Wirtschaftszweige.* Wiesbaden: Statistisches Bundesamt

Zeddies, G. (2009), 'Warum exportiert der Osten so wenig? Eine empirische Analyse der Exportaktivitäten deutscher Bundesländer'. *Wirtschafts- und Sozialstatistisches Archiv. Eine Zeitschrift der Deutschen Statistischen Gesellschaft*, 3: 241–264.

11 Mezzogiorno and Neue Bundesländer

What lessons can Germany learn from Italy?

*Francesca Bartoli, Zeno Rotondi and
Denni Tommasi*

Introduction

South Italy[1] and East Germany (hereafter respectively SI and EG) share three common and important features. First, they both have a persistent and large amount of net imports. Second, this systematic and huge deficit of the trade balance implies dependency on external funding, mainly based on public transfers. Third, they have a persistent convergence gap compared to the rest of the country which is more wealthy and industrially advanced.

Dependency on external funding from public sector is a longlasting problem for SI. Since the Second World War, great effort has been put into investing public resources in physical and human capital in the less developed South, in order to pursue per capita income convergence with the North. There exists a vast literature examining the ineffectiveness of the policies adopted.[2] On the other hand, for Germany the issue of dependency on external funding of the East area is a much more recent phenomenon, but nevertheless similar to that of SI. After the reunification in 1990, the German government had to cope with a large amount of interventions regarding different spheres – political, economic, social, demographic, cultural – and a formidable set of policies was introduced to this aim.[3] With the available resources a number of positive and distinctive results were reached, at least in comparison with the SI experience (Oliva, 2009): the quality of infrastructures and human capital is relatively better in EG than in SI; the normative framework put in place by the German federal government is more effective in ensuring the well functioning of competition and markets; contrary to SI, EG is experiencing a positive trend of exports since 1995, which has contributed to decreasing the dependency on external funding.

Although one must recognise the considerable effort made to reintegrate the eastern Länder into the unified Germany, several observers highlight that a large part of the objectives put forward at the time of unification have been disregarded (Sinn and Westermann, 2001). The fast economic growth in the first years after reunification was followed by a phase of slow growth, insufficient to fill the gaps with the western regions. The low growth rates, now, seem to be rooted and the persistence of regional imbalances represent an issue for the social and economic prospects of the area.

Something which makes EG distinctive with respect to SI is the lower banking integration of the 'Neue Bundesländer' with the 'Alte Bundesländer'. In the subsequent analysis we will examine what are the implications of this peculiar feature of EG. In particular we will examine what lessons Germany can learn from Italy in this specific context.

The present analysis is structured as follows: the first section introduces the topic; the second section examines the different patterns of dependency on external funding of SI and EG and the role played by public transfers; the third section investigates the patterns of countrywide banking integration and their implications for the financial support to the less-developed territorial economies; the fourth section provides some concluding remarks.

Patterns of dependency on external funding and public transfers

Let us first examine in detail the evolution in the last two decades of the dependency on external funding, as proxied by net imports, of SI and EG. As discussed in the introduction, they both have a persistent and large amount of net imports, which in 2006 amounted to 15 per cent of GDP in EG and 22 per cent of GDP in SI, which has reflected public transfers in the magnitude of 9.5 per cent of GDP in EG and 18 per cent of GDP in SI (Figure 11.1). In Figures 11.2–11.4 we can see the evolution over time of the total, foreign and interregional dependency on external funding for both areas.

The total dependency on external funding is measured as the total net imports computed by summing foreign to interregional net imports for each area. It is a measure of regional overall net inflows of resources.

As we can observe, during the 1991–2008 period the total net imports of SI has been stable around 20 per cent of GDP (Figure 11.2). Foreign net imports represent the smallest component of total net imports, although they have been increasing since 1998, amounting to about 3 per cent of GDP in 2008 (Figure 11.3). While interregional net imports have been stable around 20 per cent of GDP (Figure 11.4).

Concerning EG, the area started from a very high overall dependency on external funding, slightly above 70 per cent of GDP in 1991, but managed to rapidly decrease it over the period considered, halving it in 2008 compared to that of SI (Figure 11.2). This reduction has mainly been driven by a sharp reduction in interregional net imports (Figure 11.4), although it has reached a large surplus in the foreign balance of trade (Figure 11.3), with net exports equal to 8 per cent of GDP in 2008. However, even if the decrease of net imports and the positive trend of exports jointly lead to a significant reduction of public transfers, in 2008 the dependency on external funding has still remained around 10 per cent of GDP (Figure 11.2) while interregional dependency has reached a steady state value of around 20 per cent of GDP, which represents a common pattern with SI (Figure 11.4).

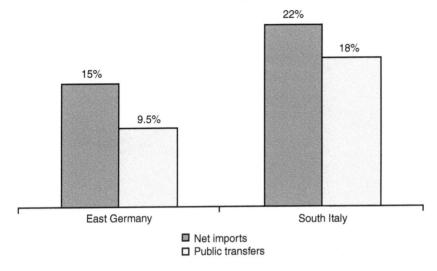

Figure 11.1 Dependency on external funding in East Germany and South Italy (total net imports and contribution of public transfers as % of GDP, 2006) (source: our elaborations on estimates from Iuzzolino (2009) and Prometeia. Data on public transfers relative to South Italy are based on Cannari and Chiri (2006), whereas data relative to East Germany are based on Sinn and Westermann (2001). Total net imports is the sum of foreign net imports plus interregional net imports).

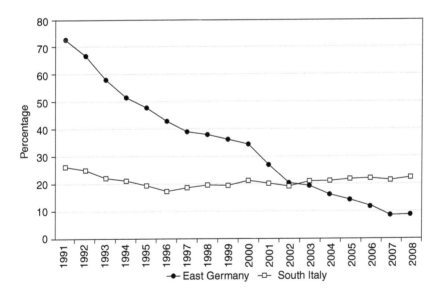

Figure 11.2 Dependency on external funding in East Germany and South Italy (total net imports as % of GDP) (source: our elaborations on estimates from Prometeia. Data source for South Italy is ISTAT; data source for East Germany is Destatis).

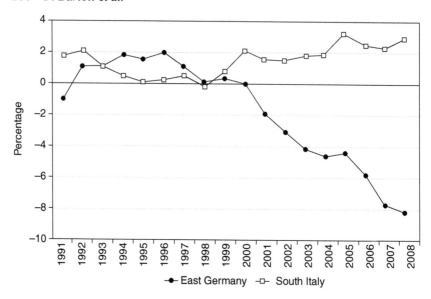

Figure 11.3 Foreign dependency on external funding in East Germany and South Italy (foreign net imports as % of GDP) (source: our elaborations on estimates from Prometeia. Data source for South Italy is ISTAT; data source for East Germany is Destatis).

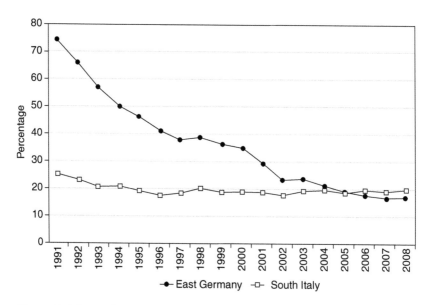

Figure 11.4 Interregional dependency on external funding in East Germany and South Italy (net imports for each area from the residual area of the country as % of GDP) (source: our elaborations on estimates from Prometeia. Data source for South Italy is ISTAT; data source for East Germany is Destatis).

Why should we be concerned about high dependency on external funding in the regional context? In order to answer this question we can recall, for instance, two alternative analytical frameworks which examine the problems arising in this context.

A first theoretical scheme, put forward by Sinn and Westermann (2001) to explain the EG situation, is the so-called 'Dutch disease' metaphor. According to this scheme the deindustrialisation post-1990 in EG had effects analogous to the well-known Dutch disease phenomenon, which occurs in countries 'affected' by a resource discovery.[4] Indeed, public transfers from the central government (the so-called *Solidarpakt*) to the new Bundesländer can be seen as a 'discovery' of natural resources. Within the Dutch disease scheme (pioneered by Salter, 1959; Swan, 1960; Meade, 1951), when a country discovers or receives a large amount of natural resources, it experiences a large currency evaluation and a subsequent decline of the tradable goods sectors (such as the manufacturing sector), followed by an increase of economic dependency on imports from foreign countries.

After the reunification of 1990, the German authorities decided not only to put in place a massive system of welfare state interventions in favour of the East, but also decided in most of the cases to use a one-to-one ratio for the conversion between the Ostmark and the Deutschmark, which resulted in an immediate and considerable real appreciation of the EG products.[5] At the same time, EG firms entered immediately into the EMU market and had to face full competition with both West German and European firms. All these effects together produced a large drop of the exports of the new Bundesländer. However, while the change in the conversion rate of the two currency had a (relatively) short-term effect, the large inflows of public resources have contributed to a medium/long-term deindustrialisation process with effects, as mentioned above, similar to the so-called 'Dutch disease' (Sinn and Westermann, 2001).

An alternative scheme, used in the context of the Italian Mezzogiorno, is the so-called 'leaky bucket' metaphor put forward by Savona (1970; 1991).[6] According to this scheme, regions with persistent high external trade deficit (and their politicians and authorities of regional policy) are affected by a 'compensation stress': i.e. they require persistent high public spending in order to compensate for structural imbalances (the 'leaky bucket'). This 'compensation stress' implies:

1 crowding out of loanable funds: i.e. lower loans to GDP ratio compared to Centre-Northern regions;
2 crowding out of private investments and weakening of local manufacturing sector compared to Centre-Northern regions;
3 worsening of local firms credit risk: i.e. higher nonperforming loans to GDP ratio compared to Centre-Northern regions.

The above effects further disadvantage local firms' access to credit and increase dependency on imports, implying lower growth.

Patterns of banking integration and financial support to territorial economies

The structure of private and public funding of a region (or a country), and in turn its degree of dependency on external funding, is strongly related to the structure of its trade balance of goods and services. De Bonis *et al.* (2010) provide an analysis of the effects of trade integration between the Centre-North and South in the case of Italy. Their conclusion is that trade integration in Italy has produced a highly 'interconnected' model of territorial funding, where the Centre-North transfers public funds to the South, for redistributive purposes, and at the same time the South transfers in similar proportion private financial resources to the Centre-North, in the form of net imports of goods and services. Indeed in Figure 11.5 we can see that SI is still highly dependent on public resources, on average 72 per cent of GDP compared to 58 per cent of the Centre-North between 1997 and 2005, while private funding is much less relevant, accounting on average for 44 per cent of GDP compared to 81 per cent of the Centre-North taken in the same period.

In order to reduce the dependency on external funding, in particular from public transfers, in SI and EG, we need to increase the importance of private funding in these two areas. This implies that we need to ensure the conditions under which the banking sector may be capable of replacing the role of the public sector in providing financial resources to the economy. In particular, we need to strengthen efficiency in the banking sector by means of greater competition.

In Italy this objective was mainly pursued by means of stronger banking integration between the South and the Centre-North. Indeed, the integration

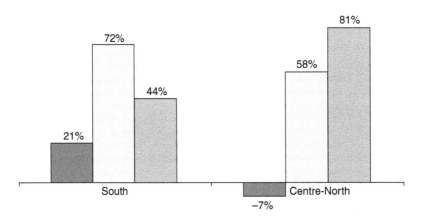

■ Net imports □ Public expenditure □ Bank loans

Figure 11.5 Dependency on external funding, public spending and bank loans in Italy (total net imports, public spending and bank loans as % of GDP, averages 1997–2005) (source: our elaborations from De Bonis *et al.*, 2010).

process should imply that the areas with the most efficient banking sector increase their banking activities in the areas with the less efficient banking sector.

In Germany, on the contrary, the East banking sector is still poorly integrated with that of the West. The Italian and German banking systems shared similar characteristics early in the 1990s in terms of a large number of banks, mainly publicly owned, but have evolved in different directions since then. Over the last decade both countries have undergone a deep process of consolidation through mergers and acquisitions. However, whereas Italy privatised its publicly owned banks, Germany kept its 'three-pillar' system of private banks, cooperative banks and publicly owned banks (De Vincenzo *et al.*, 2009). Together with the reform of public banks' ownership structure, a set of other important reforms took place in the 1990s in Italy, in part as a consequence of the implementation of the Second Banking Directive (89/646/EEC). The mandatory specialisation was gradually removed after 1990, restrictions on geographical diversification were lifted and the concept of a 'banking group' was introduced in the legislation. As a result, the share of total assets controlled by public banks and the number of banks decreased considerably, whereas the number of bank offices and the average size of banks increased. Even though Germany did not witness an analogous process of liberalisation, thanks to mergers and acquisitions the number of institutions dropped considerably and the average size of banks increased as well.

During the 1993–1997 period large banks in the South witnessed a financial crisis (Bongini and Ferri, 2005). At the end of the 1990s loans supply in SI was mainly influenced by banks in Centre-North, rigorously controlling financial flows of acquired southern banks, characterised by poor profitability and severe financial conditions.

In the present section we examine the evolution of the Italian bank integration focusing on the presence over time in SI of banks headquartered in Centre-North. Since the openness of a local credit system can be proxied by the market share of banks based outside the region, we follow Nuzzo and Oliverio (2011) and consider volume data (i.e. outstanding stocks of deposits and loans).[7] This choice bounds the analysis to a descriptive level, without taking into account advantages and disadvantages in terms of prices and profitability of the degree of integration reached in SI.

Bank integration is a means rather than an objective, while the actual objective is enhancing the access to financial services. Therefore in our analysis, taking into account our limited perspective, we focus on the size of loans available in the area compared to non-performing loans, deposits and value added or GDP of the area. The analysis of bank integration is conducted on the basis of both consolidated and unconsolidated balance sheets. In this latter case, data refer to individual banks rather than to the banking group as a whole.

In Figure 11.6 we can observe that the presence in SI of banks headquartered in the Centre-North of Italy has grown significantly since the banking

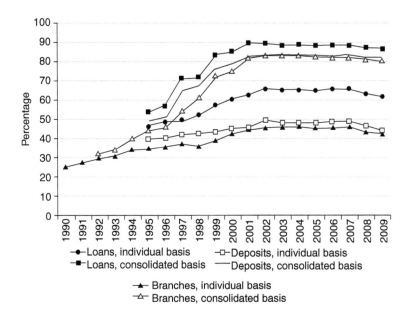

Figure 11.6 Market shares in the South of banks headquartered in the Centre-North of Italy: loans, deposits and branches (% values) (source: Nuzzo and Oliverio (2010), elaborations on data from Bank of Italy, supervisory reports. End of year stock data. Loans to households and firms based in the South including non-performing loans and net of repurchase agreements (repos). Data not adjusted for securitisations and reclassification. Deposits includes certificates of deposit and passive repos of households and firms based in the South. Share of branches with respect to total number in the area. The analysis does not include Bancoposta and the Cassa Depositi e Prestiti. Bank geographical classification is considered with respect to the location of legal headquarters of the individual bank or of the holding in case of banking groups. The analysis is conducted both on the basis of consolidated and individual balance sheets.).

liberalisation of early 1990s. On individual basis, it has reached a market share close to 60 per cent for loans and around 45 per cent for deposits; branches account for a market share of approximately 42 per cent. Once we control for banking groups, all values increase reaching a level close to 90 per cent for loans and around 80 per cent for deposits and branches.[8]

Hence, the degree of openness of the credit market in the South has significantly increased during the last two decades. The increase of market shares data on a consolidated basis compared to those on an individual basis reflects the fact that bank integration has occurred mainly through external channels, i.e. acquisitions of shares of individual banks without changing brand or legal headquarter (see Nuzzo and Oliverio, 2011).

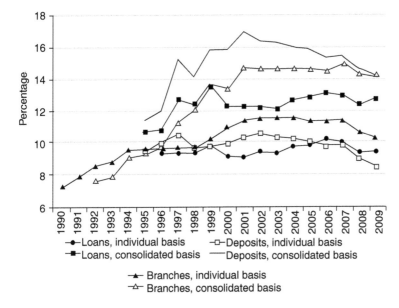

Figure 11.7 Share of activity in the South of banks based in the Centre-North of Italy (% values) (source: Nuzzo and Oliverio (2010), elaborations on data from Bank of Italy – Supervisory Reports. End of year stock data. Loans to households and firms based in the South including non-performing loans and net of repurchase agreements (repos). Data not adjusted for securitisations and reclassification. Deposits includes certificates of deposit and passive repos of households and firms based in the South. Share of branches with respect to total number in the area. The analysis does not include Bancoposta and the Cassa Depositi e Prestiti. Bank geographical classification is considered with respect to the location of legal headquarters of the individual bank or of the holding in case of banking groups. The analysis is conducted both on the basis of consolidated and individual balance sheets.).

Moreover at the end of 2009, from a consolidated point of view, the share of activity in the South of banks based in Centre-North was 15 per cent for branches and deposits, while 13 per cent for loans (Figure 11.7).

The effects of bank integration have been threefold. First there is no evidence of a drain of private funds from the South to the Centre-North. In Figure 11.8 we can see that in the South the loan to deposit ratio has remarkably increased and since 2006 is above 100 per cent. More importantly, banks based in Centre-North have contributed to the flow of financial resources to the South to a greater extent than banks headquartered in the area.

In Figure 11.9 we can see that the loan to deposit ratio for customers based in the South of banks headquartered in the Centre-North is, since 1998, above 100 per cent, whereas that of banks headquartered in the South has remained below 80 per cent for the whole period considered.

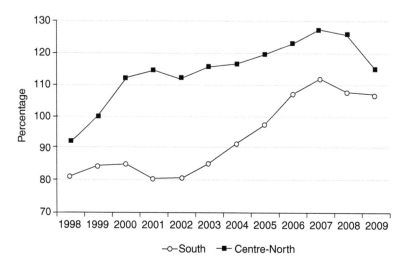

Figure 11.8 Loan to deposit ratio based on debtor's residency in Italy (% values) (source:
De Bonis *et al.* (2010), elaborations on data from Bank of Italy – Supervisory Reports. End of year stock data. Loans to households and firms based
in the South or in the Centre-North including non-performing loans and net
of repurchase agreements (repos). Data not adjusted for securitisations and
reclassification. Deposits includes certificates of deposit and passive repos of
households and firms based in the South or in the Centre-North. The analysis
does not include Bancoposta and the Cassa Depositi e Prestiti.).

Moreover, as shown in Figure 11.10 the financial support to business activities of industry and tertiary sector in SI, as measured by loan to valued added
ratio, has increased in the period 2003–2007. Finally, banking integration has
implied a more efficient credit selection process in SI. In fact, from Figure
11.11, we can see that firms' credit riskiness has converged in the two areas. In
particular, in SI the share of new non-performing loans over total loans
decreased between 1999 and 2008 from slightly above 4 per cent to around 2
per cent.

These results are important as several studies have previously pointed out that
the lower degree of banking development in SI compared to the rest of the
country has significantly contributed to the North–South divide in terms of lower
rate of entrepreneurship, fewer entries of new firms and lower rate growth of the
area (see for instance Guiso *et al.*, 2004).

Let's examine the case of East Germany banking sector. In contrast to the
case of South Italy, East Germany has not improved its banking integration with
West Germany. In particular, Figure 11.12 shows that the loan market share of
local banks in EG is remarkably higher compared to SI, about 30 per cent higher
during the 2000s. Hence, the degree of openness of the credit market in EG has

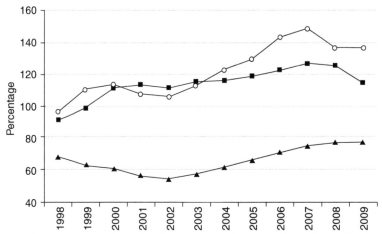

Figure 11.9 Loan to deposit ratio based on banks and customers residency in Italy (%
values) (source: De Bonis *et al.* (2010), elaborations on data from Bank of
Italy – Supervisory Reports. End of year stock data. Loans to households
and firms based in the South or in the Centre-North including non-performing loans and net of repurchase agreements (repos). Data not adjusted for
securitisations and reclassification. Deposits includes certificates of deposit
and passive repos of households and firms based in the South or in the Centre-North. The analysis does not include Bancoposta and the Cassa Depositi
e Prestiti. Bank geographical classification is considered with respect to the
location of legal headquarters of the individual bank or of the holding in case
of banking groups.).

remained relatively lower. In Figure 11.13, we can examine one implication of
this lower banking integration. While in SI bank loans as percentage of GDP
have increased from 42 per cent to 62 per cent during the 2000s, in EG they have
decreased from 49 per cent to 44 per cent.

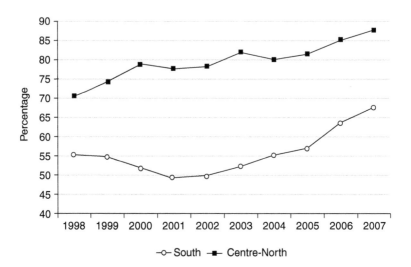

Figure 11.10 Loans to value added ratio of firms in Italy (% values) (source: De Bonis *et al.* (2010), elaborations on data from Bank of Italy – Supervisory Reports. End of year stock data. Loans to firms based in the South or in the Centre-North including non-performing loans and net of repurchase agreements (repos). Data not adjusted for securitisations and reclassification. The analysis does not include Bancoposta and the Cassa Depositi e Prestiti. Value added at current prices of manufacturing, constructions and services sectors.).

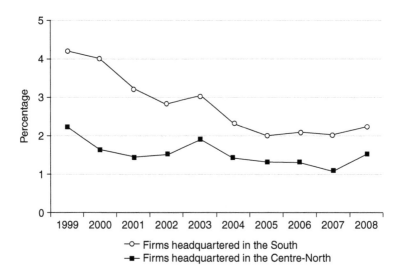

Figure 11.11 New non-performing loans of firms in Italy (as % of total loans) (source: De Bonis *et al.* (2010), elaborations on data from Bank of Italy – Credit Register. Firms' yearly flow of new non-performing loans over stock of loans at the beginning of year net of non-performing loans. Data not adjusted for securitisations and reclassification. Bancoposta and the Cassa Depositi e Prestiti are not included.).

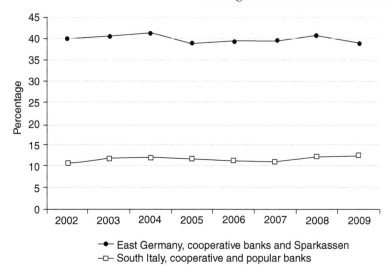

Figure 11.12 Loan market shares of local banks in East Germany and South Italy (% values) (source: Nuzzo and Oliverio (2010), elaborations on data from Bank of Italy and Bundesbank).

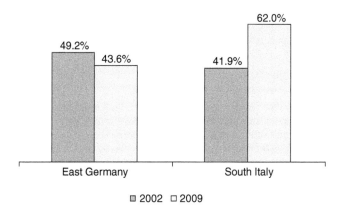

Figure 11.13 Bank loans in East Germany and South Italy (as % of GDP) (source: Nuzzo and Oliverio (2010), elaborations on data from Bank of Italy and Bundesbank).

Conclusions

In the present analysis we have argued that Germany did not experience an intensive process of banking integration like Italy, although in both countries thanks to mergers and acquisitions realised after banking liberalisation the number of institutions dropped considerably and the average size of banks increased as well. A striking difference is that East Germany banking integration with West Germany has not significantly increased compared to the case of Italy. In fact the loan market share of local banks in East Germany is remarkably higher as compared to that in South Italy.

Moreover, we have shown that in South Italy the financial support to the territorial economies has significantly increased as a consequence of the increased banking integration with the Centre-North. In contrast, in Germany lower banking integration of the Neue Bundesländer with the Alte Bundesländer has implied lower financial support to the less-developed territorial economies from the banking sector.

In order to reduce the dependency on external funding, in particular from public transfers, in SI and EG, we need to increase the importance of private funding in these two areas. This implies that we need to ensure the conditions under which the banking sector may be capable of replacing the role of the public sector in providing financial resources to the economy. In particular, we need to strengthen efficiency in the banking sector by means of greater competition.

In Italy this objective has mainly been pursued by means of stronger banking integration between the South and the Centre-North. Indeed, the integration process should imply that the areas with the most efficient banking sector increase their banking activities in the areas with the less efficient banking sector.

Therefore our findings suggest a lesson that Germany can learn from Italy by showing the potential advantages for the less-developed territorial economies deriving from higher banking integration with the more developed ones, along the lines followed in Italy.

Notes

1 Throughout the chapter we use the words 'South Italy' and 'Mezzogiorno' interchangeably. The area includes Abruzzi, Campania, Puglia, Molise, Basilicata, Calabria, Sicily and Sardinia. We refer to the rest of the country as 'Centre-North'.
2 See of instance Iuzzolino (2009) for a review of the literature.
3 Jansen (2004) estimates that for the period 1991–2003 the amount of transfers to the New Bundesländer has been over €80 billion annually. The peak occurred between 1993 and 1998, while after that period the amount of public transfers steadily declined.
4 See Corden and Neary (1982) and Sell (1988).
5 Currency holding of up to 4.000 Ostmarks per person were converted at a one-for-one ratio. Savings in excess of 4,000 Ostmarks per person were converted at a two Ostmark to one Deutschmark ratio. Currency holdings acquired shortly before unification were converted at three Ostmark to one Deutschmark ratio. Pensions were converted at a one-for-one ratio. Financial claims such as housing loans were converted at the two-for-one rate. Prices and wages were converted at a one-for-one ratio. See for instance Oliva (2009) who explains in details how the conversion process occurred.
6 More recently, De Bonis et al. (2010) have provided empirical evidence for the 'leaky bucket' metaphor in the case of the Italian Mezzogiorno.
7 For other works that analyse banks' integration considering volume data, see Manna (2004), Baele et al. (2004), Cabral et al. (2002), Hartmann et al. (2003).
8 The gap between individual and consolidated basis data is the highest for Sicily and Sardinia, since the two main banks based in the region (Banco di Sicilia and Banco di Sardegna) belong to banking groups headquartered in the north of Italy.

References

Baele, L., A. Ferrando, P. Hördahl, E. Krylova and C. Monnet (2004), 'Measuring financial integration in the Euro Area'. Occasional Papers, n.14, European Central Bank.

Bongini, P. and G. Ferri (2005), *Il sistema bancario meridionale*. Bari: Editori Laterza.

Cabral, I., F. Dierick and J. Vesala (2002), 'Banking integration in the Euro Area'. Occasional Papers 6, European Central Bank.

Cannari, L. and S. Chiri (2006), 'La bilancia dei pagamenti di parte corrente Nord–Sud: 1998–2000', in L. Cannari and F. Panetta, F. (eds), *Il sistema finanziario e il Mezzogiorno*, Bari: Cacucci Editore: 53–85.

Corden, W. and Neary, J. P. (1982), 'Booming sector and de-industrialization in a small open economy'. *Economic Journal*, 92: 825–848.

De Bonis, R., F. Farabullini and G. Nuzzo (2010), 'Prestiti e raccolta delle banche: un'analisi degli andamenti territoriali'. in R. De Bonis, Z. Rotondi and P. Savona (eds), *Sviluppo, rischio e conti con l'esterno delle regioni italiane*. Bari: Editori Laterza: 113–126.

De Vincenzo, V., E. Fiorentino, F. Heid, A. Karmann and M. Koetter (2009), 'The effects of privatization and consolidation on bank productivity: comparative evidence from Italy and Germany'. Working Papers 722, Bank of Italy.

Guiso, L., P. Sapienza and L. Zingales (2004), 'Does local financial development matter?' *Quarterly Journal of Economics*, 119: 929–969.

Hartmann, P., A. Maddaloni and S. Manganelli (2003), 'The Euro Area financial system: structure, integration and policy initiatives'. *Oxford Review of Economic Policy*, 19: 180–213.

Iuzzolino, G. (2009), 'I divari territoriali di sviluppo in Italia nel confronto internazionale', in *Mezzogiorno e politiche regionali*, Workshops and Conferences, 2. Bank of Italy: 427–478.

Jansen, H. (2004), 'Transfers to Germany's eastern Länder: a necessary price for convergence or a permanent drag?' *ECFIN Country Focus*, 16.

Manna, M. (2004), 'Developing statistical indicators of the integration of the Euro Area banking system'. Working Papers, 300, European Central Bank.

Meade, J. E. (1951), *The Theory of International Economic Policy*. Oxford: Oxford University Press.

Nuzzo, G. and E. Oliverio (2011), 'Banche locali e banche del Centro-Nord nel Mezzogiorno: evoluzione temporale e confronto con altre aree in ritardo di sviluppo'. *Rivista economica del Mezzogiorno*, 25(4): 895–918.

Oliva, J. C. M. (2009), 'Riunificazione intertedesca e politiche per la convergenza', in *Mezzogiorno e politiche regionali*, Workshops and Conferences, 2, Bank of Italy: 479–502

Salter, W. E. G. (1959), 'Internal and external balance: the role of price and expenditure effects'. *Economic Record*, 35: 226–238.

Savona, P. (1970), 'Una interpretazione finanziaria delle risorse reali per lo sviluppo regionale'. *La programmazione in Sardegna*, 28–29.

Savona, P. (1991), 'Ancora sulla "pentola bucata". Quale intervento nell'economia meridionale?' *Delta*, 46–47: 28–30.

Sell, F. L. (1988), ''The Dutch disease': Anpassungsprozesse als folge eines Ressourcenbooms'. *Das Wirtschaftsstudium*, 17: 289–94.

Sinn, H. W. and F. Westermann (2001), 'Two Mezzogiornos'. Working Papers, 8125, National Bureau of Economic Research.

Swan, T. (1960), 'Economic control in a dependent economy'. *Economic Record*, 36: 51–66.

Index

Page numbers in *italics* denote tables.

For Product Safety Concerns and Information please contact our EU
representative GPSR@taylorandfrancis.com
Taylor & Francis Verlag GmbH, Kaufingerstraße 24, 80331 München, Germany

www.ingramcontent.com/pod-product-compliance
Ingram Content Group UK Ltd.
Pitfield, Milton Keynes, MK11 3LW, UK
UKHW020958180425
457613UK00019B/742